From Sand Castles to Dream Houses

A Planner for Building or Remodeling Your Home

By Sheri Koones

Hanley-Wood, LLC.

From Sand Castles to Dream Houses:
A Planner for Building or Remodeling Your Home

Published by Hanley-Wood, LLC.
426 S. Westgate St.
Addison, IL 60101

Cover and Book Design: Phillips Design, Inc.

Publisher: Pat Carroll
Manager, Books/Educational Products: Rick Yelton
Managing Editor, Books/Educational Products: Kari Moosmann
Associate Editor, Copy/Production: Jennifer Enenstein
Contributing Editor: Pam Sourelis

Disclaimer Hanley-Wood, LLC. and its employees and agents are not engaged in the business of providing architectural or construction services, nor are they licensed to do so. The information in this book is intended for the use of individuals competent to evaluate its applicability to their situation, and who will accept responsibility for the application of the information. Hanley-Wood and the author disclaim any and all responsibility for the application of the information.

10 9 8 7 6 5 4 3 2 1

Koones, Sheri, 1949-
    From sand castles to dream houses : a planner for
    building or remodeling your home / by Sheri Koones
        p. cm.
    Includes bibliographical references and index.
    ISBN 0-924659-87-4 (hc)
    1. House constuction--Amateurs' manuals, 2. Dwellings--
Remodeling--Amateurs' manuals. 3. Contractors--Selection
and appointment--Amateurs' manuals. I. Title.

TH4815 .K66 2002
690'.837--dc21

For Rob, Alex & Jesse
I love you so

Dream House

Let there be within these phantom walls
Beauty where the hearth fire's shadow falls...
Quiet pictures-books-and welcoming chairs...
Music that the silence shares...
Kitchen windows curtained blue and white...
Shelves and cupboards built for my delight...
Little things that lure and beckon me
With their tranquil joy! And let there be
Lilt of laughter-swift-forgotten tears
Woven through the fabric of the years...
Strength to guard me-eyes to answer mine,
Mutely clear. And though without may shine
Stars of dawn or sunset's wistful glow-
All of life and love my house shall know!

Catherine Parmenter Newell

From *Poems That Touch the Heart* / Compiled by A.L. Alexander / Garden City Publishing, 1941

Acknowledgments

I owe a special gratitude to my husband Robert, who gave me the opportunity to build the house of my dreams. Not only did he have to live through the experience of building the house, he had to relive the experience for an additional two years while I worked on this book. He offered support and invaluable insight, and reminded me of details I might not have included.

My children gave me a great deal of inspiration to complete this project. They were so proud that their mother was writing a book, it inspired me to move along and to demonstrate to them that great effort and perseverance can lead to the fulfillment of very worthwhile goals.

I owe a very special gratitude to Robert Louis Stevenson III, not only a talented author, but a kind and generous person. He believed in the project from the beginning, made terrific suggestions for improving the manuscript, and showed me the means to accomplish what was only a dream. I will always be grateful to him for his kindness.

A very special thank you to Lucy Hedrick, who started out as a proposal adviser, and became a great supporter, cheerleader, and friend. She is one of the true bonuses of having written this book. I would like to thank Fran Pastore and the Women's Business Development Center, who when called for help, always responded.

I am very grateful to all of my friends and relatives who encouraged me to complete this project when the carpooling and chores seemed to take over my life and I considered tossing the project aside.

I'd also like to thank all of the many professionals who gave of their time and expertise, so generously offering invaluable insight and information. The people in all of the professional organizations offered their kind assistance: the AIA, ASID, ASLA, NARI, CEDIA, Water Quality Association, and NKBA. Architect Steve Mueller not only designed a beautiful home for our family but also gave generously of his time in professional criticism for this book. And thanks to all the magazine editors, and assistants who took the time to fill out questionnaires so that readers could better focus on this wonderful, informative medium: magazines.

A special thank you to Rick Yelton of Hanley-Wood, who believed in the book, always took a positive attitude toward it, and showed me tremendous kindness when I was most anxious. I would like to thank all the other people at Hanley-Wood who were so helpful in making this book a reality. And thank you to Pam Sourelis for her excellent editing skill, Steve Phillips for a beautiful design, Norma Ciaglia for her marketing skills, and Kari Moosmann for putting it all together.

I am very grateful for the opportunity to fulfill a lifelong dream of writing my own book and for becoming involved with a medium that I have always loved.

Contents

Introduction

For several years, my husband and I searched for our dream house. Unable to find the home we wanted, we decided to renovate a stale fifties house in a prime location in Connecticut. The house was poorly laid out and in need of updating. Although our finished home turned out to be gorgeous - far exceeding our dreams - the renovation took far longer and cost more than we ever imagined.

We made a number of errors because of our lack of experience and knowledge. For example, we called in a lighting specialist after the bidding process was complete. The additional fixtures cost a great deal more than they would have if they had been planned for in the design stage. We also didn't have a landscape plan developed until the house was complete, which created a number of additional expenses: having to bring the electrical wires to the outside, putting in a drainage system, and repaving the road. All of these procedures would have cost less if they had appeared in the original bid.

By the time the house was finally complete, I was so happy to get the builder out of the house, I failed to get information about how various systems in the house worked and what maintenance procedures we would need to follow.

It is difficult to prepare yourself for the overwhelming task of building a house. I wish I'd have had a simple, no-nonsense, easy-to-read guide.

From Sand Castles to Dream Houses: A Planner for Building or Remodeling your Home is such a guide. It gives you all the information you'll need to make informed decisions about building or renovating your home. Unlike other homebuilding books that dwell on construction and design technicalities, this guide offers advice to the average homeowner in clear, everyday language.

You'll learn about building, zoning, and wetland restrictions; general contractors; architects, interior designers, and landscape architects. You'll discover how to select a location and home design that's right for you and your family, and how to select a team of construction specialists who can work together efficiently and, even more importantly, work well with you.

The book is divided into two sections. The first is meant to inform and guide you through the process of building or renovating your home. The second is a handy Notebook to help you keep records that you will need during construction and after your home is completed.

I developed a notebook, similar to the one included here, during the construction of my own house and found it invaluable for keeping track of my project. While I was calling for references on architects and builders, I would sometimes ask if people had school and camp recommendations. I decided to include pages for those items because they can be overlooked in the rush to get the house built.

I have included a chapter on kitchens and one on bathrooms because these two rooms are among the most renovated rooms and the most complicated to construct. There are so many elements to consider for each. This book will give you an idea of all that you need to consider and plan for.

People often don't consider all of the systems (audio, water quality, and so on) needed in the house until construction has begun. Then there is a rush to find dealers and to learn everything necessary in a short time in order to get the systems installed before the dry walls go up. I've included information about various systems so you can investigate them while you are developing your plans.

Since there weren't any books available with the detailed information about systems that I was looking for, when I began writing this book I collected extensive information from manufacturers (of systems as well as manufacturers of components of systems), salespeople, and installers. Their generosity with time and data allowed me to compile information that can help you to make an intelligent decision if and when you decide to purchase a system for your home.

When I attended bimonthly meetings with the architect, general contractor, and various subcontractors, they often used terms that I was unfamiliar with. Rather than constantly asking for explanations, I would sometimes look these terms up later, missing out on their original context. So that this doesn't have to happen to you, I've included an extensive List of Terms (Appendix A). Because this book was purposely designed to be small enough to take to meetings, you can look up terms on the spot.

Having always been a magazine junkie, when we began our building project, I purchased all of the home (shelter) magazines I could find. Of course, some were more useful to me than others. When I got the idea to write this book, I sent out surveys to all of the shelter magazines in the United States and Canada, requesting information about the focus of their magazines. I hope that Appendix B, a graph compiled from this data, will help you purchase the magazines that are appropriate and relevant to your project.

I've included Web site addresses throughout the book to make your own research easier. A complete list is included in Appendix D. A list of books you may find useful is in Appendix C.

I put months of concentrated effort into renovating my home. Like most people, I was shocked by the hidden costs of construction and frustrated by constant red tape and delays.

Owning a home is the American Dream. *Sand Castles & Dream Houses* will help you avoid the common mistakes that can turn a dream house into a nightmare and will help make building or renovating your home a dream come true.

1. Always call for references before hiring any person or service.

2. Always put a completion date on all work to be done in the home. Whenever possible, there should also be a reward and penalty attached to that date.

3. Always get several bids before choosing a contractor.

4. Know what work is to be done in the house. If you don't initially understand, ask questions.

5. Never allow any work to be done on your construction without a signed agreement. Be clear in the agreement what work will be done and what will not be included.

6. Plan ahead. Even if it means delaying the project, try not to make any changes after the bid is given out. The highest and most unexpected expenses in the construction process will be from change orders or additions.

7. Never let someone talk you into something you don't want.

8. Be prepared to pay more than you expected. Even if you follow almost everything on your initial plan, the house will cost more than you expect.

9. Be organized. Arrange all the information on the project so that it is always at your fingertips. The more professional you appear, the more respect (and perhaps competitive prices) you will get from the vendors and professionals you are working with.

10. Architects will try to talk you into a trim you might not like, builders will try to talk you into doing things the way they think will look best, painters will tell you the colors you or the designer have chosen, do not look right, and so on. Custom building is not for the meek. If you are easily intimidated, look for a house that is already built.

The Ten Most Important Things to Keep in Mind Before You Build

(CHAPTER 1)

Preliminary Considerations

Selecting a Location

Real Estate brokers have always chanted the phrase, "Location, location, location," emphasizing that location is the most important aspect of selecting your home. If you are unfamiliar with an area, check out www.usacitylink.com, which lists information on many towns in the United States, including local government, the history of the town, cultural events, information about the school system, location of city departments and services, community organizations, and so on. Check with local Real Estate brokers in areas you may be considering. They are generally very knowledgeable about many aspects of the community. The following are considerations to keep in mind when selecting a location.

Proximity to transportation and services. Your house should be near locations that are important to you, such as town, school, work, shopping, public transportation, and religious institutions. Nearness to family and friends is a consideration as well.

Quality of schools. A good way of evaluating the school systems is to obtain information from the National School Reporting Services. They can be contacted via the Internet at www.TheSchoolReport.com. Some Realtors subscribe to their services and have software which can provide a comparative analysis of several school districts you may be considering as well as information about private schools. You can also get information from the U.S. Department of Education by using the School

5

Locator on their Web site at www.nces.ed.gov/ccdweb/school/school.asp. All you need to enter is the zip code, county, or city and state to search for information about schools across the country. www.usacitylink.com lists public and private school information as well.

Taxes. High taxes can add an additional burden to the expense of owning a home. Find out what the local taxes are and how your future home will be assessed after it is built or remodeled. Although the current taxes may seem relatively low, you should find out what they are likely to be when your project is complete. You can obtain this information from the building office in the town or city hall in most towns.

Association and government fees for building. Check to see if you will be required to pay community association deposits to assure the community that you will abide by their construction restrictions and conditions. These will later be refunded if all conditions are met. Some associations assess fees on a monthly or yearly basis. Find out what those expenses will be before you purchase the house or property.

Building permits can be costly, so you need to call the local building permit or inspection department to determine the cost. All fee schedules are set by the municipality. In Greenwich, Connecticut, for example, a fee of $10 per $1,000 of work is stipulated on the permit. Commonly, the fee is determined by an amount per square foot.

In the case of a major renovation or new construction, the person who is responsible for doing the whole construction, usually the general contractor, is responsible for obtaining a building permit for any improvement in the house. If it is a minor renovation, the homeowner may be responsible for obtaining the permit. Typically, the tradespeople (plumber, electrician) will get their own additional permits for their portion of the job. Some areas charge for a certificate of occupancy and for re-inspections. It is helpful to be aware of these costs before starting a construction project. These can be obtained at the town or city hall. There is usually a "building" office in the local town or city hall with an officer who can give you the information on the cost of permits and zoning. They can also direct you to the correct person or persons to speak with regarding other building concerns.

Zoning Laws. Different areas have different lot requirements. If you prefer to live in a more isolated area, you may want to select an area with larger lot sizes. Smaller lot requirements can offer less-expensive lots to build on. Various regulations will determine:

The percentage of land that can be covered by a structure.
The required setback from the edge of the property.
The allowable height of the structure.

The required size of the lot.

The required minimum or maximum size of the house.

The foliage that can be cut down, if necessary.

How the land can be used: for farming, residential housing, industrial, and so on.

Water and sewer systems. It can be costly to dig a well (depending on how accessible the water is) and to put in a septic system. The size of a septic system is determined by the number of bedrooms in the house. If you are planning to expand the number of bedrooms, you should check to see if the current septic system is adequate. It could be very costly to expand the system, and there may not be enough property for the expansion.

The health departments in some locations require secondary septic systems, designed on paper, in the event the first system fails. If property is needed for expansion of the first system (if you are adding bedrooms), for the backup system (if you need to expand on the land reserved for the secondary septic site), and the required setback, you may have extreme limitations on the area you can build or expand onto. If the area you select has water and sewerage service available, but your home is not hooked up to it, find out how much it will cost to connect these services to your home. Find out-before purchasing the property-if there are any additional fees for the service or if you will incur any added expenses. Consider the cost of maintaining a septic system, which requires annual servicing.

Neighbors. To find out the demographics of any neighborhood in the country, you can log onto www.iplacepro.com and order a CD that will give you information on all aspects of the neighborhoods you might be considering: whether the community is child-or adult-oriented, whether it's a growing community, as well as

Rob Leanna

socioeconomic data. This Web site also offers information about climate, houses of worship, schools, crime, and other neighborhood facts.

Visit the area on different days and times. Do you see children? Toys left outside? Also look to see if the neighbors do a good job of maintaining their houses. Is there peeling paint? Are the lawns mowed?

Environmental restrictions. Make sure to get a lot survey before purchasing any property. Even if wetlands are shown on an existing survey, you should have a soil engineer (if possible the person who did the original one) reevaluate the property and flag the areas that are wetlands. Drawings should be made to update the wetland locations. It is possible that the wetlands are so excessive that there is little room to build the house.

The architect must also adhere to zoning setbacks (the distance that you must set back the front, rear, and sides of house on the property) and also to **wetland*** setbacks (the distance the house must be from the wetlands). Consider these conditions, along with well and septic setbacks in determining the practicality of building or renovating a house on a particular lot.

In addition, in making determinations regarding permits, the commission could hold your project up for several weeks or months if you need a **variance** (exception to the zoning regulations) or if you are in a coastal area and need a CAM (coastal area management) review to determine particular construction capabilities. It is therefore important to know what the requirements are in advance and the time necessary to get these issues in order. The cost of the soil engineer and the correction of conditions deemed necessary by the commission could be very high. These are factors that you need to know so you can determine whether you want to get involved in a particular property. If time is a tremendous factor, you may not want to get involved with a property that has potential problems requiring time to solve.

When the wetlands commission determined that there were wetlands on our property (by using past surveys), we were forced to agree never to build on that portion of the property even though we discovered there were no longer any wetlands. We had to comply with additional demands (removing fill, planting ground cover, and so on) before they would grant us our required permit to complete our house. Without prior knowledge of the ecological conditions and the local requirements, you could unknowingly waste valuable construction time as well as property you were counting on using for your construction.

Find out if you will be able to remove trees that are blocking your construction site or view. If you are considering purchasing property on a lake, for example, consider that the view might be impeded considerably by not cutting down trees. Find out what the restrictions are before purchasing the property.

The future of the area. Is your house located in a growing area? Will it be overcrowded in several years? Are there traffic problems and overcrowded schools? If there is a great deal of vacant land surrounding the site, will there be construction on that land? How much? You can get this information by asking at the local real estate office, asking people that work in the building department at the local town hall, asking people that live in the area, or by logging on to www.ipacepro.com.

Fitting into the neighborhood. The size and style of the house you are dreaming of may be totally inappropriate for the neighborhood. Having the largest house on the block is always a disadvantage because when you sell it, the price of your house might be determined by the surrounding houses, which are smaller and thus less expensive. On the other hand, you don't want to buy a house that looks disproportionately small and is overpowered by the houses that surround it.

Find out if there is a lot coverage code (the percentage of the lot that can be used to construct the house) or a floor-area ratio (the size of the house that can be built on a particular lot) in the area that you are considering building in. The town may prevent you from enlarging and renovating an old house or building a large new house. You must find out the construction limitations before you purchase the property.

Site improvements. Rock removal can be costly. If you plan to locate the house where there is rock, it will have to be blasted out before the construction of the foundation can begin. If you plan to put in a pool in the future, blasting the rock will add expense as well. Roads and utility lines are also very costly to add. Often it is necessary to build retaining walls to prevent excessive runoff. Depending on the topography of the property, this can add a huge additional expense to the cost. Lack of adequate drainage is a problem; fixing it will be expensive. The property often has to be **regraded**, and **catch basins** and **seepage drains** installed. This can also add additional expense to the project.

Topography of the lot and surrounding area. You should like the physical characteristics of the property you select as well as the surrounding area. The contour of the land you select could determine the location and design of the configuration of the house. See if it will be possible to have the landscaping sloping away from the house's foundation to avoid future drainage problems. If there are visual indications (such as with rock outcroppings) that there may be ledge, have a soil scientist do test borings of the soil. The cost of rock removal would have to be added to the cost of construction. If there is no septic system on the property, have a percolation test (perc test) done to determine how quickly water will drain from the septic system you will install. Make sure there is a flat area where you can put in a pool if you want one or swings and a play area. A pool can be put in on a sloping terrain; this is, however, a more complicated installation.

Views. See whether the property offers views that you like. Consider how you can situate the house to best take advantage of the view. Architects can be helpful in siting (or locating) the house so that you take advantage of beautiful foliage, mountains, bodies of water, and so on. They can also design the house so that you can avoid the view of neighboring houses, roads, and the like if that's what you prefer.

Local services. Find out if there is adequate fire and police protection. Is the crime rate low? Also check on whether there is garbage collection in the area. Payments to a private refuse company will add to your monthly expenses. Is there a public library? Are there parks? Is there local mail service? Find out whether you will have to pay to bring electrical, gas, or telephone lines to your property. Occasionally, telephone and electrical poles are located in areas where you've planned expansion of the house **footprint**. Find out what it will cost you to move or bury the wiring.

Covenants. Find out whether there are restrictions established by the neighborhood (homeowners associations) or the local government (architectural review board) on the style of house you can build. Some areas, for example, require you to build the house without the garage doors or skylights visible to the street. Make sure you feel comfortable with any local requirements.

Some towns have restrictions on tearing down old houses. You may need written notification to neighbors before you can do so. Check with the town in advance of your purchase.

Homeowner associations can try to restrict the style, color, or materials you use for the house. They may suggest design requirements, which can be fought. Architectural review boards are sanctioned by local governments and are enforceable by the town. Find out about these restrictions before you buy your house or property.

Easements. An easement is a right of use that an individual or government gives to a tract of land. These can be recorded or unrecorded. An unrecorded easement might involve a neighbor using a piece of your land for a driveway to access his or her house. A recorded easement could arise when a utility company needs access to a piece of property to install a pole. A recent property survey should include this information, as well as on the deed and/or the **title insurance** policy (which is required by most lenders to protect the new owner of a property against people who might later appear and say they are the rightful owners).

Getting Started Creating Your Home

Early on, you should develop a reasonable idea of what you would like your house to look like. If you are building from scratch, your only restrictions will be the configuration of the lot and the town regulations. If you are renovating an existing house, there are many more limitations. Consider how much of the existing house you want to keep. If you want to keep most of it, you will be somewhat restricted by the footprint and, for the most part, the style and layout of the existing structure.

We opted to extend the footprint, alter the roofline, and totally gut the interior of the house we bought. In our case, as is the case for those who are building from scratch, the design possibilities were almost endless.

There are many ways to prepare, even before you consider meeting with an architect, so that your house will ultimately reflect your style, not someone else's. Take the time to look through magazines, Web sites, and so on so that you can clarify for yourself what you like (and don't like) in houses. See what styles, colors, details, and materials you would like to incorporate into your home. Exploring other houses and pictures of houses will help you decide what you really like. Collect as many pictures as possible so you will be able to best convey this information to the people who will be working with you on the design.

Beginning the Process

Doing the research before you begin the design process will make your job easier and cause fewer changes later. You should be clear before you proceed as to what styles, materials, colors, and details you like and which you don't. As you begin to tear out pictures of items and details you like, you might begin to see a trend-which will be helpful in pinpointing what you would like you house to look like.

Take photographs. Take pictures of houses, or aspects of houses, that you like. If you take enough pictures of parts of houses-entrances or roofs, for example-you will eventually be clearer about the style you like. We had always noted houses in our travels, but when we began to think about building, we returned to them and took pictures. We reviewed the pictures to ascertain what it was about them that we had liked, then noted those aspects for later design decision making. Our architect incorporated several of the elements that were in our pictures, including a southwestern-type hearth and a stucco finish on the exterior.

Look through magazines. Magazines are an invaluable source of data on home styles, new materials, and new products. They also contain great decorating ideas, which may give you a better sense of the overall look you would like for your home. I found myself pawing through every house design magazine I could find. I tore out pictures and set up files to keep them in an organized way. I collected information on new products, as well as styles and examples of beautiful old and new ways to construct and decorate a house. In Appendix B, you will find an extensive list of home building and decorating magazines to make your search simpler.

Read books. New books are always coming out about construction, decorating, and landscaping. These can be found at the library; in neighborhood bookstores; in online bookstores, such as www.amazon.com, www.barnesandnoble.com, and www.chapters.indigo.ca; as well as at the many independent online bookstores, such as www.booksmith.com.

We were interested in exploring the style of the Southwest and California, and found several books about that area. We were also interested in finding some casual looks for our bathrooms that would be consistent with the design of the rest of the house. We found several excellent books with great ideas for bathrooms.

Collect brochures and product catalogs. Many product brochures are listed in the back of magazines and books. Some of the brochures are quite easy to obtain, merely by returning a product card enclosed in the magazine; for others you might have to contact the company. I found some terrific design ideas in product catalogs. When designing the powder room in my house, I found a terrific model for a carved wooden counter in a Kohler sink brochure. Although they were featuring the sink, I used the picture to build a custom counter. Company brochures can give you great design inspiration as well as familiarizing you with materials you might otherwise not know about. There are always new products coming out and it's good to stay on top of them so your new construction will be as up-to-date as possible.

If you want a specific manufacturer's catalog, you can usually locate them on the Internet by searching for their company's name and then requesting product information at their Web site.

Read newspapers. Often, you can find up-to-date construction and home design information in daily newspapers as well as the special weekend home design sections. When you see something of interest, pull it out and file it for future use.

Check out Web sites. Several excellent Web sites offer valuable information for the home builder or renovator regarding products, style options, planning, budgeting, resources, and so on. It is worth the time to scan these sites (listed in the following table) to find information relevant to your own project.

Homeportfolio	www.homeportfolio.com
Improvenet	www.improvenet.com
B4U Build	www.B4Ubuild.com
Eplans-The Houseplan Superstore	www.eplans.com
ServiceMagic	www.servicemagic.com

Go on tours. If possible, go on house and kitchen tours. You will see beautiful houses, get great ideas, and obtain sources for locating suppliers. If source information is offered by the owner or the organization sponsoring the tour, take it for future reference. If you see something that you particularly like on the tour, such as beautiful kitchen cabinets, ask the guides for information on the supplier. I went on a kitchen tour, and although I wasn't able to take photographs, I made some quick sketches and took notes on items of interest.

Talk to construction professionals. Ask the construction people you come in contact with as many questions as you can. When you're talking with brokers, architects, and builders, ask them questions. When you meet people who might be knowledgeable about home building, pick their brains. Several years ago, I was looking at a house with a broker and loved the faux painting on the walls. I asked the broker for the name of the painter and filed it away for the future. While building our house, I contacted that painter. I already knew I liked his work, and he did a superb job in our house. While interviewing builders, I often asked them which professionals or companies they liked to use for various systems and supplies. I used all of this information in comparative shopping for our house.

Get organized. Once you start collecting information, you will need an organized way of keeping all the little tidbits. There are obviously many ways of doing this. In the back of this book, is a Notebook where you can jot down all the information you will need during the project and after the project is complete. I still use my Notebook to locate contractors and suppliers now that my house is complete.

Another important organizational tool is a set of files. You will need a place to put all the pictures you've found in magazines, the brochures from suppliers, and later on contracts, manuals, and photos from people you have purchased from. It is a good idea to have a file for each category of rooms that you will be designing; you will then be able to find trends in the various pictures and compare them for specifics. You will also need files for each professional that you employ and a separate file for contracts, receipts, and manuals.

List your preferences. Develop a wish list. Some of these wishes will be fulfilled; some will have to be forfeited because of more crucial or practical considerations. We had hoped to have a sitting room outside our children's bedrooms that would serve as both a television viewing area and a computer area. In developing our usable space, the architect was not able to accommodate this particular wish. In another case, I was adamant about wanting an office off the master bedroom. I was able to get an office, but it had to be very small to fit into the scheme of the footprint.

In order to develop a usable plan, you will have to work with the architect to decide what your priorities will be. It is a good idea to bring your well-thought-out wishes and priorities to the architect, even if you think you won't be able to get everything you want.

Examine your current home. List the things that you like and dislike about your current home. Do you have lighting that feels particularly comfortable or totally inadequate? Are your kitchen and bathroom cabinets at a comfortable height? Chances are, unless you have built your current home, these cabinets are a standard height. When you are building or remodeling your home, you have the opportunity to do things the way you would like. Measure the size of various rooms in the house. Should they be larger, differently shaped? Will you be taking furniture and equipment from your old house to your new house? Measure those pieces. We loved our beautiful, old dining table so much, we designed our new kitchen around it.

Selecting a Good Team

The quality, beauty, and speed of construction will depend on the team you put together to work on the project. If all of the contractors work well together, the project will run smoothly. If just one or two of the people you choose are not team players, it can slow down your job immensely.

The following are important factors to consider when hiring the people who will work on your project:

■ Will they be people that you and the other people on your job will be able to work with? Do they have pleasant personalities? Are they respectful of other people and their schedules? Are they able to convey their ideas and listen to the ideas of others? Are they punctual?
■ Do they seem enthusiastic about getting involved with your job?
■ Do they have experience working on a job of your size?
■ Do they have good references?
■ Do they show up on time for your preliminary meetings?
■ Is it difficult for them to set up meetings?
■ Do you feel they know what they are talking about?

■ Do they talk about the work they have done with pride?

■ Will they come back to the job when problems occur?

Some of this information will come from references. If the answer to any of these questions is no, you should think carefully about hiring this person. If you decide to hire him or her anyway, be prepared for potential problems.

Sometimes even though you get good references you still shouldn't hire a particular contractor. Use your instinct and consider whether your job is similar or more difficult, more complex or messier (in the case of a building site) than the jobs the contractor has done for the reference you called.

We hired a carpenter who had done a great job on our friends' house and was highly recommended. But he was always difficult to talk to and either came late or didn't show up for prearranged preliminary meetings. We excused his behavior because we believed he would do quality work. We paid him a percentage of the project so that he could purchase the supplies and believed that if we were patient, the job would come out great.

We were very wrong. He never showed up at regularly scheduled team meetings, and none of the other people on the job could get feedback from him. He was late installing our bathroom cabinets, which held up the plumber and ultimately the painter and mason. This one person delayed our entire project. Our job was too large for him, and he was not used to working on construction sites. He ended up leaving the job unfinished and disappeared with our money.

In retrospect, we should have gotten more information about the types of projects the carpenter had worked on previously and taken clues from his earlier behavior. When he showed up late for preliminary meetings, we should have realized that he might have difficulty keeping to a work schedule as well. He was difficult to deal with in the early stages of the project, and that should have alerted us to problems in dealing with him later on. Although good craftsmanship is important, it should not overshadow other potential problems that can occur with various professionals. This error in judgment was costly and aggravating. Fortunately, we used better judgment in hiring all of the other professionals who worked on our house.

Before you begin the actual task of hiring the architect, builder, and other designers, consider carefully what your budget will be. Look at all that is involved and make sure you will be financially able to build the type of house you want, in the location you want. There are so many expenses that people just don't consider and then find themselves under tremendous financial strain after the construction has begun. Before you proceed, review all of the possible expenses you are apt to incur and then make an educated decision about whether to continue. If you do decide to go on with your project, try to find professionals who will work within your budget and make the experience a pleasant one.

CHAPTER 2

Budget Considerations

I once heard it said that if you want to know what your new house will cost, take the highest bid and the lowest bid and add them together. Unfortunately, this bit of humor very often isn't far from the truth. One of the biggest problems home builders encounter, particularly first-time home builders, is going way over budget. I have met people who were forced to sell their newly built homes because they went broke from construction expenses.

In order to complete your home without experiencing financial ruin, spend time in the early stages finding out what various construction elements cost (such as roofing, siding, fireplaces), considering how much time you will devote to selecting items for the project, and what items you will compromise on.

Your Participation in the Project

A major decision you need to make is how much of the construction you will choose to handle and how much you will turn over to the general contractor (GC). As a homeowner, you have the option of selecting those items (floorings, tiles, kitchen cabinets) and services (systems, painting) that you want to purchase on your own. It is best to make that decision before you or the architect send out the plans from which potential general contractors can create their best bid. The more complete these documents, the less likely there will be any later misunderstandings. You must let the general contractor know what these items are before the bidding process.

Those items will then be left out of the **bid**. Since general contractors approach each contract negotiation as a package, any unforeseen change upsets the project costs. This is easy to understand as you start to interview the bidders. Some GCs are more efficient in framing, others in concrete, and others may have great kitchen crews. Thus, not all general contractors will review your change in the same way.

It's unfair to the GC to suggest a major change after you accept the bid. If items are deleted from the contract after the initial bid is complete, the GC may have the legal right to withdraw the bid. It is best to be up front initially and let the GC know that some items are provisional, so that there are no surprises later. Many standard contracts contain provisions for substitutions that can carry a hefty surcharge to the owner.

The extent of your involvement will depend on the time you have to devote to the project and the extent of your budget. It takes a great deal of time to research and bid out the various materials and systems you may want to purchase on your own. Bidding out is requesting a price for a particular item or aspect of the construction project or an entire project, usually from several companies, in order to get a comparative cost. This requires a great deal of shopping, asking questions, and getting prices. Following up on products and services is also time-consuming and will be the homeowner's responsibility if he or she chooses to handle aspects of the construction. Late deliveries will be the homeowner's responsibility and may delay the completion of the house. If there is a problem with any aspect of the subcontractor's work, the homeowner will have to deal with the problem. If the GC is handling the subs, it is his responsibility and he may have more leverage in dealing with them since it is likely that the sub would like to work on future projects with the GC. The homeowner may incur the risk of charge backs from the GC if the sub doesn't follow the GCs' normal procedure. If, for example, the sub damages the dry wall, the owner may be charged with the wall repair. Additional clean-up work necessitated by the sub can be costly and will also have to be paid by the homeowner.

The positive side of this process is that you, the homeowner will become an educated consumer. As you shop around, you will get a better idea of what is available and what you want. An added advantage is the possible savings in costs and commissions.

Some GCs will require you to pay them a commission on the things you purchase on your own. Their rationale is that they are supervising and scheduling the installation and delivery of these items and that they should be compensated for their time and effort. Some GCs will only work under these conditions, although their rate of commission will vary by individual and location of the house. This percentage must be negotiated and included in the contract. Other general contractors may be willing to have you purchase certain items on your own and not insist on a commission. I was willing to pay a fee on those items I felt were essential for

the GC to supervise-such as the masonry work, where scheduling could have been a nightmare. On many other items, I did not pay a commission to the builder. You must establish this with the GC before he bids your job so there are no misunderstandings or ill feelings.

When we built our house, I opted to buy my own flooring. I had my heart set on antique, wide plank, heart pine floors for the common areas. Prior to the bidding process I discussed this with the GC and told him that I would be purchasing the wood and hiring an installer on my own. I proceeded to do extensive research in the wood industry, since I was unfamiliar with the many varieties of wood. I went to a number of lumberyards to explore my options, pricing out wood and getting quotes from installers. My GC one day presented me with a sample of new southern yellow pine wood that he had distressed, suggesting this as an alternative to antique pine. Having shopped the wood market, I knew I could get one-hundred-year-old beautiful, heart pine, naturally distressed and installed for less than the figure he quoted us for "new" wood. I did save a substantial amount of money and got what I wanted. When, later on, there was a problem with a few of the planks, the sub was not willing to come back and fix them. Again, it was my responsibility to handle the problem and find another sub to fix the problem, instead of having the builder handle this. You have to weigh all factors before deciding to take on this work.

If you plan to have the GC build the entire house, you must establish a budget for him to adhere to. You can either select every item in the house (with or without the architect) prior to the bidding process or allow the GC to select the items that fit into your budget.

When constructing our home, we took many of the interior items (flooring, tiles, lighting fixtures, and so on) out of the bid. (These are listed in Table 2-1 as "optional" items.) We kept the interior doors in the bid. It was one of the optional items that we opted to have our GC purchase for us. Having the time to price out the doors, I discovered that I could buy them for a substantially lower price than the price that was in the contract. This seemed like a wonderful opportunity to save some money. When I approached the GC with this information, he told me I still had to pay the figure in the contract. If I had kept the doors out of the contract, I would still have had to pay him for the installation of the doors, but I could have saved a substantial amount on the doors themselves.

Understand that the dollar figures given in the contract are the ones you will most likely have to adhere to. If you choose to have the GC include those items, they will most likely not be negotiable later.

If the GC finds that an item costs more than the figure in the contract, he may request that you pay the additional cost if the item is not definitively described in the contract. Discuss this issue before you sign the contract with a GC. Be clear about who handles what and who pays for what. Hire a GC that you feel will be honest with you.

Building Expenses-Estimated and Actual

Consider all the expenses of the construction, large and small. If money is no object, you might not need to be as diligent in preparing yourself for all expenses. If you are like most people, however, and have a budget, you need to find out what everything will cost and consider making some compromises early on. You must also allow for contingencies in the budget. Even if you plan extremely carefully, expenses will arise that you won't be able to predict-so be prepared.

Use tables 2-1 through 2-5 to evaluate the expenses that you can expect to have in constructing your home. You may find some that you hadn't considered. It is important to begin the process with a clear understanding of what is involved. You can then begin to consider compromising on certain items or delaying part of the project. Although it is nearly impossible to predict the exact cost of the project, careful planning will allow you to come close to your budget.

You can later fill in the actual costs-to keep a running record of the final cost of the house.

Table 2-1 Basic Construction Expenses

Basic Building Costs	Quantity	Estimated Cost	Actual Cost
General conditions*			
Site work			
Demolition (if renovating)			
Foundation			
Concrete			
Masonry			
Structural steel			
Rough framing			

Basic Building Costs	Quantity	Estimated Cost	Actual Cost
Exterior architectural woodwork			
Interior architectural woodwork			
Roofing & gutters			
Insulation			
Mill work			
Siding			
Exterior doors and garage			
Windows			
Drywall			
HVAC system			
Electrical work			
Skylights			
Staircase & railings			
Paving			
Well			
Septic			
Plumbing			
Surveys			
Permits			

*General conditions include costs associated with operating a job and preparing the site. Examples of these expenses are temporary facilities (office, telephone, heat, toilets, and so on), refuse removal (big containers), soil testing, cost of a supervisor, silk fencing, and so on. These are expenses that do not directly affect the construction of the structure.

Table 2-2 Optional Items (Which the Builder May or May Not Purchase)

Optional Items	Quantity	Estimated Cost	Actual Cost
Kitchen cabinets			
Installation			
Appliances			
Refrigerator			
Stove			
Microwave			
Dishwasher			
Trash compactor			
Garbage disposal			
Instant hot water			
Range hood			
Washer			

Optional Items	Quantity	Estimated Cost	Actual Cost
Dryer			
Installation			
Lighting fixtures			
Installation			
Hardware			
Floorings			
Kitchen			
Installation			
Bathrooms			
Installation			
Common areas			
Installation			
Bedrooms			
Installation			
Mud room			
Installation			
Playroom			
Installation			
Den			
Installation			
Other			
Installation			
Other			
Installation			
Bathroom fixtures			
Toilets			
Sinks			
Showers			
Bathtubs			
Spas			
Installation			
Hardware			
Mirrors			
Tile			
Bathroom 1			
Installation			
Bathroom 2			
Installation			

Optional Items	Quantity	Estimated Cost	Actual Cost
Bathroom 3			
Installation			
Bathroom 4			
Installation			
Bathroom 5			
Installation			
Bathroom accessories			
Stone counter tops			
Stone decking(bath)			
Cabinetry			
Interior doors			
Installation			
Stairs and railings			
Installation			
Interior painting			
Trim and stain			
Interior decorations			
Fireplaces			
Exterior Expenses			
Landscaping			
Interior decorations			
Exterior painting			
Trim and stain			
Backup generator			
Installation			
Site improvements			
Site lighting			
Light fixtures			
Installation			
Paving			
Material			
Installation			
Curbing			
Walks			
Planting			
Plants			
Labor			
Finish grading			

Optional Items	Quantity	Estimated Cost	Actual Cost
Seeding			
Pool decking			
Material			
Installation			
Pool			
Entertainment decking			
Drainage system			
Pest control			

Table 2-5a Furnishings

	Playroom	Bedroom 1	Bedroom 2
Window treatments			
Flooring			
Built-ins			
Furniture			
Fabric			
Accessories			
Hardware			
Wall treatment			
Linen & pillows			
Light fixtures & lamps			

Table 2-5b Furnishings - Continued

	Living Room	Dining Room	Kitchen	Den
Window treatments				
Flooring				
Built-ins				
Furniture				
Fabric				
Accessories				
Hardware				
Wall treatment				
Linen & pillows				
Light fixtures & lamps				

Home!
My very heart's contentment lies
Within thy walls

Home by Nellie Womack Hines from Poems that Touch the Heart

Bedroom 3	Bedroom 4	Bedroom 5	Optional

Media Room	Office	Gym	Optional

Table 2-3 Systems Expenses*

Systems	Estimated Cost	Actual Cost
Water-conditioning		
Lighting		
Security		
Telephone		
Audiovisual		
Central vacuum		

* See Chapter 9 for a discussion of systems.

Table 2-4 Professional Expenses

Additional Expenses	Estimated Cost	Actual Cost
Architect		
Structural engineer		
Landscape professional		
Water specialist		
Interior designer		
Surveyor		
Soil specialist		
Attorney		

Hidden Costs

When trying to estimate the cost of your home, always include the cost of installation. People often think these will be insignificant expenses, but they can add up to be major ones. The floor tile that we installed in our kitchen was costly in itself. Because the tile was very thick, we had to lower the floor to accommodate the tile. We never bothered to ask about the cost of installation, and it ended up being a major added expense that we didn't anticipate. The tile had to be washed several times, mud laid, and given several coats of sealer. The total cost of the floor ended up being exorbitant, but we had no idea what we were getting into when we bought it. If we'd have known what this floor would ultimately cost, we would have used a different material. Always ask about the cost of installation.

Delivery charges are another hidden cost. When added to the various items purchased, delivery charges will be a major expense. You will need to retain the services of a consolidator in order to receive wholesale furnishings and supplies (such as tile) because commercial companies will not deliver to private homes. A consolidator is employed to receive all items, check on the merchandise, and then deliver the shipments to the home. They use various methods of charging the consumer: by the pound, by the mile, and/or by the time they have to store the merchandise between deliveries.

If you are renovating your home and will be adding bedrooms, you may be faced with enlarging the septic system (if you are not on the city system). You must find out the capacity of your current system and what the cost will be to put in a new one if necessary.

Look on the Internet and shop the stores to get an idea of what various items cost. Use preliminary costs you receive from the builders and add in all the additional costs listed in the previous tables, as well as some of the potential hidden costs. Consider alternative size plans and alternative items that might bring the cost of the construction within your budget. Try to account for the fact that there will be additional costs that you had not planned for.

Check the Improvenet web site (www.improvenet.com). This site offers a service, in addition to others that will be mentioned in Chapter 3, in which estimators evaluate the cost of your pending project by zip code.

Make a decision to renovate or build with an educated understanding of what will be involved. Building a house can be a joyous experience, but it can also be a painful one-if it empties your bank account, puts undue pressure on you and alters your lifestyle, preventing you from doing all the other things you enjoy. Consider the financial aspect of the project carefully before proceeding.

Notes

Architects

ARCHITECTS

What Architects Do

Architects can help you complete the construction of the house in many ways. Most architects are capable of helping with the following tasks:

1. Conceptualizing the project.
2. Evaluating and selecting a site.
3. Helping you decide whether to renovate or rebuild.
4. Executing the design of the house or redesigning what exists of the space that you want to renovate.
5. Siting the house properly to take the best possible advantage of views and orientation of the sun.
6. Planning where the approach or road entering the house will be.
7. Developing a program that accommodates the residents' lifestyles, takes the best advantage of the space, and creates a comfortable relationship between rooms.
8. Selecting construction materials and details.
9. Developing construction drawings.
10. Helping select and negotiate with a builder.
11. Determining potential problems with construction and maintaining quality control while the house is being built.
12. Reviewing the builder's bills and evaluating whether the items being charged are satisfactory.
13. Evaluating the completed house against the contract requirements.

Each construction situation is different. The owner and architect should decide ahead of time to what extent the architect will be involved in the project.

Not everyone will opt to employ an architect. Each state has its own rules regarding the need to submit architect's plans to the town or city and the square footage for which plans are required. The state of Connecticut, for example, requires architectural plans for all projects over 5,000 square feet. In some states, either an architect or an engineer can submit the plans.

How to Locate an Architect

There are many ways to find an architect. It is important, however, to explore as many means as possible so that you will find an architect that both meets your design needs and makes the experience pleasant. The architect we selected designed a beautiful house, made the project more enjoyable, and was even helpful in dealing with other professionals hired to work on the project. Although it is not necessarily the role of the architect, ours served as our "team" leader-working with the builder, interior designer, lighting specialist, and at times subcontractors and suppliers. His easy personality made him well suited for smoothing out minor disputes when they occurred. The architect can be an important factor in the ultimate beauty and practicality of your home, as well as your personal sanity during the process. Here are four ways to find an architect:

1. **Get referrals.** The best way to locate an architect is by referrals from relatives and friends. They can give you important information about an architect's previous projects or personal integrity. Other associated professionals, such as real estate brokers and interior designers, can be a good source of information as well. If you know people related to the construction field, such as brokers, interior designers, suppliers, or lighting specialists, they can often recommend architects they have worked with and have been impressed with.

2. **Scan architectural, as well as, local magazines for houses that you like.** If the architect isn't listed in the credits, contact the magazine for this information.

3. **Contact the local office of the American Institute of Architects (AIA).** If you are unable to find the local chapter in the phone book, you can contact the central office at 1735 New York Ave. NW, Washington, DC 20006-5292, phone them at 202-626-7300, or visit their Web site at www.aia.org. The AIA will supply you with the names of all the architects in your area who have indicated that they design the type of project you are inquiring about-most likely a single-family residence. Their Web site also has a link to local chapters across the country. A large percentage of the working architects in the country do belong to the AIA, so this is an excellent way to find an architect.

4. **Check the Improvenet web site (www.improvenet.com) and the ServiceMagic**

web site (www.servicemagic.com). These sites offer a free service, identifying architects (as well as contractors and designers) in requested locations. Both companies have their own screening methods, which are supposed to eliminate companies with poor legal and credit records. Consumers should still check references, however. These sites also offer valuable information on various materials, contracts, design planning, and so on.

We found our architect in a more unusual manner. While we were looking at a custom-built-homes development, we met an architect who was working in the construction office for another client. We chatted briefly about design and a house that we had considered building. He asked if he could send literature about his office. When he made a follow-up call several weeks later, we told him we hadn't found any suitable property to build on or houses that we wanted to renovate.

Soon after, he put us in contact with a realtor who helped us find the property that we eventually purchased. He also helped us make the decision to purchase the house by helping evaluate its potential for renovation. Although we later interviewed other architects, Steve was a clear choice, having met the criteria discussed in the next section.

How to Select an Architect

You will spend a great deal of time with the architect, so try to find someone you will enjoy working with. Building or remodeling a house is an expensive project; it should be an enjoyable one. During or after your meeting with each architect, enter notes in the Notebook at the back of this book so that you will later be able to evaluate each one without totally depending on your memory. Be sure to answer the following questions as you shop for an architect:

1. **Is there good chemistry between you and the architect?** The design process will be so much more pleasant if you have a good relationship with the architect. There should be a commonality of design sense as well as a respect for each other's opinions.

2. **Is the architect a good listener?** It is extremely frustrating to give a lot of information to a person and then find out it was a waste of time. Before we found Steve, my husband and I had begun working on another project with another architect. We met with him for several hours, then waited several weeks to receive the proposed plans. The plan we received had no relationship to what we had spent hours describing to him. From the disparity, we

could only assume that he had pulled an old plan out of the drawer and offered it to us. When we complained, he said, "This time I'm really going to listen to you." Three weeks later, we received the second plan, which was not much better than the first. This architect obviously wasn't a good listener.

3. **Has the architect provided you with a list of references?**
   Call these people and ask them the following questions:
   - Were you happy working with this architect?
   - Did you feel that this architect was listening to you when you were describing your needs?
   - Did the architect work in an organized and professional manner?
   - Did the architect ultimately do the drawings for your house himself?
   - Did you encounter any problems with the architect or his or her plans?
   - Were the plans technically correct, so that the builder was able to construct a house with them?
   - Did you need to make any changes in the architect's design?
   - Did you need many revisions?
   - Did the architect execute plans that were within your budget?
   - Did the architect help you select materials to be used in the house? Were you happy with those selections?
   - Were there any additional fees after the initial contract? Were the fees fair?
   - Was the architect available when there were problems or when there were scheduled meetings?
   - Was the architect responsive to problems brought out by other people working on your project?
   - Was the architect helpful in finding and selecting a builder?
   - Did the architect work well with the builder?
   - Would you hire this architect again?
   - Would you recommend this architect?

4. **Is the architect able to relate to other people who will be working on your project?** Does he communicate well? He will have to work with the general contractor, subcontractors, and suppliers. It will be a more pleasant experience if he works well with all of the other people you bring to the project. It is common to have weekly, bi-monthly, or some regularly scheduled meetings before and during the construction of the house. These will go more smoothly and be more productive if the architect, as well as the other team members, communicate well.

5. **Is the architect creative?** Will the architect make valid contributions to the

design of the project? Do you have confidence in his or her judgment and respect his or her opinions?

6. **Is the architect comfortable discussing money?** These discussions will come up throughout the project, regarding the architect's payments, payment to other people on the project, and your budget for various items and services that will be necessary to complete the house. You should feel that the architect is comfortable in dealing with money issues with you as well as with the other people on the team.

7. **Are you comfortable with the architect's fees?** Do the fees fit your budget? Be sure that you are clear what you will be paying for.

8. **Do you feel comfortable with the terms of the architect's contract?** Find out what the terms will be and make sure they are consistent with your expectations. When will payments be required? How many plans will be executed? The contract that many architects use is the AIA document B141. This contract is fine as long as you feel that your interests are met.

9. **Is the architect knowledgeable about local codes and regulations?** These can vary from town to town, so the architect must be current on zoning codes and building regulations for the location where you plan to build. When possible, it is preferable to work with someone who is already familiar with these.

10. **Will the architect be available for on-site consultations?** These may include regular meetings or informal consultations. If the architect works locally, it may be easier to schedule meetings and/or have him or her available for questions or problems that may arise.

11. **Does the architect have problems with other professionals reviewing the plans?** Will the architect be willing to alter the plans in accordance with the recommendations of other professionals on the project? Our interior designer and kitchen specialists had very valid ideas for changing the original plans. Our architect didn't always agree with the changes, but he was adaptable, and when he saw we were determined to make the changes, he made them willingly.

12. **Does your architect use a computer program to design houses?** This allows you to "walk through" the entire house before it is built. Several professionals working on the same project can share these programs. If everyone is using the same program, it can save the home builder a great deal of money. We had an interior designer in Seattle, Washington, who did most of her work on the CAD system. Because our architect worked manually on the plans, the interior designer had to enter all the dimensions into her computer in order to develop the design plans. We had to pay for the time it took her to enter this information.

13. **Does the architect have the technical ability to execute plans, whichever method he or she uses?** It is important that the plans can easily be read by the

other people working on the project and that the plans are technically correct.

14. **Does the architect have the time to devote to your project?** Find out if she or he is working on many other projects that will delay the completion of your project. Will the architect be available if problems occur and he or she is needed on site? Will the architect take your phone calls and not be too busy to talk with you on a timely basis?

15. **If the firm you are talking to has several architects, who will be working on your project?** Will your project be executed by a senior partner or be handed to a more junior person? Are you satisfied with this person's level of experience? Do you feel this person understands what you are trying to achieve? Who will be your contact person? Who will be supervising the construction?

16. **What is the architect's level of education and experience?** Where did this architect go to school? What types of projects has the architect worked on in the past? Has he or she ever worked on a project as large (or small) as yours?

17. **Does the architect carry professional liability insurance-called errors and omissions insurance?** This protects clients against blatant errors that can have long-lasting repercussions after the house is complete.

18. **Is the architect able to include minimal requirements for all mechanical items in the house, as well as materials to be used?** Architects are not always knowledgeable in these areas, but it is important to seek one out that can specify minimum requirements for items, even if he or she doesn't know all the brand names. In the selection of mechanicals and materials, as little as possible should be left up to the builder.

Initial Meetings with Several Architects

Before making your final choice, you need to set up a formal consultation with one or several architects. You should check in advance to see if there will be a fee. In the initial meeting, you should discuss the site, your vision of your home, and your basic requirements. This is an opportunity to see the architect's office, look at the portfolio of houses he or she has designed, and observe his or her personal style and manner.

Be prepared to ask a lot of questions. You want to know how knowledgeable he is about the style and size house you have in mind, his time schedule, his availability to work on your project, his fees, and so on. Evaluate his talent and creativity. You generally want to get to know him and see if he is someone you feel comfortable working with. You should share a design and style sense. The architect should also be evaluating you to see if he feels comfortable with you, comfortable with the proposed plan and feels he can do a good job. You will be spending a great deal of time with this person, developing your project; if you have positive feelings about each other it should be an enjoyable experience.

While looking through the architect's portfolio, see if you like the houses she has designed. Look at the detail work. If there are aspects of the house you don't like, question her about it. We didn't like a particular deck that our architect had put on a house, and we asked him about it. He told us that he had tried to discourage the client from building that particular porch, but the client had insisted on it. This comment said to us that the architect understood that it was the client's house, and he was adaptable to their wishes. If possible, ask the architect if you can visit one or two of the homes she has worked on. This will give you the opportunity to see the quality of her designs, as well as the quality of work of a potential builder.

Just because the architect doesn't show you any houses she has done in the style that you are considering doesn't mean she is incapable of doing so. Ask her if she has any interest in working in this style. We did not see any homes in our architect's portfolio that indicated he was familiar with the Mediterranean style. When we asked about his knowledge of this style, he brought out several books about it and seemed genuinely excited about the prospect of designing in this style.

If you are dealing with a large architectural company, you will also want to know who will be working on your project. Meet the person who will be working on your account and see how you feel about his or her competence, creativity, and personality. We met several excellent architects, but the overriding factor in selecting our architect was that he was local. We felt he had talent, was a good listener, had good references, would be easy to work with, and as a local architect, would be tuned in to the local building requirements. With this professional, as with all of the others who work with you on your home, there are bound to be problems sometime down the road. If you start out liking your architect, it will be a lot easier to work through the problems.

Optional Areas of Design for Architects

Architects have expertise in different areas. The architect should tell you which areas he feels competent designing and what input he will have in the total plan. Find out if he has the ability and experience to design the kitchen, the landscape, the lighting, and so on. Discuss those areas that the architect will not be directly responsible for designing. You should try to find other professionals who will coordinate with the architect on those items before the final drawings are complete.

Consider the following:

1. **If your architect does not have the expertise to design a lighting plan, con-**

sult a lighting specialist before the plans go out to bid. We sent out our initial bid with the architect's lighting plan, which we modified later, after having it reviewed by a lighting specialist. This increased the cost for our electrician substantially. It is better to have the correct items in the bid, not put them there after the bid is accepted. Those prices that you get after the bid is accepted will not be competitively established and will almost always be higher.

2. **You should consider including the landscape design or a part of the landscape design as part of the architect's responsibility, if you feel he or she is capable.** The architect knows the property and its overall design and may be the best qualified to design the retaining walls, recontouring of the property, drainage, patios, terraces, pool area, outside lighting, sprinkler system, backup generator, outside audio equipment, outside electrical needs, telephone wiring, and roads. You should look at work the architect has already done in this area if you are considering having him or her be responsible for it. If the architect doesn't feel comfortable with this area of design or if you prefer he or she doesn't work on this area of your project, you should bring in a landscape professional to develop plans before the bidding is sent out to contractors. Whomever you consider hiring to design the exterior areas of the house should document their recommendations on paper. Get bids on all aspects of the exterior while you are in the bidding stage. You will save a tremendous amount of money if the builder does some of this work rather than having to bid the work out later. Often, people delay this part of their project because they are overwhelmed with the expenses of completing the house. The expense will usually be greater later on.

   You can have this part of the project bid by specialists other than the builder. It is easier to have the outside lighting done, however, while the electrician is installing the inside lighting. It will be less costly if you get prices this way, rather than piecemeal. While considering the landscape plan, it is a good idea to plan the placement of the outside spigots or water sources; it is sometimes very difficult to bring water lines to the outside after the project is completed. These kinds of items should be included in the architectural design.

3. **Does the architect have the expertise to design the kitchen and the cabinetry?** If you are working with an architect who has demonstrated that she is particularly proficient in this area, you may want to have her do these designs for you. However, in most cases, I would suggest having kitchen specialists design the kitchen and cabinets. This is a very important area of the house and one that requires a particular expertise. The kitchen in particular must be functional as well as attractive. There are many excellent and qualified people in this area. In most circumstances, I would suggest getting independent bids from specialists in this area to do this work. Find out, how-

ever, who will install the appliances. Often, kitchen specialists will include this service. If you find they won't, make sure the appliance installation is included in your bid with the builder.

What Architects Would Like You to Know

When I spoke with architects, they had the following suggestions for making the client/architect relationship run more smoothly. These suggestions will also expedite the project and make it a more pleasant experience for you.

1. **Architects can only design for two people when they agree on what they want.** Couples should agree on what they want before meeting with the architect. If a couple comes to an architect with two sets of ideas, one of the people will not be happy with the ultimate design. Do not assume that the architect will act as a psychologist-give the architect one clear design agenda.

2. **Architects would like clients to communicate what they want as clearly as possible.** They would like clients to be prepared to verbalize and illustrate what they want in the early stages of the design phase. This can be achieved by sharing the items in your files (see Chapter 1), such as photographs of houses you like, pictures from magazines, and so on.

3. **Architects would like clients who are knowledgeable about fees.** When clients are comparing the fees of several architects, they should be sure they are comparing like services. Clients have to be clear on the services of each architect to make a fair comparison. For example, will the architect design the plans and then leave the project, or will the architect be attending regular meetings and helping to supervise the project?

4. **Architects would like clients to understand the importance of spending adequate time on the design stage.** Steven Mueller, the architect on our project, told us, "Design slow; build fast." Spend the time getting the design and budget as close to perfect as you can and then spare no time in getting the project built. If the project is rushed into construction, the cost for changes and revisions could be enormous.

Procedures for Working with Architects

You have already had a preliminary meeting with the architect, both of you have decided that you want to work together and have negotiated a contract. Now it is time to begin planning your "castle". The procedure is outlined below.

1. **You and the architect should have a working meeting.** After you have selected the architect and agreed on terms, you should have an intensive working meeting. Bring all of your magazine clippings and photographs, and any
books that will help to describe what you want. The better you are able to
describe your vision, the closer the architect will be able to come to creating
that design. If possible, you should describe not only the rooms you want,
but also the flow of the rooms into each other. It can be helpful to look
through books of architectural plans to find the aspects (exterior look, flow
of rooms, types of rooms, and so on) that you like.

You will also want to give the architect an idea of the size you would like
the rooms to be. You should have already measured the rooms in your current residence, so that you have a visual idea of particular spatial areas. If the
dining room in your current house is 12 feet by 12 feet, you can tell the architect that this is too small and needs to be substantially larger, less square,
and so on. Looking at model homes and prepared plans can be helpful in deciding which rooms you would like to include in your plan and what relationship you would like them to have to other rooms.

You need to consider your lifestyle and decide what the ideal home would
be for you. You will probably not be able to have everything you want, unless you have an unlimited budget, but you can have a great deal of what you
want if your architect is creative with the available space.

At this time, the architect should let you know if your desires are inconsistent with your budget. It is a waste of time for the architect to begin plans
that he knows you will never be able to afford to build. Discuss priorities and
compromises early on. For example, would you be happy with less space if
you could have a tile roof? By the end of the meeting, the architect should
have a good idea of what you are looking for in terms of:

- Style.
- Space.
- Number of rooms.
- Spatial relationship of the rooms.
- Details that you like: moldings, types of materials, and so on.
- Number of closets.
- Views you hope to take advantage of.
- Any other information you can give.

The more information you communicate with the architect (both verbally and
with pictures), the quicker the architect will be able to arrive at a design resolution
that you'll be happy with.

2. **The architect will then begin to formulate a "program" for the client.** This program will outline all the components, material elements, and special features that the client has communicated. You will receive a list of the rooms that will be designed (all of the rooms in the case of a new house), the approximate size they will be, the number of closets they will have, how they will relate to other rooms in the house, the flow of the rooms into each other, and important details that you have conveyed to the architect about the overall look of the house.

   Depending on the architect, this process should take two to three weeks. When you receive the program, you will know how well the architect was listening to you. You should let the architect know if there are any errors. The architect should send you a revised program and then you will be ready to proceed to the next phase. Select an architect who will give you a outlined program before doing the actual layout. If your architect skips this procedure, he or she will surely waste time later with extra redrawing.

3. **The architect will do rough drawings or computer renderings to show you the general layout of the house and its position on the site.** By the time the architect begins these preliminary schematic drawings, she or he should have an excellent idea of what you are hoping to achieve. In a renovation, the architect will go out to the site at this time and begin to document the condition of the property. This includes survey acquisition, collection of data, and a photographic study.

If you are not happy with this first plan, you will discuss alternatives. The architect will have to modify the plan until you can agree on a plan that meets your needs. The architect will show you preliminary drawings and might show you a three-dimensional rendering or stake out the site so that you can visualize the important features of the house.

4. **The architect will seek construction estimates on the preliminary plan with several builders that you might potentially employ.** When the initial design phase is completed and you have approved the design, the architect will have this plan estimated by builders who you would like to later have bid on your project. Sending the initial plan out for estimates will give you a good sense of whether the plan will fit into your budget. If you have been working with an experienced architect, she or he should have developed a plan that is close to your stated budget or informed you earlier if your expectations were unrealistic. A compromise plan should then have been developed.

   Local square footage costs, for major renovation and new construction, can be applied as a quick reference point for preliminary purposes. (These footage costs will vary in different parts of the country.) The architect has an obligation to let the owners know early on if the budget is unrealistic for their expectations. This may require owners to modify their expectations or request that the architect provide a design response to their program to establish a true preliminary estimate of construction costs. At that point, qualitative and quantitative changes can be applied to modify the design so that it will meet the budget requirements. If the estimates all come back much too high, you will have to begin the design phase again, with a plan that is perhaps more of a compromise, but realistic.

5. **The architect should discuss a variety of components (style, interior and exterior materials, color, and so on) with the client while he or she is designing the house.** Many decisions have to be made regarding the construction of your house. The architect should suggest various alternatives before the final drawings are complete. Specifications for interior and exterior windows and doors, for example, should be made by the time the final documents are complete. The type and color of the roofing and siding should be discussed, as well as the trim.

6. **The architects should discuss amenities you will want to consider.** The architect can help you select amenities that will affect the long-term value of your home. You might want to wire the house, for example, for a lighting system. If you should opt to sell your home in the near future, this feature could enhance its value. You may want to consider options that protect your home against the elements. There are window films that protect your furniture from ultraviolet rays and filtration systems that remove the minerals from

the water. The architect should be familiar with the newest technologies and help you to explore the ones that may be important for you.

7. **The architect will then begin to develop construction documents.** When you and the architect feel that the plan meets the design intent and works for the site and your budget, it is time for the architect to begin working on the construction documents. These include detailed or working drawings (which show the spaces in the correct proportions and include details) and specifications (also called specs).

The drawing should show the following:
- Site plan.
- Dimensioned floor plans.
- **Elevations.**
- Foundation plans.
- Structural framing plans.
- Roof plans.
- Plumbing plans.
- Electrical/lighting plans.
- Mechanical systems (HVAC).
- Details/sections of complicated elements.
- **Renderings.**

These drawings will be used in the following ways:
- To bid the house with the builder.
- To get the construction permits.
- To construct the house.

Be sure the specs indicate which products (materials, brands, sizes of materials, type of warranty, manufacturer, quality, and so on) should be used and any other relevant information about them. This should include minimal construction requirements, such as the width of the wood used and details of the job site. Be sure that such things as brand and length of warranty are specified for mechanical items. (A water heater, for example, should be selected, that carries a 10-year warranty.) If these types of items are left up to the contractor, he might select a less expensive model with a three-year warranty in order to cut corners. The architect should be as specific as possible.

At this point, the architect will often consult with a structural engineer to confirm what will be required to make the house structurally sound. The engineer will often review the documents when they are complete to make sure that everything has been done to protect the homeowners. Often the engineer will then take responsibility for this part of the project. Be aware in advance that there may be an additional cost for this consultation. The architect may incorporate this expense into his price or may tell you that this will be a separate cost. Make sure that an engineer will be consulted, unless the architectural firm you employ has its own engineer on staff.

This phase, depending on the particular architect you are working with, may be very time-consuming. You can, however, use this time to put together interior components, interview other possible team members, and call their references. In the initial meeting with the architect, she or he should have supplied you with a time schedule, so you can anticipate what to expect. Be sure that the architect includes the practical, but often forgotten, details of the house, such as where the garbage will be stored for pickup and where the wood for the fireplace (if there is one) will be kept.

8. **Final changes should be made in the construction documents.** This is the best time to make any changes. If you have been shopping around for products and speaking with other professionals associated with your project, you might want to make some alterations in the plan. After having shopped for bathroom fixtures, I discovered that I needed to move a door in one of the bathrooms in order to accommodate a bathtub. After developing kitchen plans with several specialists, I discovered that I had to make several changes in the initial plan to accommodate everything I hoped to fit into the kitchen. I ended up eliminating a window and a door.

It is much less expensive to make revisions such as these on paper than in the field. Review the electrical plan with the architect or lighting specialist to be sure you have included enough telephone jacks and outlets, and that they are in the proper locations. Anticipate that you will need more computer and fax lines in the future. Consider including outside lighting and phone jacks in the plan. While the GC will be digging around the outside, it will be easier to lay **conduits** for future lighting. It is also wise to review the plumbing plan for future sinks and for refrigerators with icemakers in a wet bar. It is relatively simple to include these in the **rough-in** stage but much more complicated when the sheetrock has been installed. If you are planning window treatments, consult a window specialist. Shutters, for example, require an alternate form of trim. This can be anticipated in the design stages.

9. **You and the architect should select several builders to competitively bid the job of constructing your house.** The architect can be helpful in recommending builders that he or she has worked with in the past. Consider using some of the builders that gave you preliminary estimates. During the documentation development stage, you should have been looking around for other

builders you might be interested in. Calling for references on the builders could clarify your decision. You should visit projects completed or under construction by each contractor to see the quality of their work.

10. **Four bids will give you a good selection to choose from.** When you send out the bids, I suggest including a reasonable completion date for their return. Speak with the builders before you send them the documents to be sure they can comply with the date. If they cannot, this may be an indication that they are too busy to take on the project or are not interested in it. During this phase, the architect should be starting to get approvals from the building department as well as environment and health departments, and building permits from the town or city.

11. **The architect will help in the selection and negotiation with the builders.** Not all of the bids will arrive in the same format. Although the architect will probably be specific about what prices he or she will require, broken down in a specific way (demolition, concrete, rough carpentry, and so on), the builder will often change the format when putting in a bid. The architect should help you understand the various formats given by the various builders. He or she should discuss the attributes of each builder to help you make a decision. You should then meet with all of the builders that have bid the project (with or without the architect present) to get final answers to any questions you have. The owners will have to make the final decision, but relevant information from the architect will be very helpful. It is then time to negotiate with the builder, or general contractor you have selected. This will be discussed further in Chapter 4.

12. **The architect should be involved with the project while the house is being constructed or renovated (construction observation).** The architect should attend regular meetings with the owner and general contractor so that questions can be answered about any conditions that are not clear on the drawings and to make sure that the construction is going according to plan. Often the architect is asked to approve all of the general contractor's bills so the owners feel secure that all work that is being billed for is actually complete and that the materials that they are being billed for were in the original specs.

The Schedule

It is helpful to know in advance approximately how long it will be before construction can actually begin. The following table suggests possible times for various phases of design development and contractor selection. Being informed will avoid frustration. You can then use the time effectively to collect information on various aspects of the house, such as interior design.

Table 3-1 indicates the time schedule you should expect your architect to adhere to.

Table 3-1 Time Schedule	
Suggested Times	Your Architect's Plan
Existing conditions	2-4 weeks
Design development	4-6 weeks
Preliminary estimate	2-3 weeks
Second initial plan	4-6 weeks
Preliminary estimate (optional)	2-3 weeks
Construction documentation	4-8 weeks
Bidding process	2-3 weeks
Selecting a contractor	1-2 weeks

The schedule will vary depending on how quickly the architect works, how quickly the contractors respond to the bid, and how quickly you are able to make decisions. You can speed up the entire construction process by shopping around for tile, flooring, bathroom fixtures, and whatever items you have chosen to purchase independently while the architect is working on the plans. It is also a good time to begin interviewing and hiring any other professionals you are considering bringing in on the job-landscape architects, interior designers, and so on-so that you will be able to put together a team quickly.

Doing all of this preliminary work gives you the opportunity to better coordinate the house, hasten the building process, and make changes in the architectural plans before they are complete. If items are selected, and the architectural plans are altered early, it cuts down on the expense of change orders with the contractor later on.

We consulted with a lighting specialist after we selected a contractor. We decided on a number of additional fixtures, which added a large cost to the electrical plan. It would have cost us far less if these fixtures had been included in the initial bid. We are grateful that we didn't make a great many of these errors, but we did make enough to teach us a very important lesson: any late changes cost more than they would in the initial plan, so try very hard to plan ahead. Use the time, during which the architect is completing the documents, to do your own research.

The Contract

Be sure to include these conditions in the contract:

1. **A program of requirements from the architect.** This is generally done in

outline form and lists all the rooms that you want, the flow of the rooms, what is needed in each room, and what the style will be inside and outside. When the program is complete, if it corresponds to what you have described to the architect, you will know he has been listening to you and you are on the right track. If the list is not even close to what you described, you could have a serious problem down the road and should reconsider whether you want to use the architect's services at all. An architect may be incredibly creative, but if he or she cannot listen and design the house that you want, you should find an architect who can.

2. **An adequate number of plans (I suggest three) that meet the criteria of budget and requirements that you and the architect have already agreed on.** An experienced architect should be able to design a plan that meets the clients' program, style, and budget. Many clients prefer to find out what their "dream house" will cost before they begin altering their ideal. In this case, they need to be prepared to pay additional architectural fees (and perhaps waste valuable time) for what may be extravagant, overly expensive designs.

   If you are like most people and do not have unlimited funds and are on a tight schedule, you must tell the architect that you want to be alerted early on if the program and budget are inconsistent, even before a **schematic** drawing is done. The program should then be altered quantitatively (by removing square footage, taking out a fireplace) or qualitatively (changing the materials, changing the quality of windows) to meet your needs. At that point, you will have to decide if you are willing to sacrifice aspects of your original concept so that the plan will work within your budget.

   If the architect presents you with the predetermined two or three plans and they do not meet the established criteria (for budget and program), the architect should then be obligated to do additional plans at no added cost. People often get the false impression that the architect will continue designing plans until the client is happy with one; do not expect this will happen unless you have agreed on parameters for a valid plan in the contract.

3. **Clearly state what parts of the plan the architect will be responsible for.** The previous section contains an extensive discussion of some of those areas.

4. **The number of hours or visits the architect will make to the construction site.** You should have weekly or semimonthly meetings with the general contractor, subcontractors, and other professionals working on the project, in order to coordinate all those working on your house. The architect should be present at these meetings to answer questions and watch over the project, to see that construction is going the way it's supposed to, and to check that the quality of work is being maintained. Know in advance what the architect will charge for these on-site meetings. Before you sign the contract with the

architect, be sure you understand what services are covered and what additional fees you will be required to pay.

How Architects Charge for their Services

Fees will depend on the extent you want the architect to get involved in your project and how large the project is. Define the architect's responsibilities and make sure they are clearly stated in the contract. This will help prevent surprise charges after the construction has begun. Fees are negotiable, so the best time to make your arrangements with the architect is before you have hired him or her. Whatever deal you make you will have to live with, so spend time with the contract and be sure you are happy with it before you sign your name. Architects charge for their services in three ways:

1. **Fixed fees for different phases of construction.** This type of contract breaks down the payments so that each phase (design, construction documentation, construction, observation) are listed and given a price. With this type of contract, you know what you have to pay and at what phase of the project. You can budget for architectural fees before you even begin. If necessary, you can discontinue the relationship with the architect at any phase and know exactly what you owe.
2. **A percentage (an average of 10% to 15%) of the construction costs.** Architects sometimes work on a percentage basis because they don't know how large the project will be when they sign a contract with the client. This payment method could encourage an architect to choose, or influence you to choose, high bids on the construction of your project.
3. **An hourly rate.** This method of payment should be used when an architect is a consultant on a project or will be involved in just a small project, such as remodeling a bathroom. It would not be a reasonable method of payment for an architect involved in a large project.

Architect/Builder Teams

Sometimes, you have the option of employing a builder/architect team. I don't believe this is a good choice for the home builder. Most often, in this situation you are required to use the architect that the builder has chosen. The selected architect may not meet the criteria discussed earlier in the chapter: experience with your type of project, excellent references, easy to work with, a good listener, and so on. You do not have an opportunity to competitively bid this project. You can never be sure that you are getting the best house for your money.

If, however, the builder/architect team is building several homes, they may be getting excellent prices from the subcontractors and suppliers. In this case, it might be worthwhile for you to get involved in this kind of purchase. You will definitely not have the control you would have had if you put the project out to bid, but it might work out financially and emotionally in your favor in some situations. As long as you know the pros and cons of each alternative, you will feel that you have made an educated decision.

Alternatives to Employing an Architect

There is often a large cost reduction in choosing an alternative method of designing or remodeling your house. Considerations other than budget include the terrain of your building lot, the size of the house you wish to build, or the size of the renovation. Evaluate all of the alternatives before deciding which method you will employ.

1. **It is becoming increasingly popular to purchase ready-made architectural plans.** Several well-known architects (for example, Robert A.M. Stern and Michael Graves) are getting involved in designing ready-to-build plans. The advantage of purchasing this type of plan is that you may get a very well-designed house at a modest fee (anywhere from about $200 to $600). The disadvantages, however, are plentiful. The cost of altering the plans to meet your personal needs can be substantial, and the plans may contain errors. The architect will often stand behind the plans and send revisions, but this might not work very well if the errors are found in the middle of construction.

   The largest drawback to using these plans is that they are not prepared with the individual construction site in mind; making changes to meet these differences and local codes can be costly. As with custom plans, a structural engineer will probably have to be brought in to check for structural reliability. The supplier of the plans may suggest the cost of building the house. This cost may vary, depending on the area of the country where the project will be constructed. The architect may not be available to make changes in the plan or to help with on-site meetings. For renovations, it is impossible to adapt these plans to what remains of the structure.

   If you are interested in using this method, however, you can contact:
   ■ Home Planners magazine at 800-521-6797 (www.homeplanners.com).
   ■ Fine Homebuilding magazine at 800-2837252

An example of the current sophistication of modular houses.

(www.finehomebuilding.com).

Garlinghouse Publishers at 800-235-5700 (www.garlinghouse.com).
Consult other magazines listed in the back of this book that
contain floor plans.

Check out the www.B4UBUILD.com Web site, which features floor plans
that can be ordered online. (This site also offers a large variety of other
construction information, such as recommended books, contracts,
landscaping and gardening topics, and links to other relevant sites.)

2. **You can purchase a modular home, which is produced in a factory and
transported to the job site.** Several companies across the country manufacture modular homes. In New England, Westchester Modular Homes is a large
supplier. An in-house design team designs the home or adapts one of the 40
to 50 design plans that the company owns. It is then OK'd and stamped by
a structural engineer so that a permit can be issued. From 80% to 90% of the
house will be manufactured at the factory; from 10% to 20% will be completed by one of the company's network of builders. The builder will put in
the foundation and connect the plumbing and electricity to outside sources.

The advantages of modular construction are:

- A 15% reduction in cost.
- A finished product in less time. (Homes take approximately 7 days to 8 weeks to produce.) The length of time it takes to install your home will depend on the contractor you employ to put in the foundation and complete the installation.
- Fewer environmental hazards (less settling because the job site is not exposed to the elements; weather does not hold up construction.)
- Generally low maintenance.
- A 10-year structural warranty.
- Most plans are flawless because they have been used so frequently.

The disadvantages of modular construction are:

- A lack of design options. Floor plans cannot be too intricate or detailed.
- A lack of flexibility in terms of materials.
- A lack of flexibility in terms of last-minute changes.
- There are few checks and balances in this type of construction. One company is handling most of the process. When you are building your own house, you have architects, builders, interior designers, and so on scrutinizing the project.
- Labor is so inexpensive in some areas that modular manufacturers cannot compete adequately.
- Contemporary style homes are difficult for modular builders to construct because of the great variation in rooflines.

Modular construction can be used for renovations, usually for second-floor additions. It is a fast and economical method of constructing weekend and resort homes. For more information, contact Westchester Modular Homes at 800-832-3888. For a listing of other modular manufacturers, contact the National Association of Home Builders at 800-368-5242 extension 663 or the Modular Building Systems Association at www.modularhousing.com (or telephone 717-238-9130).

Creating a design for your home can be an extremely exciting experience-an opportunity to meet your physical needs as well as your and your family's unique tastes. If possible, try to take the time to select an architect you will still want to know when your home is complete and be proud to introduce as its architect. I can't say that I didn't have problems with my architect during the course of my project, but I am very pleased with the end result, which he had a very large hand in creating. The best compliment I can give him is that I would not hesitate to call on him again or to recommend him to others.

Notes

CHAPTER 4

General Contractors

All of the people you hire to build your house are important to the success of the project. But perhaps the most important person is the general contractor, or builder. The builder has to be able to make your house structurally sound and economically feasible as well as have a personality that won't cause you a nervous breakdown.

The term builder is sometimes used synonymously with general contractor. Builder, (or production builder) however, can refer to a person who purchases property, has a house designed (by his own selected or in-house architect) and constructs it, selecting all materials and hiring all subcontractors. He then sells the house and property as a package deal. The general contractor (or GC) as used in this book (and sometimes referred to as a custom builder) constructs the house with input from the architect and the owner. The owner purchases the property, selects the design, and decides on the types of materials to be used. Builder and GC are very loose terms, however, and in this book they will be used interchangeably.

The architect's drawings, even when technically well done, are just a starting point in constructing a house. The architectural construction documents and the specifications graphically communicate to the GC what to build. They don't, however, tell the builder how to build the house. For this, you will have to depend on the contractor's expertise and experience in executing the plans.

We wanted to build a hearth in the center of our living room, which is a typical design feature in the Southwest, but not something commonly done on the East Coast. I gave the architect a picture I'd clipped from a magazine of the type of hearth I wanted. He, in turn, executed the drawings and specs needed to build the fireplace components based on his assumptions about the existing conditions of the house. However, after the demolition was complete and structural unknowns were uncovered, the builder then had to analyze and review the conditions and then modify the house to make the architectural design work. Our GC did a great job of finding a way to build a very complicated structure while also modifying the house to make the plans work. Particularly in renovations, the builder must be able to adapt the house to execute the architect's drawings and specs.

What General Contractors Do

The general contractor's responsibilities will depend on who you select and the terms that you agree on. GCs perform a variety of functions, not all of which will be performed by each one:

- Preparing a schedule.
- Getting permits.
- Being familiar with the building codes and carrying them out.
- Establishing a way to carry out the plans.
- Supervising the other workers and subcontractors.
- Participating in the construction.
- Dealing with local inspectors.
- Communicating progress and problems with the owner and architect.

Although to some extent you will depend on the architect to oversee your project, he will not be on your job every day. It's the contractor who will be dealing with the other workers and the town inspectors, and watching out for your interests on a day-to-day basis. You will have to depend on his knowledge, his ability to do construction, his honesty in looking after your interests, and his ability to coordinate with any other people you decide to bring on the job. You will be spending a great deal of time with this person or group of people. You want to build an efficient, strong, beautiful home, but you don't want to have a nervous breakdown or go broke, so selecting the appropriate person to build your house is a very important decision.

Finding a General Contractor

While you are looking for an architect, you can also be compiling a list of recommended contractors. The methods for finding both are similar. The following are some possible methods:

1. **Family and friends are good sources for recommendations.** Let them recommend contractors they have worked with and have had a positive experiences with.

2. **Architects, who have worked with various general contractors in the past, can make excellent suggestions for builders.** If the GC and architect already have a working relationship, they will most likely be able to work well together. The architect is already familiar with the quality of the contractor's work. On the other hand, you do want the architect to keep an eye on the contractor; this may or may not be possible if they already know each other. Each situation will be different. You will have to evaluate your comfort level in each case.

3. **Real-estate brokers are often familiar with excellent GCs.** They may be able to recommend GCs who have remodeled or built homes for past clients.

4. **The National Association of Home Builders (NAHB) can offer recommendations on local builders and general contractors.** You can contact the national office in Washington, DC, by telephone at 800-368-5242 or on the Internet at www.nahb.com. State and local chapters can offer information as well as directories of homebuilders and the price ranges of the homes they build.

5. **Several other Web sites (in addition to the NAHB's) provide information on contractors.** www.remodeltoday.com is the Web site of the National Association of the Remodeling Industry (NARI). They list names of contractors in specified locations. www.contractor.com also offers a comprehensive directory of contractors, who are rated according to their ability to stay on time and budget, the quality of their work, and their overall performance. This site offers valuable tips for hiring home professionals and contractors.

   www.improvenet.com also provides names of contractors. As noted in Chapter 3, they use their own screening techniques before making recommendations. Another web site offering referrals is www.servicemagic.com which also screens contractors before making recommendations. www.homebuilder.com is sponsored by the National Association of Home Builders (NAHB) and lists custom builders by location and includes links to some of them. The

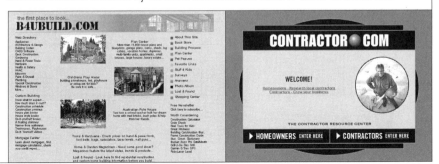

Canadian Home Builders' Association provides construction advice and names of contractors on their Web site, www.chba.ca.

Although a listing on any of these sites demonstrates a level of commitment to the building trade on the part of the contractor, a contractor's membership in these organizations in no way ensures reliability or a high level of professionalism. You need to thoroughly check out any contractor that you're considering hiring.

6. **Go on house tours and collect information about the builders, kitchen designers, and so on.** If you see things you like on the tour, ask for information. Most home owners or tour operators will be happy to give you whatever information you request.

7. **Find out who built the homes that grab your attention in magazines and newspapers.** Magazines will rarely list the contractor's name or company, but the architect is often listed and you can contact him or her for the information you need. If the architect's name is not available, often the magazine will get you this information.

8. **When you see a house in the area that you like, ask the owners about their GC.** People are generally flattered if you ask for the name of their builder. A well-built house and a satisfied customer is the best recommendation you can get.

9. **When speaking with or interviewing other professionals, such as architects, ask them to recommend general contractors they have worked with.** I actually found my contractor when I was calling for references on another contractor. I had briefly considered bypassing the bidding process and hiring a contractor that I'd met through my architect. He had been very helpful during the development stages of our project and appeared to be very knowledgeable and pleasant. The project was already taking more time than I wanted it to, and I was anxious to move the project along so my children could begin the school year in their new home. I asked for and received a list of recommendations from the contractor and called most of the people on the list.

I received an incredible education in everything that can go wrong with a GC. People complained about everything, from faulty plumbing to incomplete work. The architect was surprised and embarrassed when I shared this information with him. After that experience, I learned the importance of checking references. I also realized the importance of the bidding process. You need to go through the whole process of bidding, which includes interviewing prospective contractors, checking their references, and getting several prices before selecting one of them. I would never consider bypassing this process again. One of the references told me that although he was very unhappy with his GC, whom I was calling about, his close friend was very satisfied with his. I called his friend and ultimately hired that GC, although I did bid the project with three other contractors as well.

Criteria for Hiring a General Contractor

While interviewing several GCs, find out as much as possible about them. The following are some guidelines to consider while interviewing each one:

1. **Does the GC have a manner that you and all the other people working on the job will have an easy time with?** The GC will most likely have to deal with an architect and many subcontractors. You want a person who will make the project go smoothly, not someone who will create a war zone.

2. **Is the GC a good communicator?** He should keep you apprised of the progress on the job. When problems arise, he has to be able to discuss them with you. He must be accustomed to putting **change orders** (documents describing alterations or additions to the original contract between the owner and the general contractor) in writing.

3. **Do you want a "hands-on" GC or a managerial company doing construction supervision?** A hands-on contractor will most likely be on the job every day doing the work along with his workers. A managerial-type company usually employs a supervisor or foreman to watch individual jobs while the management staff does the purchasing and hiring. We preferred to have the builder on the construction site at all times, giving us the ability to interact with him on a regular basis. A managerial company may have more clout in hiring talented subcontractors and have more time to shop for materials for your home. Because they have the ability to build several homes at one time, they may be more professional as well. You will have to decide which you prefer.

4. **Has the GC worked on homes in the price range that you are considering?** A builder who is accustomed to building low-budget homes may not be fa-

miliar with higher-end products or have the same quality expectations.

5. **Is the GC knowledgeable about a variety of products, local codes, and building techniques?** When you are interviewing the builder, ask him about the houses he has built in the local area. Question him about products he used as well as his techniques for a difficult or unusual construction. Our builder was not familiar with the technique necessary to build our hearth, so he communicated with a builder on the Internet and found out how it should be done. His excellent knowledge of general building techniques made it possible to adapt to this unfamiliar construction.

6. **Which subcontractors does the GC generally work with? Do they do quality work?** For how long do they guarantee their work? Subcontractors are plumbers, electricians, painters, and so on who are hired by the builder (or the owner) to complete a portion of the construction on the house. If the builder hires them, find out how often the builder has used them, the types of homes they have worked on, and what type of guarantee they will give on the workmanship and materials. The roof is a particularly vulnerable part of the house and if not done properly can cause leaks, creating further interior problems. Find out how long the subcontractor/contractor will guarantee the roof.

7. **If the GC is a hands-on GC, does he know about all aspects of building the house?** He should know how to do all the aspects of construction himself as well as be able to instruct the other workers how to do the work correctly. Ask the builder about his experience doing various aspects of the construction and ask his references about his ability as well.

8. **Is the GC available to work on your home on a timely basis?** Most people are on a schedule and would like to finish construction on their house as quickly as possible. If the builder already has a great deal of work to do and won't be able to get started on your house for awhile, he might not be the right person for your job. If, however, you are building a second home or are not in a rush to complete your project, you might want to wait for a builder you prefer but who is busy and not immediately available.

9. **Does the GC have good references?** The following are some questions you should ask when requesting information about the contractor:

- Was the GC easy to work with?
- Did he work well with your architect?
- Were you happy with the quality of his work? With the subcontractors' work?
- Did he take responsibility for the work of his subcontractors?
- Did he work at a good pace?
- Was the completion of the house close to schedule?

- Did the house come in close to the original bid?
- Did he put all change orders in writing?
- Was he fair on his change order costs?
- Did he work in an organized and clean manner?
- Did he take precautions to preserve the landscape?
- Did you have any problem passing the local codes?
- Did he schedule and attend regular meetings?
- Was he responsive to suggestions by other professionals on the job?
- If the contractor is a supervisory one, was the foreman competent? Was the supervisor on the job enough?
- Were you unhappy about anything the builder did?
- Did you have any problems with the house after you moved in?
- Did the GC come back to correct the problems quickly?
- Did you have to replace anything in the house prematurely because of shoddy work or poor-quality materials?
- Would you consider hiring the GC again if you were building another house?

If you ask specific questions, people will usually give you more information than they had planned. If you agree to keep this information confidential, most people will be very helpful.

It would be wise to ask the contractor for the names of the people he did his last four jobs for. It should be easy for a contractor to find three or four people who would give him recommendations over the span of his career, but it would be useful to find out what the last several people had to say.

10. **Does the GC have adequate funding?** The owner can ask the GC to supply financial statements, tax returns, and so on to substantiate his solvency. If the builder runs out of funds or goes bankrupt in the middle of your construction, he may not be able to complete your home.

11. **Look at homes the GC has built and check the quality of the construction.** Does the workmanship appear to be good? Are moldings straight? Are there any visible signs of leaking? Do you see cracks in walls or basement floors?

12. **Consider the GC's level of training and experience.** Did he apprentice with other builders? Has he ever supervised a project of the magnitude and complexity of yours?

13. **Make sure the GC is licensed by the state.** All of his subcontractors (plumber, electrician, HVAC) must be licensed as well. You can ask to see their licenses.

14. **Is the GC accustomed to making detailed schedules?** It is a difficult task to keep a project working in terms of receiving construction materials and having subcontractors arrive at the appropriate time. The builder must be able

to construct a detailed schedule so that you and he can schedule arrivals of materials and subcontractors appropriately.

15. **Is the GC comfortable with your intended involvement on the project, either doing some of the work yourself or hiring some of your own subcontractors?** Builders generally prefer to hire all subcontractors themselves and purchase all building materials. Make sure that if you intend to hire several of the subcontractors or purchase materials such as floorings, doors, tile, and so on, that the builder will feel comfortable with this. Be sure to let him know the extent of your involvement before you sign a contract.

What General Contractors Would Like You to Know

It is helpful if the client is knowledgeable about what is involved in altering plans and how payment schedules work. The better your understanding of issues that concern builders, the more potential you have for getting along with them.

Altering the Plans

Because many people are not knowledgeable about construction, they tend to underestimate the complexity of a change order in the project and sometimes feel that that they are being overbilled. It is possible that they are. However, very often the job is bigger than the layperson may assume. The owner should ask a lot of questions and try to find out what the change involves.

The Payment Schedule

The GC should take the time to review the payment schedule with the owner so she knows what she is paying for and how she can plan out these payments. The owner and GC will decide how often payments will be made; usually it will be bimonthly or monthly. The GC will bill the owner for the percentage of each phase of responsibility he has completed minus the 5% to 10% retainer (the part of the contractor's payment that the owner holds back until the project is sufficiently complete).

If, for example, the builder has completed 60% of the demolition (which is broken down in the bid) and 10% of the site work, the owner will be charged for the percentage of the items completed. The schedule that the GC has supplied shows what percentage of each area he expects to complete each week. Chances are, he will not work exactly by that schedule, but it will give the owner an idea of how she can plan her building expenses. The architect should review each bill to be sure it is accurate and that the percentage of work has been completed. He must then sign off on the GC'S application for payment.

If the contractor will be working on a smaller project, such as repaving the road to the house, it is important to ask him what extras might come up. Will extra drains have to be installed? Will masonry work need to be redone? Will extra soil need to be brought in? If part of the road will be eliminated, will you require a landscaper to seed the ground, or will the contractor include that portion of the job in the contract? Be very clear about what is included in the estimate and what additional variables will probably be necessary. It is the extras that put most people over budget.

How Long Construction Will Take

Most people want their houses to be built immediately. They want to get their children into school in September; they want to enjoy the summer months at their lakeside home; and so on. The time it will take the builder to complete the construction, even if he is working on it diligently, will depend on several factors:

- The difficulty of the construction site.
- The size of the house.
- The size of the crew working.
- The complexity of the project.
- How organized the project is. (Have the materials been ordered to arrive on a timely basis and have the subcontractors been hired to arrive at the correct time?)
- The weather.

Smaller projects that are 1,000 to 4,000 square feet can take 3 to 5 months to build. Larger homes that are 4,000 square feet and up will generally take 4 to 10 months, and sometimes longer, to build.

Financial Arrangements with General Contractors

A variety of financial arrangements can be made with a general contractor. Which arrangement you choose will depend on budget considerations, time restraints, and the amount of involvement you would like to have in the project. The following are some of the possible contracts that can be made.

Fixed-Fee Contracts

With a fixed-fee contract, the GC reviews the construction documents, evaluates the total cost and labor, and gives the homeowner a total price to build the house. Once the owner and GC agree on the price, a contract is signed and the contractor assumes responsibility for all of the construction. The owner can select everything that will go into the contract prior to the bidding process or put in **allowances** for certain items. An allowance is the amount of money provided by the general contractor or builder, in the contract, for the buyer to purchase certain items or products that they have not pre-selected. The owner will have to pay the extra cost of any item that is more expensive than the contracted allowance price.

The owner should be informed about what the allowance is for. If for example, there is a $10,000 allowance for appliances, does that figure represent installation as well? Installation fees can be very costly. The owner must find out what is not included in the contract.

The builder is responsible for the supervision, construction, and purchasing of all items he contracts for or purchases that are specified in the contract. This arrangement puts the least amount of wear and tear on the owner but is potentially the most expensive method of working with a GC.

Modified Fixed-Fee Contracts

In this arrangement, the owner selects the items that will not be included in the contract. The owner can eliminate any items, systems, or subcontract work from the original bid or after the bidding process. Depending on the GC, you may or may not pay a supervisory percentage on these items.

We opted to work with our GC using this arrangement. We eliminated most of the interior items from our contract, including most of the systems, including the central vacuum system and lighting system (see Chapter 8 for a discussion of systems); the entire kitchen; and all floorings, bathroom fixtures, and tiles. This worked out well for us because we had the opportunity to take our time to become educated about the various systems and products, to select what we wanted, and to negotiate the best prices on those items. All of this took a great deal of time and effort. Arranging for the arrival of materials and coordination of subcontractors was sometimes the most difficult part of the process. We did, however, pay the builder to supervise several of the subcontractors because of the complexity of the work and limitations in scheduling flexibility when so many subcontractors are involved.

It is difficult to make all the arrangements (getting materials and subcontractors at the appropriate time) necessary to keep to a construction schedule. When I had trouble with my carpenter, the plumber and the mason were also held up. It was my responsibility to get the carpenter in to  finish his work, which was a very frustrating task. If you hire your own subcontractors, be very careful that scheduling will not be a problem, particularly if you have a **penalty clause** in your contract with the GC. A penalty clause spells out the amount that a GC or other worker will be penalized if a project isn't completed by the agreed-upon date. Because we had problems with the carpenter, our project ran over schedule and our GC was able to get out of the penalty clause by pointing out that the carpenter had delayed the project. If you do hire your own contractors, try to make sure they are flexible and will be able to stay on a schedule.

GCs have ongoing relationships with some contractors, which gives them more clout when problems (such as scheduling) occur. A subcontractor might be more apt to be flexible because of his ongoing relationship with the builder. He might hope to get future work, which can be assured of by doing an excellent job and helping with problems. It is possible that the quality of the work you find on your own may surpass that of the builders' subcontractors because you are shopping around for the subcontractor who does the highest-quality work. As much as the builder may be concerned about quality, he may be working with subcontractors because they are trying to keep the cost within a particular budget where there is more room for profit and/or because they feel the subcontractor is reliable and will be available when needed.

Selecting materials gives the owner the opportunity to explore all of the options and negotiate the best prices. It took a great deal of time for me to go through lumberyards and visit antique flooring contractors to find the wood flooring I wanted. But it was worth the effort because I was able to find the most beautiful wood at a reasonable price.

GCs will generally prefer to have more control of the project and to purchase everything for the house themselves. It is therefore imperative to tell the GC up front what your involvement in the house will be. The GC can then decide if this is a situation he wants to get involved with. For the owners, this type of arrangement is an opportunity to get what they want, at the best possible price.

Cost-Plus Contracts

In this arrangement, the owner bids out the supervision and coordination of the project. The builder will give the owner an overall price for supervising all the subcontractors and purchasing all the materials. The GC will estimate the cost of all labor and supplies but will not be responsible for those costs. The owner will have the opportunity to bid out all contracted work and all supplies, along with the builder. Sometimes the GC will request a 10% to 15% mark-up fee on all subcontract work and all supplies.

Generally, with the cost-plus contract, the owner will set up a joint checking account with the GC so that both parties can pay bills. This situation puts a great deal of responsibility on the owner and is very time-consuming. It is an opportunity, however, to vastly reduce the cost of building the house. It also eliminates the huge expense of change orders. The owner will absorb any additional cost for labor and materials without a penalty for altering the plan. The owner has time to make decisions on a timely basis and the flexibility to alter his or her choices as the construction goes along. This is an excellent way to build a house if the owner has the time and stamina to do it. If, however, the owner does not have the time to spend doing this work, it should not be an option. It may also encourage the contractor to hire higher-priced subcontractors and purchase unnecessarily expensive supplies.

Conditions You Should Include in the Contract

The contract that you make with the builder is the one you will have to live with throughout the construction and after the project is complete. Make sure to consider the following:

1. **Be sure you receive a warranty on both the work the GC will do himself and the work he will supervise.** I recommend you get a one-year warranty on all the work performed or supervised by the GC, in writing, in the contract. Contractors should give more than a one-year contract on some items, such as the roof, where 5 to 30 years is traditional. If the GC is responsible, he should be available to fix whatever he can or ask the subcontractors to fix the problems in their areas of expertise. If the owner will be responsible for hiring and supervising the subcontractor, a written warranty should be given for that work as well.

    I hired a subcontractor who came highly recommended by the lumber supplier to lay the floor. When several boards began to come up, the contractor would not come back to fix the problem. Unfortunately, we had not thought to get a written warranty. I had no other recourse but to hire someone else, at additional expense, to fix the boards. The warranty will not ensure the return of an unscrupulous contractor, but it will give you legal recourse.

2. **The contractor and all his subcontractors should sign a Release of Liens form (AIA Document 706A).** This is necessary for any owner working on a fixed-fee or modified fixed-fee arrangement. This protects the owner if the GC does not pay his subcontractors or suppliers. They could put a "mechanic's lien" or a "materialman's lien" against the owners' property. The subcontractor could then claim a piece of the property or a portion of the money the owner receives when the property is sold. A lien release is a document signed by the subcontractor or supplier promising that the subcontractors have been paid and that they will not file a lien against the property.

3. **Insist on a reasonable completion date with a penalty and possibly a bonus clause.** If time is an important factor, as it is for most people, there must be some arrangement that will ensure that your project will be completed on a timely basis. A bonus can be specified in the contract for the completion of the house before a particular date. If, however, the house is completed after the predetermined date, the builder will have to forfeit a set amount for each day that he goes over it. Most people would be delighted to pay the bonus if the house is completed early. They may be without permanent housing during the construction or need to get in for such reasons as schooling. If you will get involved in the construction, be sure you don't become a factor in delaying the job, or you will not benefit from the penalty clause.

4. **If you hire a supervisory builder, put in the contract how often the supervisor will be visiting your property.** There may be an excellent foreman on the job, but if the person hiring the subcontractors and buying all the materials for the project is not around, there is potential for problems. Find out in advance how often the builder will be there and what experience the foreman has.

5. **Insist that all change orders (AIA Document G701) be in writing and signed by the GC and the owner (and possibly the architect).** The cost and effect on the completion date should be noted on each change order. If, for example, you have decided to add an additional bathroom to your house after the contract is signed, the extra cost as well as the additional time it will take must be listed on the change order.

6. **There must be an agreement that approximately 10% of the cost of the work completed will be withheld for retainage.** This assures the owner that the builder and the other workers on the job will complete the work.

7. **Make a provision for unexpected site conditions.** Pre-establish a dollar amount for any conditions that may come up in the course of constructing

the house. Establish a unit cost or price for quantity-for example, the price per cubic yard to remove rock (also referred to as ledge). All possible conditions should be listed in the contract so that the GC doesn't overcharge for conditions that aren't initially discovered.

Most builders use the AIA Document A101 (the Standard Form of Agreement Between Owner and Contractor) with the A201 Supplement (which states general conditions of the contract for construction) as the contracts between themselves and the owner. This contract can also be used as a guideline for a more personalized contract. Be sure you and the GC feel comfortable with its terms. Whichever type of agreement you make with the general contractor, be sure to have an attorney review the contract. You want to be sure that it serves your interests and that your liabilities on the project are minimized.

Procedures for Working with the General Contractor

Once you have narrowed down your search, it is time to make sure you want to work with a particular builder and time to negotiate terms and prices with him. Make sure you feel comfortable with all aspects of this relationship. You will be spending a great deal of time with the builder, it will cost you a lot of money, and you will live with the results for a long time.

1. **Set up a meeting with the GC you have selected as your first choice.** Having reviewed all the bids, you may feel that some of the GC's items are incongruous with those on other bids. You will have a much better idea of the costs of various items after reviewing those of all the bidders. This is the time to negotiate with the GC and to make the best deal possible. You may want to alter some aspects or get the GC to reduce the cost of particular items. Make sure you can agree on the terms of the contract and the type of financial relationship you will have. Be sure you feel comfortable working with this person or company and that the GC seems anxious to get involved with you and your project. Check that the timing will work out for both of you.

    If you cannot agree on terms, consider speaking to your second bid choice. Set up a meeting with that GC and try to work out an arrangement that will be comfortable for all involved. I want to emphasize again that the person you select and the deal you make will be with you for a long time, so choose very carefully. Don't necessarily choose the lowest bidder. Use the criteria, mentioned earlier in the chapter ("Criteria for Hiring a GC") keeping in mind personality, expertise, and availability, and considering the flexibility of the builder in the final negotiation and specifically in altering his bid.

2. **If the architect has not applied for building permits and worker's comp, the GC will have to do it at this point.** The GC needs to receive several approvals before applying for the building permit: planning and zoning, health department (if the house will require a septic system), and the inland wetlands and watercourses agency (if there is any chance there are wetlands on the property.) The GC takes the construction documents to the town hall. Each of the above offices will review the documents for compliance with the local codes and ordinances. The GC will then apply for the permit. There are three national building codes. Each state has the option of selecting one of these codes. The BOCA (Building Officials and Code Administrators) rewrites these codes every 2 years, so it is very important that the builder stay current on these codes in order to gain approvals from the various departments.(The architect will sometimes begin the permit process during the bidding period if time is an important factor. If this is the case, the general contractor will later finish the process of obtaining the permit and put the permit in his or her name.)

   Permits. The cost of the permit is based on a percentage of the construction costs or the square footage of the structure. Permits must be obtained from the county building inspector's office before construction can begin. If the construction is not begun within six months of the permit being issued, the permit will have to be renewed. If the construction has not begun in three years, the architect or GC will have to apply for a new permit. Various inspections will be scheduled during the construction, including building, electrical, plumbing, and HVAC (heating, ventilation, and air-conditioning). The inspector will check to see that the contractor has complied with local codes and ordinances. The permit takes about 3 weeks to obtain, which is about the time the bidding process will take. You will save several weeks by having the architect begin this process.

   Workers' Compensation Insurance. Most states require the builder to obtain workers' comp to provide workers with hospitalization insurance for all job-related injuries. The owner should find out if this is a requirement and make sure that the GC meets the state conditions. Some states require coverage of subcontractors as well; other states require the subcontractors own companies to give them coverage. Make sure that the GC covers the subcontractors with compensation and liability insurance. If the architect applies for the permits, he will apply for the compensation in the owners' name, which will be changed when a builder is hired. If the GC will be hiring and paying the subcontractors, it will be his responsibility to pay for the workers' compensation. If the owner will be paying the subcontractors, it will be her or his responsibility.

3. **The GC should provide you with a schedule.** The owners will want to know

Category	1/17	1/31	2/14	2/28	3/14	3/28	4/11	4/25	5/9	5/23	6/6	6/20	7/4	7/18
General Conditions	8%	8%	7%	7%	7%	7%	7%	7%	7%	7%	7%	7%	7%	7%
Site Work:	33.3%	33.3%	33.4%											
Demolition	33.3%	33.3%	33.4%											
Concrete		50%	50%											
Masonry:		33.3%	33.3%	33.4%										
Structural Steel:				100%										
Rough Framing (Ext./Int.)			50%	12.5%	12.5%	12.5%	12.5%							
Exterior Architectural Woodwork						50%	50%							
Interior Architectural Woodwork										33.3%	33.3%	33.4%		
Wood Shingle Roofing						25%	25%	25%	25%					
Insulation							100%							
E.F.I.S. System							25%	25%	25%	25%				
Interior Doors							50%			50%				
Exterior Doors									100%					
Garage Doors/Operators							100%							
Windows		50%			50%									
Glass/Glazing					100%									
Gypsum Drywall								50%	50%					
Exterior Painting								50%	50%					
Interior Painting										33.3%	33.3%	33.4%		
Prefabricated Fireplace							100%							
Electrical Work					50%								25%	25%
HVAC System					50%							25%	25%	
Plumbing System								33.3%			33.3%		33.4%	
Floor Tile											33.3%	33.3%	33.4%	
Wall Tile											33.3%	33.3%	33.4%	
Wood Flooring									75%					25%
Exterior Pavers										50%	50%			
Carpet														100%
Cabinetry				20%		20%		20%		20%		20%		
Counter Tops											50%	50%		
Appliances					5%									95%
Accessories														100%
Fixtures [Plumbing]								25%					75%	
Fixtures [Lighting]											50%	50%		
Hardware														100%
Security System					50%									50%
Landscape Improvements									50%	50%				

An example of a builder's schedule

when they can expect to move into their home. Rarely are builders able to stay on schedule. However, if there is a penalty clause, it is possible that they will complete the house close to schedule. The owners may be concerned with leases on temporary housing, school, and scheduling money outlay. Subcontractors, painters, glaciers, carpets, window treatments, and so on will have to be scheduled. Therefore, it is important that a realistic schedule is made and that the builder tries hard to adhere to it. An example of a builder's schedule above.

4. **The GC should be ordering the supplies that he needs and putting together a crew. He should begin construction as soon as possible.** Starting the con-

struction requires setting up some type of office; getting a phone line; and securing portable toilets, waste containers, and the like. It will also take time to begin ordering materials needed to begin the demolition or construction. A crew will have to be hired if they are not already on staff, and subcontractors will have to be lined up.

5. **If you are renovating, the demolition will begin; if this is to be a new construction, the GC will begin preparing the site.** For a new construction, soil tests will be done in preparation for the septic system. The land will have to be cleared of vegetation, trees, and bushes where the house will be sited, to provide for access to the site, for the septic system, and for the well. For a major renovation, if there are additional bedrooms and/or bathrooms (depending on the area) you may have to expand the septic system. In some towns, if you have to alter the system to accommodate additional rooms, you may then be required to design a secondary backup system. Find out what the local requirements are before you purchase the land or consider renovating an existing house.

6. **Regular meetings should be planned throughout the construction phase.** The meetings should be planned for each week, every other week, or whatever interval you have agreed upon, when everyone involved will be available. The owners, the GC, the foreman (if there is one), and the architect should attend all meetings if possible. The GC should schedule various subcontractors to attend meetings on a timely basis. If you are beginning to **rough-in** the electricity, the electrical contractor and fixture supplier/designer should be present to offer their input. One of the regular participants at the meetings should keep notes and distribute them to the other attendees. The architect usually takes responsibility for this. The meetings will keep everyone informed and avoid potential problems.

   If plans need to be altered, change orders should be issued as soon as possible. Everyone in the group can decide on alternative solutions to the various problems that come up. Meetings also provide an opportunity for subcontractors to communicate with each other. If, for example, the plumber and carpenter attend the same meeting, they can work out the placement of water lines behind cabinets. There are sometimes several possible ways this can be done, and it is better if the owner is there to make the decision. If the owner will be involved in ordering certain materials (for example, flooring) or hiring certain subcontractors (for example, telephone systems), the GC should alert the owner at these meetings about scheduling.

7. **The owner needs to stay in communication with the GC and the other professionals who are working on the job.** Even when everything is going according to plan, the owners may not like the way a particular aspect of the con-

struction looks in reality, as opposed to on paper. Therefore, it is imperative that the owner visit the site on a regular basis, know what is being done, and try to make alterations while it is still possible. Owners should communicate any changes they want with the GC or the foreman, not the workers or subcontractors. Bringing donuts and coffee to the job site creates goodwill among the workers and can make them want to do their best for the owner. However, complaining to workers directly can anger both the GC and the subcontractors.

8. **The builder must make sure that all required inspections are performed during the course of the construction.** Each town has different requirements, which must be strictly adhered to. It is imperative that the contractor calls the inspector on a timely basis, so as not to hold up the job.

9. **When the house is nearly complete, the GC and the owner (and perhaps the architect) should compile a list of items that still need to be completed.** This is called a **punch list**. As each item is completed, it is checked off. Make sure that all of the items are checked off.

10. **The GC should schedule final inspections (electrical, plumbing, building, and so on) so that a certificate of occupancy can be issued.** Final verification of surveys are sometimes required by the town, to make sure that the house was sited according to the original survey and that all zoning regulations were met. When the certificate has been issued, the house should be considered complete.

11. **The owner should get a list of required maintenance procedures.** If the owner must follow certain procedures to maintain the house, the contractor must clearly state them before leaving the job. These procedures might include removing leaves from gutters on flat roofs, adding salt to a water-conditioning apparatus, and so on. Failure to do many of these procedures could result in damage to the house. For example, not removing leaves from a flat roof could cause a buildup of water around the **parapet** and a leak in the ceiling. Failure to add salt to a hard water tank could cause a buildup of calcium in the pipes and eventual clogging of pipes and drains. It is wise for the owner to ask the contractor for these instructions before he has left the job. Otherwise, the contractor might incorrectly assume that the owner knows what has to be done.

12. **The GC should supply the owner with the names of all subcontractors who worked on the construction.** The work of the subcontractors should be under warranty with the GC for a year. However, if the GC disappears or is unwilling to correct a problem, the owner must know who to call. Even if the GC is responsible and handles problems the first year, that year will go by quickly. The owner needs to know who to call if there is a problem later on, if the GC is not available. The subcontractors who worked on your house will be the most familiar with the various systems and in the best position to rec-

ommend solutions to problems.

13. **The GC should supply the owner with all operation and maintenance manuals, as well as warranties.** The contractor should put together all of the instruction and maintenance manuals that come with appliances, heating units, and so on for future reference. Printed warranties should be handed over to the owner as well.

14. **The owner needs to pay the GC the retainage.** When all of the above items are complete-all punch lists items are corrected, maintenance has been reviewed, names of subcontractors have been turned over, manuals and warranties have been given to the owner and the Certificate of Occupancy has been issued, the owner should give the builder the retainage.

Record Keeping

While it may be difficult, it is imperative to keep good records during construction. You may be in cramped quarters, and will probably be trying to go on with your regular routine during this time. You need to set up a special drawer or temporary filing cabinet with the following items:

1. Contracts with the architect, builder, and so on.
2. Construction documents.
3. Construction receipts.
4. Financing agreements.
5. Photographs of the work in progress.
6. Warranties.
7. Notes from meetings.
8. Change orders.
9. All communications regarding the project.
10. Proposals and estimates.

Entering information in the Notebook at the end of this book will help you keep track of data needed during construction and will make it easy to retrieve that information when a problem occurs down the road.

When the construction is complete and you and your family have moved into your home, ideally you will still have a good relationship with the GC. If you have chosen carefully and the GC is competent and honest, both of you will be in a winning situation. He can depend on you to give him a good recommendation for future projects, and you will have someone to call on when there are problems. By the time it's complete, no one will be more familiar with your house than the GC.

Notes

CHAPTER 5

Interior Designers

It is surprising how many people spend an enormous amount of money renovating or building a new home only to ignore the interior, using furniture that doesn't fit the style of the house or the dimensions of the rooms. The beauty and comfort of a home is derived from the compatibility of the furniture with the house and from the comfort and ease of lifestyle the furnishings provide.

Some people have an incredible talent for design. Over the years, my sister-in-law has pulled her various homes together with the same ease that she pulls her beautiful wardrobe together. She is one of the very talented few. The rest of us have trouble with correct proportion, symmetry, and pulling a house together so that it is both comfortable and cohesive. Although people sometimes believe that working with interior designers will make it more expensive to decorate the interior space, this is not necessarily the case. If you buy furnishings that don't fit with the dimensions of the room or aesthetically don't work, you will not have saved any money by purchasing them yourself. Designers also have access to many more resources than non-professionals do and are sometimes able to purchase branded and/or unbranded items below what may be available at retail.

Designing the interior of the house should be an enjoyable experience. You have the opportunity to purchase items that will not only make your house more attractive and fulfill your design fantasies, but also make it comfortable and efficient. While working with the designer, be sure to make notes in the Notebook in the back of this book. This will not only help keep you organized during the design stage but also later on when you need a record of some item, such as paint color.

What Interior Designers Do

Interior designers offer a wide range of services. Their involvement will depend on the size of your project and the point at which they are brought in. If you are building a new house or remodeling an existing one, it is a good idea to include the designer in the planning stage before the architect completes the working documents. They can be helpful in taking a beautiful architectural design and making sure it is also practical in terms of personal comfort, storage, placement of furnishings, and even moving the placement of doors, windows and electric outlets if necessary. The designer's input will be more limited if the drawings are completed and the placement of walls and windows, for example, are already in the final plan. Depending on the expertise of the individual you hire, a designer can provide services such as these:

1. Suggest alterations to the architect's plans to provide for better placement of furnishings and more practical use of space.
2. Design the interior space, including moldings, cabinetry, lighting, floorings, bathroom layouts, tile, kitchens, and so on.
3. Develop a theme for the house, including style, period, and color.
4. Design and have custom furniture made.
5. Design a floor plan for the placement of all furnishings.
6. Draw elevations for designing wall units or trim and for the placement of wall coverings.
7. Select the fabric and furnishings.
8. Select paint colors and wall coverings.
9. Select window treatments.
10. Incorporate furniture you already own into the new plan.
11. Accessorize the house to give it a "finished" look.

How to Find an Interior Designer

Your search for an interior designer will not vary from that of the other professionals you bring to the job. When you are building a house or remodeling one, you should always be looking for recommendations for interior designers at the same time you are looking for architects, general contractors, and all other home

professionals. While you are looking for ideas for the exterior of your home in newspapers and magazines, you can also be looking for designers who have done interiors that you admire. Here are several ways to begin your search:

1. **Ask family and friends to recommend designers they have previously employed or that their friends have employed.** They can tell you how the designer works, how satisfied they were with the designer's services, and so on.

2. **Look through "shelter" or home-oriented magazines.** Local home resource magazines, if available, can be particularly helpful for locating capable designers in your area. If you find designs that interest you, see if the magazine has specified the designer. If not, you can call the magazine and request this information. While shopping for designers, you can also be looking for design ideas or furnishings that appeal to you.

3. **Visit model homes.** Visiting model homes will provide you with good ideas as well as insight into a particular designers' ability. If you like the interior in the model, ask for the designer's name.

4. **Go on house tours.** This is good method of gathering ideas for your own home and getting familiar with the work of excellent designers.

5. **Call the national office of the American Society of Interior Designers (ASID).** The number is 800-775-2743. Or you can visit their Web site at www.interior.org to obtain the names of members from their worldwide referral service.

When to Bring an Interior Designer in on Your Project

Interior designers are often brought onto the job when the construction is complete. That is fine if they will only be assisting you with the selection of fabric and furnishings. If, however, you want more design input, you should bring the designer onto the project during the development stage, when you are working with the architect.

The designer should review the placement of electrical layouts. He or she can help locate the best places to put outlets and fixtures so that they will be hidden and allow the easiest furniture placement. The designer can contribute to the architectural design by adding beams, moldings, and built-ins. Our designer moved doors on the original drawings to offer the best possible flow of space and rearranged the interior layout of a bathroom to create the most attractive and practical arrangement of components.

Selecting an Interior Designer

When you have found several designers you are considering working with, set up a consultation with each one. If an assistant is going to be working on your project, be sure to meet this person and look through her or his portfolio. Discuss the designer's fee arrangements and your own budget. Call recent references. Before making your final choice, be sure to consider the following:

1. **Consider whether you like the designer's sense of design.** It is irrelevant what style you have seen a designer work in on other projects; a good designer is generally capable of working in most any style. You must look at how they use the space, how they handle conversation areas, how well they use color, how unified the various rooms are, how well the furniture is scaled to the size of the room, and so on.

2. **Consider whether the designer is a good listener.** Find a designer who understands the look and feel you want to achieve. He or she must be attentive to the practical considerations which concern you. If durability is a priority, make sure the designer won't be suggesting delicate antiques and glass coffee tables. When the designer leaves your home, you will live with the results of his or her work for a long time.

3. **Consider the designer's experience.** The designer may be creative, but experience could make her or him a more seasoned, effective professional. Find

out how long the designer has been working in the field and has worked on the types of projects that are similar in size and complexity to yours.

4. **Find out who will be doing the shopping.** Will the designer expect you to shop with him or her, or will the designer pick out furnishings, fabric, wall coverings, floorings, and paint samples for you to select from? Some people prefer to see all of their options and enjoy the shopping. Others prefer to work with someone who will do all the legwork for them. You must select a designer who works in a way you feel comfortable with.

5. **See if the designer will be open to your suggestions and those of the other professionals working on the project.** You will get the best results if you, the designer, and the other professionals on the project can positively interact as a team. The designer may suggest, for example, eliminating one window to expand the wall area in the guest/office space. The architect can be helpful in determining if this will compromise the look of the exterior; the lighting specialist can tell you if there will be enough light and if additional fixtures should be planned.

6. **Consider the designer's knowledge of resources and current innovations.** Ask what resources the designer uses and if the designer is continually seeking new ones. Designers should be familiar with a wide range of materials (tiles, floorings, wall and window coverings), furnishings (tables, sofas, chairs), and craftspeople available to make custom furniture. If the designer keeps up with current trends and spends time shopping for new resources, he or she will be better equipped to recommend what is available. The designer I worked with recommended small copper tiles that could be interspersed with slate tiles on the bathroom floor. This was a look that she had seen in her travels and sought out for her clients. It was not a look that I had seen on my own.

7. **Consider the designer's knowledge of various periods and styles.** Find out if the designer is familiar with the particular style you would like for your home. If you have decided to design your home in French country, for example, see if the designer understands the furnishings from that area.

   If a designer has a good sense of symmetry, design, and color, they should be able to adapt their talent to any style. Most talented interior designers are capable of working in any style with good taste, although there may be a period or style they are not comfortable working with. Discuss the style you are considering, to be sure the designer is comfortable with that particular one.

8. **Check to see how the designer executes his or her plans.** See if they are done by hand or with the use of computer-aided design (CAD) or computer-aided design and drafting (CADD) software. If possible, try to find a designer and an architect who use the same method. This will save you money and time.

9. **Find out if the designer has worked on projects similar in size to yours.**

You don't want to hire someone who will be either overwhelmed by the size of your project or unhappy with the limitations of your budget or the size of your home.

10. **Be clear about who will be doing most of the work.** If you are hiring a design company, be clear about who will be working on designing the space and who will be supervising installations. Make sure both people (if there is more than one) are qualified. Find out what level of involvement the person you hire will have.

11. **Make sure the designer has the time to work on your home.** You don't want your project delayed because the designer is too busy to work on it. You may need to make a quick decision and want the designer's input. Find out if the designer will be available to you on a timely basis.

12. **Make sure the designer has good references.** Be sure that the previous clients were satisfied with the designer's performance, attitude, integrity, honesty, and creativity.

13. **Decide whether close proximity to the designer is important to you.** There are excellent designers all over the country. It is possible to find a designer who does not live in your area, comes highly recommended, and has great regional resources and craftspeople to create furnishings.

There are several drawbacks to working with a designer out of your regional area. The designer may not be able to be present when the furnishings arrive, so he or she can place them. They may not be available for onsite consultations on a timely basis or to help with the ongoing decisions that have to be made during the construction process.

However, I've worked with a designer from across the country on my last two projects. I have so much confidence in this designer that I am happy to sacrifice proximity for her great skill, knowledge, and professionalism. This designer is accustomed to working with clients at a distance and has worked with clients from as far away as Japan. Before hiring a designer from a distance, though, find out if he or she is accustomed to working in this way. This situation is not for everyone, but it's one you may want to consider.

14. **As with other professionals you choose to work with on your house, make sure you have a good rapport with the designer.** You will spend a great deal of time with the designer, either on the phone or face-to-face. Having a good relationship with your designer will make the experience much more pleasurable.

15. **Make sure the designer is able to work within your budget.** Let the designer know what your budget is and what areas you hope to complete in your home. Find out if the designer feels that your proposed budget is realistic for the size of your project. If a designer is experienced, he or she should be able to give you a preliminary estimate as to what your project should cost given your wish list.

16. **Be sure the designer prepares carefully executed plans.** It's important that you and other people working on your project will be able to read and work with the plans. When you are calling for references, ask previous clients if the plans were carefully executed. Ask the designer to see plans that she or he prepared for other clients.

17. **Find out what professional training the designer has had.** The terms interior decorator and designer are sometimes used interchangeably. Almost anyone can be a decorator, with or without a certificate.

A designer is someone who has completed a degree program from an accredited university.

18. **Find out the designer's policy on your selecting items on your own.** You may find items in your travels that you would like to purchase while you are working with the designer. Find out if the designer will have a problem with this and whether there will be a charge for accepting the items into her or his plan.

19. **Make sure the designer will be able to work within your time schedule.** If you are hoping to move into a beach house for the summer, you might be on a tight schedule. Find out if the designer can complete the project by your requested date.

Preparing to Work with an Interior Designer

After you have selected a designer, you should set up a working meeting with him or her to further discuss your project.

Be prepared for this meeting, and bring the following:

1. **Pictures.** Bring magazine or newspaper clippings, or photos of items or details you like. You may like the overall look of a room or a specific part. Organize the pictures into categories, either by room or by materials: flooring, wall covering, window treatments, and so on. The more pictures you can show the designer, the better she or he will understand what you want to achieve.

2. **A list of furnishings you own.** Prepare a list of all of the furnishings you currently own that you plan to incorporate into your new home.

3. **A list of space priorities.** Let the designer know if storage is a priority, whether the use of rooms for dual purposes is important, and so on. Make a list of every room in the house and the function it will serve.

4. **A list of color preferences.** List specific colors you prefer and those you don't like. You might also let the designer know if you prefer warm colors (red and orange), cool colors (green and blue), primary colors (red, blue, and yellow), secondary colors (orange, green, and purple), pastel colors (baby pink and powder blue), or earth tones (rust and olive). There are several excellent books on the market that can help you focus on color.

5. **A list of fabric preferences.** Let the designer know what types of prints, textures, weaves, and so on you prefer. You should take the time to visit fabric stores to get an idea of the type of fabrics you like. You can also scan books and magazines for pictures that appeal to you.

Information an Interior Designer Should Have

The designer should ask you many questions before beginning to design your home. To do a good job, your designer should know about:

1. **Your lifestyle.**
   - Whether anyone works at home and will require room for equipment, storage, and work space.
   - What room you watch television in.
   - How you entertain (formally or informally).
   - Where computers will be kept.
   - Whether anyone will require space for crafting.
   - Whether there will be any large instruments (such as a piano or a harp) that require space and/or quiet for practice.
   - For a weekend house, there may be special requirements, such as the storage of skis or extra sleeping facilities.
   - How many children you have and their ages. Where they will play, do homework, and sleep.
   - Whether anyone living in the house or visiting has special needs, such as an older adult or a person with a disability.
2. **The importance of durability.**
3. **How much maintenance you are willing to do.**
4. **If you own artwork that must be worked into the plan.**
5. **Furniture that you own that you plan to have in your new home.**
6. **Your budget for the project.** Make sure the designer can work within your proposed budget. If not, you have the option of expanding the budget, modifying the plan, or finding another designer.
7. **The style you prefer.** Contemporary, modern, period furnishings, and so on.
8. **Your preferences in design.** Color, pattern, texture, style.
9. **The type of mood or ambiance you would like to create.** Mellow, vibrant, earthy, and so on.
10. **The importance of storage.** In what parts of the house you need it.
11. **Collections.** Where you would like them displayed.

How Interior Designers Charge for Their Services

The method of payment will depend on the area of the country in which the designer works, the designer's expertise, and the size of the project. Speak with several potential designers and find out the going rate in your area (unless you plan to employ a designer from outside your area). Select a designer who not only meets all of your other criteria for personality, professionalism, and design ability, but who has fees you will feel comfortable with. Often fees will consist of a combination of more than one of the following types:

1. **Straight design fee.** The designer gives you a price for the total job or breaks the project down into stages with a price for each stage. The advantage of this pay schedule is that you know in advance what the design services will cost. If you should choose to terminate the project with the designer, you can do so at any stage and know in advance what your financial responsibility will be.

2. **Hourly fee.** The client is charged for the time it takes to draft plans, shop for furnishings, coordinate the furnishings, consult with other professionals on the job, supervise construction, and so on. Rates often vary within a design company, based on the expertise of the individuals who work on the project. This fee is often combined with a percentage of purchases.

3. **Percentage of purchases.** The designer generally buys furnishings at wholesale prices; they mark up these prices anywhere from 10% to 100%. This percentage will be added to all purchases.

Find a designer that you trust professionally. Be sure you're comfortable that the designer's fees are in line with his or her expertise and that you feel the designer has the integrity to be fair and honest.

The Contract

The contract or letter of agreement between the designer and client should include the following information:

1. **The location of the project.**
2. **The specific areas of the house that will be designed.**
3. **The services to be included.** Designing the space (working up a floor plan and/or elevations), purchasing furnishings, hiring and supervising workers (such as painters and carpenters), and supervising the installation of furnishings.
4. **The expenses that the client will be responsible for.** Telephone calls, postage, traveling expenses, and so on.
5. **A preliminary estimate of the cost of the project.** A professional designer should be able to give you a fair estimate of what your project should cost. Don't expect this to be exact; a ballpark figure is appropriate.

6. **Design fees.** The type of fees and the rates should be included.
7. **How the client will be charged for furnishings they purchase themselves.** Designers may charge their full percentage, a modified percentage, or possibly no fee at all.
8. **How often and in what manner the client will be billed.**
9. **A stipulation that the client will approve all items purchased by the designer for their home.** Make sure you will have the opportunity to approve all items before they are purchased.

Periodic Statements

Statements are usually issued monthly. Find out how the person you hire handles this. Expenses that you should expect to see are:

- Design expenses.
- Deposit costs on purchased items.
- Final costs on purchased items.
- Labor costs on custom-made items.
- Commission percentages on purchased items (depending on the agreement you have made).

The owner should scrutinize the statements to be sure there are no errors, not only in accounting but also with items incorrectly ordered. The designer may have unknowingly ordered an item that you don't want. This can be picked up quickly by reviewing the statements.

Selecting interior furnishings and details can be the most enjoyable part of the project. It may come after months or years of arduous construction. Working with a compatible designer can be a great joy. If you select well, you can develop a relationship that can extend to future projects, large and small.

Notes

CHAPTER 6

Landscape Professionals

The outdoor area of your house should be as livable and enjoyable as its interior. It should meet your needs in terms of recreation (swimming pools, tennis courts, and so on), entertainment (areas for cooking and dining, lawns, decking, patios), a place for children to play (swing sets, playhouses, grounds to run around on), and gardens. An attractive outdoor area will enhance, not only your enjoyment of the grounds, but the value of your home. Take the time to develop this part of your "kingdom."

The landscape should relate to and be consistent with the style and tone of the house. If you are designing the landscape at the same time as you are designing the house, you have the opportunity to integrate the style of the two. At the same time, you can incorporate the audio, telephone, and lighting systems into the landscape. The extent of the participation of the landscape professional (LP) will depend on how large your project is and how much you want the LP to be involved in it. The type of professional that you hire will depend on what aspects of the landscape will be attended to and how much of the job you will do yourself. If you are renovating or enhancing your home, it might be a small job; if you are building a new house, the property may be relatively undeveloped and it will be a much larger project.

Types of Landscape Professionals

The type of landscape professional you hire depends on the type of project you will be undertaking, how much of it you will do yourself, and what you budget is. First decide want you want to accomplish and then interview several landscape professionals; select the person you feel meets your criteria. (Suggested criteria are listed later in the chapter.)

Landscape architects are licensed professionals who have gone through a bachelors program (BLA-Bachelors of Landscape Architecture) and/or a masters program (MLA-Masters of Landscape Architecture) at an accredited college and have studied horticulture along with landscape architecture, geology, art history, and a variety of related courses. They have a broad education that encompasses all aspects of the landscape, not just plantings. They have to be licensed by the state, which requires passing an exam and serving an apprenticeship. They are able to create a design and draft a plan for all aspects of your outdoor design. They can:

1. Help site (or position) the house to take the best advantage of the sunlight and views.
2. Design pools, tennis courts, and gazebos.
3. Design terraces and patios that are either attached to the house or apart from it.
4. Plan plantings that are appropriate to your location and house style, including trees, plants, vegetables, and herbs.
5. Help select fountains and sculptures for the garden.
6. Plan roads that enter the house, walkways, and paths.
7. Design outside lighting. You will need lights for security around the house and for the safety of your family and guests. Lights are needed for convenience if you want to sit out in the evening, and lights may be needed to illuminate tennis courts or swimming pools. Lighting can illuminate your house and plantings in the evening to enhance their beauty.
8. Plan grading and drainage to avoid flooding and water from pooling in an area around the house. Water can ice up in the winter to create a safety hazard.
9. Plan an irrigation system, which will help to maintain the plantings with sprinklers in the spring and summer.
10. Help to plan recreation areas where children can play or use play apparatus, such as swing sets and trampolines.
11. Plan retaining walls to prevent the soil from eroding or to create areas for plantings. Steps

can be designed to link several areas on different levels.

12. Design and suggest fencing for privacy, decoration, or safety around a pool.

13. Plan areas that may be used for cooking (such as a built-in barbecue or outdoor refrigerator)and dining (picnic tables and the like).

14. Help to plan structures such as pool houses.

15. Help plan for the maintenance of the property. They should give you the names of several contractors or individuals who can help maintain the pool and plantings. If you spend a great deal on plantings, for example, you don't want someone inadvertently removing flowers that are mistaken for weeds.

16. Contract for and supervise all or part of the landscape work.

Landscape designers may have had the same education as landscape architects but have not gone through the process of becoming licensed. Typically, however, the landscape designer has gone though a basic horticulture program geared toward the design of plantings. They can design a garden, which you might execute yourself or contract out. If you are planning to design or enhance your garden, a landscape designer may be very qualified and artistic. Before you hire anyone, however, find out about his or her qualifications and expertise.

Design/build contractors usually have a landscape designer on staff (who can design a total concept), as well as a crew of people who will execute the entire landscape plan or supervise their own contractors to complete the project. They purchase the materials and plants, which they will have to guarantee. A big advantage to this arrangement is the wear and tear it takes off the homeowner. It is a lot of work to hire contractors and then to schedule, supervise, and coordinate all of them. If, for example, you were putting in new gardens, you would want to have the irrigation system installed before you put in the plantings. The installation of a pool should coordinate with lighting, decking, plantings around the pool, and the installation of a cooking area.

Design/build services may be more costly than if you bid each portion of the project out with the individual contractors. For a large project, however, this type of arrangement will certainly simplify your life. You will have to decide which type of service you need based on the complexity of your project and your budget.

When to Hire a Landscape Professional

Often landscape professionals are hired after the construction is complete. It is far more practical, however, to bring the LP to the project before the architect has completed the working drawings. The LP can help to position or site the house, as well as design a plan that will integrate the landscape with the house. A plan should be worked out even if you don't intend to complete this work immediately. It would save money in the long run if you were able to include at least some aspects of the landscape in the general contractor's bid, such as outside lighting and the pavement of roads. If you later choose not to have the general contractor do any of this work, at least you will an idea of costs for future reference and can include these costs in your overall budget. If possible, the GC should execute at least the preliminary work necessary for the preparation of your future plans-such as installing conduits in the ground to carry wiring for lighting and outdoor telephones, and installing the underground components of an irrigation system-while the ground is already being disturbed.

How to Find a Landscape Professional

After you identify the type of professional you want to hire, take the time to use all of the available resources to find several people to interview. You want to hire someone who will best meet your needs and make it a pleasant experience. Where do you get names? Start with these suggestions:

1. As with other professionals, the best recommendations come from family and friends who have a personal experience with a particular landscape designer.
2. Other professionals, such as architects and general contractors, can very often make excellent recommendations. If they have worked with a landscape designer in the past, they are familiar with their work and can attest to their reliability and artistry.
3. Nurseries can sometimes recommend landscape designers they have successfully worked with.
4. You can contact the American Society of Landscape Architects (ASLA) by telephone at 202-898-2444 to get the number for the local chapter. Most chapters publish a statewide directory of landscape professionals. Several states also publish profiles on various members. You can visit the ASLA Web site at www.asla.org for the names of landscape designers in various cities.
5. Often landscape professionals advertise in local magazines. Check out these ads as well as any pictures of their projects that may be included.

Criteria for Selecting a Landscape Professional

Designing the landscape will be an enjoyable experience if you take the time to select an individual or company who meets most of the following criteria.

1. **Try to select someone you will enjoy working with and who you feel you can connect with.** As with the architect, you should feel that you have a commonality in your design sense with the landscape professional.

2. **Make sure the person you select is experienced and competent in residential architectural design.** Commercial projects can vary a great deal from residential ones, so find someone who predominantly works on residential projects.

3. **Check the credentials of the person you are considering.** See if the landscape architect is a member of the ASLA (American Society of Landscape Architects), which requires a degree and apprenticeship. Most states require landscape architects to take an exam, which generally conforms to the standards of the Council of Landscape Architectural Boards (CLARB), with variations in different states.

4. **Make sure the landscape professional is creative.** Check the designer's portfolio to see the work she has done. Visit some of the sites she has recently worked on. Look to see if all of her work looks the same. If you like that particular style, that may work for you. But try to find a landscape designer that adapts her ideas to individual houses, various terrains, and different styles. See that she is competent in designing in a variety of styles: contemporary, natural, historic, formal, informal, or Asian gardens, particularly if you are not sure what your landscape should look like. Try to find someone who can offer options that are appropriate to your house. If you prefer a style that the landscape designer cannot do, look for another designer.

5. **Make sure the designer is a good listener**. Be sure he is able to listen to what you want and will design what you have in mind, rather than what he has in mind.

6. **Make sure the designer is a team player.** Be sure the designer feels comfortable taking suggestions from the other members of the team. This is especially important if you hire the landscape designer at the beginning of the project, when the team might include the architect, interior designer, lighting specialist, and so on.

7. **Make sure the landscape designer has knowledge of all the aspects of the landscaping that you will need.** Make sure she has knowledge about gardens, walkways, pools, grading, patios, lighting, drainage, tennis courts, and

any other aspect that may be included in your plan. If she is not able to plan outside lighting, for example, consult a lighting specialist.

8. **Be sure the landscape designer is familiar with your region.** The landscape designer should know what will grow in the area. If there are deer or other animals, he should know what plantings the animals are likely to eat, so that you can avoid those species of plants. Also be sure he is familiar with local codes. If he will be putting in a pool, he will have to get a permit, and local regulations will prevail.

9. **Make sure the landscape designer has good references.** Check with previous clients to make sure the landscape designer was easy to work with, made workable plans, executed the project well, was fair with fees, was creative, completed the project on a timely basis, and so on.

10. **Find someone who will be on the job or closely supervise their workers so that the job not only goes according to plan, but also that there is no damage caused by the workers.** You want to make sure that wires that are already in the ground are not cut and other items already present are not damaged.

Things to Consider When Planning the Landscape

All of the following are important considerations when you plan your landscaping. The landscaper should meet all of these criteria if he or she is to establish a workable plan for you.

1. **Practicality.** This should be your first concern. Be sure there is room to comfortably park your car and those of your guests. Access to the house should be easy and well lit. There should be an accessible and unobtrusive area for trash and the storage of wood (if you have fireplaces).

2. **Budget.** Be clear about what you are prepared to spend on the project. The landscape professional should suggest alternatives to items that are too costly. If you have the time, try to shop around for prices on some of the items you plan to include in the landscaper's responsibility. It is always an advantage to have an idea what items and services cost before negotiating a final price.

3. **Consistency.** The landscape should be consistent with the style of the house and its interior.

4. **Future.** Care should be taken to plant trees, shrubs, and flowers that will blossom at various times of the year so that the land will not look barren. Consider what plantings will look like in 10 years. Will trees grow so large they will hide the house?

5. **Maintenance.**

- Consider how much work you plan to do to maintain the plantings, pool, and so on.
- Consider whether you plan to hire professionals to do the maintenance or if you will do it yourself.
- Plan the landscape so that it is manageable for you if you will be doing the maintenance. Plan for self-cleaning apparatus (such as a Polaris)if you will be maintaining the pool yourself. These devices are not maintenance-free but will limit the work you will have to do. Consider installing an irrigation system (or sprinkler system) for watering the plantings.

6. **Children.** Be sure space has been reserved for swing sets and any other play options. Fencing, which is usually required around pools by local codes, should be planned, especially when there are young children living there. There should be plantings in front of steep areas of the terrain to protect children from falling down.

7. **Demands of the land.** Check to see if you will need retaining walls. Also check for areas where trees will have to be cut down to make room for future roads or construction.

8. **Aesthetics.** Plant flowers, trees, and shrubs that will enhance the beauty of your property and that you will enjoy looking at.

Conditions You Should Include in the Contract

Be clear in advance that everything that you and the landscape professional agreed upon verbally will be in your contract. Include the following items as well:

1. Be clear about the landscaper designer's responsibility. Know in advance exactly what you are paying for and what the cost will be. Find out how you will be billed and at what points in the work plan. Find out if you will be paying for the initial consultation.

2. If the landscape professional will be purchasing the plants and trees, find out if he or she will guarantee them, and for how long.

3. Make sure the contractor will be responsible for any damages caused by his or her work.

4. Make sure the landscape designer specifies what materials or plants will be used, along with the cost.

5. Find out how extra charges will be determined. These are items that might not have been on the initial contract but were added later on.

6. Make sure the contractor will provide insurance for all laborers on the job. The law requires that the contractor carry workers' comp and general liabil-

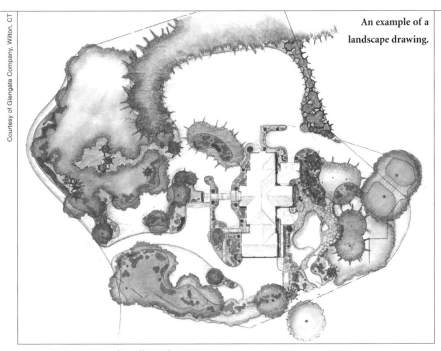

An example of a landscape drawing.

ity insurance for all workers.

7. Designate who will pay the subcontractors and who will be responsible for guaranteeing their work.

8. Find out if the landscape designer will execute drawings. Make sure it is noted who will own the drawings. This is necessary if you decide to terminate your contract with the landscaper. Sometimes the landscaper will work up design drawings for a fee, which will later be taken off the cost of the actual work.

9. Make sure there is an opportunity to end the contract if you are unhappy with the services or decide to put this phase of the project on hold.

10. Make sure that if you hire a contractor they will secure all permits and certificates and arrange for necessary inspections.

The methods of payment to landscape professionals are numerous, as are the responsibilities they take for the project. The LP can design just the plan or take responsibility for the plan and the execution of all aspects of it. There are also an enormous number of alternatives between these two ends of the spectrum. Some landscapers will charge a fee for the plan and a percentage of the work or an overall charge for the entire plan. Costs will vary greatly with location. You should interview several landscape professionals and see what the going rate is, then decide to what extent you want the LP involved in the project. The sooner you decide what the landscape plan will be, the more efficiently you will be able to plan for this part of the project.

CHAPTER 7

Kitchen Essentials

The kitchen is one of the most important rooms in most homes. It is the hub of family life: the place where everyone in the family gathers for dinner, where homework is done, where guests are entertained, where the family just sits and relaxes.

The kitchen is by far the most complicated room in the house to construct; it is also the room that can cause many delays in completing the construction of a house. When the kitchen is part of a larger renovation or house construction project, careful attention should be paid to delays that may occur in other areas of the house, which could in turn delay the completion of the kitchen. If the construction is taking longer than expected, suppliers should be informed as quickly as possible, so they can reschedule deliveries and installations.

For renovations of just the kitchen, you and your family will most likely be living in the house while the work is being done. Pre-planning is necessary so the family will be inconvenienced as little as possible. Work done on the kitchen is a tremendous intrusion, particularly if it drags on for several months. All of the components should be selected and purchased before the demolition is begun. A bonus and penalty clause should be incorporated into the contract if a general contractor is working on the job. Many GCs are working on several projects at the same time and don't share your sense of urgency to complete your home. If there is a bonus for finishing by a particular date, they are apt to work more diligently. In the same way, they won't be happy to lose money with a penalty.

If you are renovating an existing kitchen, you may extend its size by pushing out exterior walls and/or extending the walls of the current kitchen to integrate with other rooms, such as an adjacent den. You will then have to hire an architect and a general contractor to complete the project. By extending the walls of your current kitchen, you may have the option of adding to the functions of the kitchen by adding a sitting room, laundry room, office space, and so on. If you don't plan to extend the walls of the kitchen, you will have more restrictions on your design plan and the functions the kitchen will serve.

If you are planning a facelift for your kitchen, you can do as little or as much as you like. Your decision will be based on how long you plan to live in your home, the budget you've allotted for the project, and how much you feel it will increase the value of your home. Sometimes a new coat of paint, new wallpaper, new hardware, a new kitchen table or a new appliance will give your kitchen a fresh look. Refinishing kitchen cabinets is also an option. This may cost from one half to one third the cost of new cabinets. Many custom cabinet makers will not refinish cabinets, so unless you plan to refinish them yourself, you may have to find another professional to do the job. Many of them will prefer to finish cabinets in their workshops because a more precise, even job will result.

Be aware that the domino effect sometimes occurs in the case of kitchen facelifts. Put in a new sink and the counter top will need to be replaced. When the counter top is replaced, often the backsplash will also need to be replaced. Try to get as much information as possible before embarking on such a project.

This chapter is not meant to be an exhaustive study of kitchen design but a directory of the many components to consider when planning a kitchen. For inspiration and information on available options, review some of the many books, magazines, newspapers, and Web sites listed in the appendixes.

Preliminary Considerations

The following are important factors to consider before planning the kitchen with the architect or kitchen specialist:

1. **Functions.** Besides the obvious cooking functions, kitchens today also serve as play areas, media centers, dining rooms, offices, hobby rooms, and so on. Consider what functions you want your kitchen to serve.

2. **Proximity to outside areas or other rooms.** Decide whether it is important to have access to the outside: a play area, patio, and/or swimming pool. Consider whether the kitchen should open to other interior rooms: the dining room, playroom, office, and so on.

3. **Accommodating furniture.** We planned our kitchen around a beautiful old table that we'd grown quite fond of and wanted to use in our new house.

Decide if there are any pieces of furniture that you own or have seen in a magazine or store, or on a house tour that you would like to incorporate into your kitchen design.

4. **Style.** The kitchen should be in a style that works with the rest of the house. Whether your home is formal, country, or modern, the kitchen should be integrated with the other rooms, particularly those adjacent to the kitchen.

5. **Budget.** How much do you plan to spend on the kitchen? Take into consideration all the components involved, including cabinets, appliances, flooring, wall treatment, window treatment, furniture, lighting, and any relevant professional fees.

6. **Aspects of your current kitchen that you like and dislike.** Look at your current kitchen and see if there are aspects you would like such as a window above the sink. Consider those aspects that you would like to change, such as size, amount of counter space, and types of storage space.

7. **How many people will be cooking in the kitchen at the same time.** Will one person be cooking at a time or will several likely be cooking together? This may make a difference in the number of sinks you plan for and the amount of counter space you will need.

8. **Health Risks of Cabinets.** There is a great deal of formaldehyde in the glues and resins, as well as the plywood, MDF, and particleboard used to make cabinets. If you have concerns about allergies, buy factory-produced products, which are already cured in the factory and are much safer. Choose cabinets that are totally sealed on the edges and on the backs to prevent the seepage of toxic gases. If you have cabinets that will be painted on site, ask that they use paint that has fewer health risks, such as water-based paint. Find out how long it will take for the cabinets to cure and consider staying away for that period of time, which may be anywhere from 3 days to 2 weeks. Ask the cabinet company salesperson whether they generally use a neutralizing chemical on their plywood and particleboard to lessen the effects of the formaldehyde. Discuss your concerns and find out what measures the individual companies take to prevent health risks.

9. **Appliances.** You will have to select the appliances you prefer. The possibilities are numerous. You will also have to decide which small appliances you will have and if they will be put away or stored on top of counters.

10. **Eating areas.** Will you choose to have a table, counter, fold-down table, or a combination? If you decide to have a table, what size will be appropriate for the room?

11. **Cabinetry.** What style and color cabinets do you like? What items do you plan to store in them?

12. **Shelving.** Decide if you prefer open or closed shelves.

13. **Grocery storage.** Consider how many groceries you will need to store. Do you generally buy in bulk or just what you need each day?

14. **Cookbooks.** Think about how many cookbooks you will need to store in the kitchen. Then plan for shelves to accommodate them.

15. **Electronics.** Will you want a telephone? A television? A computer? You will have to plan where they, and the outlets for them, will be.

16. **Islands.** Decide if you want to have an island and what its functions will be. It may have a counter for eating, counter space for working, storage for various items, a place for appliances, and so on.

17. **Storage.** What items do you need to store in the kitchen? Do you have several sets of dishes? Many large pots? Platters? If there will be a television viewing area, will you need a place to store tapes?

The Kitchen Specialist

If you are renovating a large part of your house or building a new one, you may want your architect to plan the kitchen design. Some architects excel in this area. Most, however, will prefer that you consult a kitchen specialist for the design. Kitchen cabinet suppliers generally have kitchen designers on staff who will help you design the kitchen as an accommodation. There is sometimes a charge, which is deducted from the cost of the cabinets. Some stores, such as large hardware chains, have designers who will show you instantly how a variety of kitchens will look on the computer. Getting input from several sources will help you to decide what you will or will not like for your new kitchen. Kitchen cabinet suppliers generally install the cabinets and will sometimes install the appliances as well.

Many of the same methods of finding other professionals apply here. There are several national kitchen cabinet companies with local representation, and there are many local companies and private designers around the country. The following are suggestions for how to get an idea of what is available:

1. Ask friends and neighbors; they are the best source.

2. Ask the architect, general contractor, and other professionals on the job for referrals.

3. Look for advertisements in local publications.

4. Check the phone directory.

5. Go on house tours and take notes.

6. Contact the National Kitchen and Bath Association (NKBA) at their Web site www.nkba.org. Call their consumer line at 800-367-6522 and ask for a listing of kitchen designers in your area.

7. Books and magazines are an excellent source of inspiration. Magazines generally have the most current trends and product information. Take advantage of the easy-to-order brochures available in many of the home magazines. Check Appendix B for recommendations relevant to your situation.

Initial Planning

You will begin to speak with kitchen designers, look through catalogs, magazines, books, and newspapers and you will begin to develop preferences in these areas. The following are the many aspects of the kitchen that will have to be coordinated:

1. Cabinets and hardware.
2. Appliances.
3. Ventilation.
4. Counter tops.
5. Lighting.
6. Furniture.
7. Pot rack.
8. Window treatment.
9. Flooring.
10. Sink(s) and plumbing fixtures.
11. Electrical lines (outlets, telephone, and cable lines).

If you have the space, try to plan for a separate pantry and utility closet. Both of these spaces will give you great additional storage space. These spaces should be worked out with the architect, if there is one, and can later be fitted either by the GC or the cabinet manufacturer.

For new construction or extensive house renovation, all of the above items will have to be coordinated with the general contractor along with the rest of the house. Begin plans for the kitchen at the earliest possible time. Put together a budget, shop for all of the above items, and try to put together a plan before the final architectural drawings are complete.

Make sure the GC obtains a permit from the local building department, on a timely basis, so there are no delays in beginning construction. Have the GC give you a schedule or work one out together. If you are purchasing the cabinets, flooring, and so on, you must make sure that everything will be delivered in time for the GC to meet his target date. Completion dates must be put on all items ordered for the kitchen. You must call periodically to make sure everything will be on time. Being on top of the project will help to make it move along smoothly and on schedule.

If you are on a tight budget or merely want a face-lift for your kitchen, consider refinishing the existing cabinets. You can replace doors, drawers, cabinet finish, hardware, and/or counters and get a new look. You should shop around for the cabinets/counters that will work best with your existing framework. Try to redesign the kitchen so that you maintain the same locations for the sink, stove and refrigerator, if possible, to save on plumbing costs. A kitchen specialist should be able to redesign the existing kitchen to better meet your current needs and update its look and functionality.

For one-room renovations, you may opt not to hire an architect, in which case you probably will not have a floor plan of the room. It is therefore important to develop a plan yourself so that you can speak to dealers and get a preliminary plan and price estimate. Some dealers will charge a fee for coming to your house to take measurements of your kitchen. Others will not come to your house unless you have given them a deposit and signed a contract. It is therefore helpful to develop your own floor plan to bring along with you when you are shopping for cabinets.

Creating Preliminary Kitchen Drawings

Drawing a floor plan (an overhead view) of the room is not difficult and requires no professional training or experience. Begin with a large piece of graph paper that can be purchased at most stationery stores. A simple scale-four squares to a foot-makes

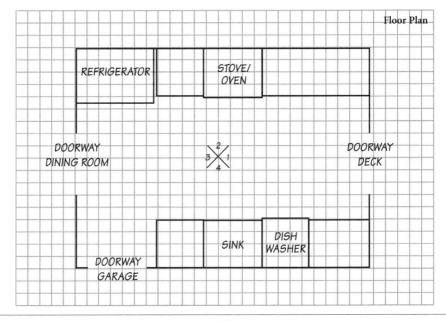

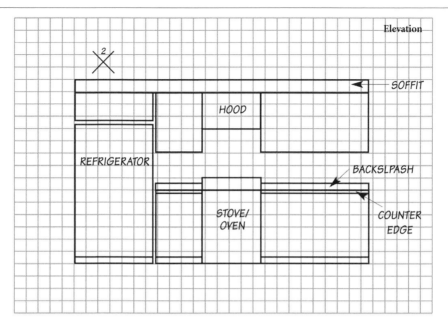

it easy to draw quarters of a foot or 3 inches with each box. Measure as many walls as there are in the kitchen and draw these lines on the graph paper. Then measure the distance from the walls to the windows and doors and include those features in the plan. You should also include your appliances and sink so the designer will know where the water lines are. An example of a simple floor plan is shown in the diagram on the facing page.

If you have mastered this drawing, you should attempt an elevation drawing, which is a drawing of a wall as you would see it straight on. You would measure the height of the room and draw vertical lines on the graph paper using a similar scale as above. Then measure the length of a particular wall and draw horizontal lines for the ceiling and floor. A drawing should be done for each of the relevant walls. You can then include items currently in the kitchen. An example is shown in the diagram above.

This might seem like an overwhelming project if you haven't done it before, but if you take some time, it is not difficult. These drawings will be tremendously useful in working with potential kitchen dealers.

Possible Kitchen Layouts

Kitchen designers often recommend that the following three work areas form a triangle in the kitchen. This is meant to be a useful guide rather than the rule. According to the NKBA (National Kitchen and Bath Association) the total distance between the points of the triangle should not exceed 26 inches. The three areas are:

- **Food storage:** refrigerator.
- **Food preparation:** range and oven.
- **Cleanup:** sink and dishwasher.

Several basic layouts accommodate this triangular layout:

- **Straight line.** This is stretching the triangle idea with the sink in the center and the refrigerator and range on opposite sides. Consider using all under counter appliances with this layout, such as an under-counter refrigerator/freezer in order to give you extra workspace. Pull-out carts (with storage underneath) and counter on top will also give you additional work space, which can be used by an additional person working in the kitchen. If you have the space, try to make the base cabinets deeper than the usual 24 inches so the rear of the counter can be used for storage.

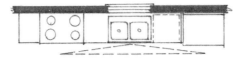

- **Galley.** This configuration consists of two walls facing each other. The sink should be in the center of one wall, the refrigerator and range on the opposite wall, separated by counter space. Everything is close at hand, but it could be crowded with more than one cook in the kitchen. Make sure the distance between facing cabinets is at least 42 inches so you can use appliances and also have room to pass. If you want to eat in the kitchen, a pull-down table can be included in the design.

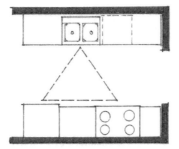

L-shape. This is a common design that lends itself to a center island and a dining table. It is sometimes tricky to make the right angle in this configuration functional. Full and half lazy Susan cabinets work well in corner spaces. Some cabinet makers have devised unusual pull-out cabinets to take advantage of the space. Appliance garages can be used to take advantage of a large corner counter space. Find out how the various cabinet companies deal with this area.

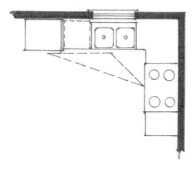

Broken U- or G-shape. In this design, a peninsula is added to the U-shape design, which can be used as an eating counter, a cooktop, or additional counter space. This is another popular kitchen configuration.

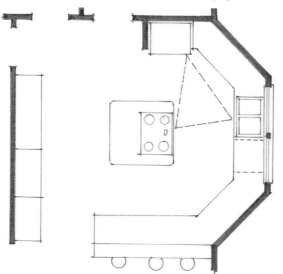

U-shape. The most common kitchen design, this layout has three walls to work with. In a wide U shape, there is room for an island in the center. The end of the U is a good place for a breakfast nook or table. Because it has two corners, care should be taken to make good use of that space.

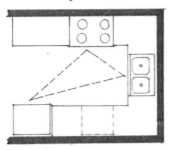

Box shape. Cabinets or counter space can be situated on four sides. If the triangular configuration is adhered to, this is a very efficient and comfortable room to work in. An island is usually used in the center of this design.

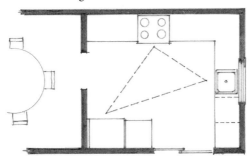

Many other configurations are possible, particularly in large kitchens. It will be up to the kitchen designer to come up with the best design to meet your needs and take the best advantage of your available space.

Basic Specifications

Check to see that the kitchen plan, developed by the kitchen designer, has a well-planned work center and also meets the basic specifications listed below. If it does-n't, ask why! Obviously, if you opt to have the cabinets custom made, you can make them any size you want. These specifications are offered as a guideline.

- Counter space should be adjacent to the open side of the refrigerator. Counters should be at least 15 inches to 18 inches on the opening side of the refrigerator or have 15 inches to 18 inches of counter space on an island that is not more than 48 inches away.
- Counters should be at least 15 inches on one side of a built-in oven/range or have access to counter space on an island that is no more than 48 inches away from it.
- Counters should be at least 18 inches on one side and 24 inches to 36 inches on the other side of the sink.
- There should be a 42-inch to 48-inch clearance in front of a dishwasher.
- There should be a 48-inch clearance in front of an oven.
- There must be a minimum of 36 inches between a dining table and the wall.

General specifications:
- Base cabinets are 36 inches high and 24 inches deep.
- Wall cabinets are 18 inches above the base cabinets, 30 inches high, and 12 inches deep.

Kitchen Components

The kitchen is composed of a number of essential components, including cabinets, countertops, sinks, appliances, ventilation, lighting, electrical lines, flooring, window treatments, and furniture. The best way to become an educated consumer is to shop around and explore as many options as possible. You will formulate a better idea of what you want-both in terms of style and price-after exploring many alternatives.

The variety of available kitchen styles has grown in the last several years; you have many more options than ever before. People are now using mismatched cabinets, antique units in place of some cabinets, and freestanding pieces in place of islands. By shopping around and perusing the current magazines and books, you will find a variety of unusual and innovative looks that you might want to incorporate into your own kitchen.

Cabinets

Your cabinet selection will depend on the size of your room, your budget, your design preferences, and available features. If you would like to have an unusual type of design, you may have to have your cabinets custom-made. If you are on a tight budget, stock cabinets may be the most practical.

You can find beautiful cabinetry in all price ranges if you spend time shopping around and apply your creativity. A particular company may economize, for example, by offering inexpensive handles. Companies sometimes offer alternatives for an upcharge. If they don't, you can request a discount and buy the handles of your choice elsewhere.

You will find mail-in cards in the back of some magazines that will help you get easy access to literature about various cabinets; magazines that specialize in kitchens are listed in Appendix B.

How Cabinets Are Sold

Cabinets can be purchased in the following ways:

1. **Mass produced or stock cabinets.** Dealers of stock cabinets represent one or more factories, which manufacture a range of cabinets in specific sizes. Generally, there is a wide range of sizes, materials, designs, and finishes to accommodate most tastes. Stock cabinets are generally the most reasonably priced cabinets as well. Ready-to-assemble (RTA) cabinets are available for handy do-it-yourselfers. The dealer usually provides a design plan of the kitchen as a bonus for purchasing their cabinets. Sometimes, however, they do charge for this service, which will be deducted from the purchase price. In some home centers, designs are done on a computer (on a CAD system) while you are there.

2. **Custom factory-made cabinets.** The company builds the cabinets to order according to client specifications. They offer specific sizes and designs that are adapted to the individual kitchen space. The factory may be represented by many dealers or by just one or two. They usually offer a larger selection of materials, colors, finishes, and styles than are available from stock companies. Custom factory-made cabinets are generally more expensive than stock cabinets as well. The dealer usually provides a design plan for these cabinets, deducting the design fee when the cabinets are purchased.

3. **Custom-made cabinets.** These cabinets are built to order by a carpenter, according to the home owner's specifications, in his or her own shop or on site. They are hand-made to the customer's specifications. The design and material options are unlimited, except for those imposed by the carpenter. If your needs are unusual, custom-made cabinets are a good option, but they are usually the most expensive and not necessarily of any better quality than the custom factory-made cabinets. Also, keep in mind that the carpenter will generally not design the kitchen; you must have a kitchen planner or architect,

supply the carpenter with shop drawings.

Selecting a Kitchen Dealer or Carpenter

Make sure you do your homework in this area when selecting a kitchen dealer or carpenter. Meet with a variety of dealers and craftspeople before making a decision. Compare all of the following factors before selecting cabinets.

1. **The dealer's reputation for quality and service.** If possible, work with a principal of the company or a manager. Salespeople often leave in the middle of projects, which can cause confusion and delay. Owners and managers are also often more anxious to please the customer. Check to see how long the company has been in business. Try to make sure that the company that takes your deposit will still be in business when the time comes to deliver the cabinets.

2. **The creativity of the designer employed by the dealer.** Dealers will work up a plan based on the floor plan that you or the architect has provided. (Occasionally the company will go to the house to measure the room before working up a plan.) The dealer will ask you about your requirements and preferences, then create a plan on the computer or by hand. There are usually many possible designs that can be done for any kitchen; the creativity of the designer in coming up with an attractive and efficient kitchen may determine which company you choose to work with.

3. **The eagerness of the dealer to work with you.** Early on, you should eliminate dealers who forget to call you back and seem uninterested when you are shopping around. Chances are they won't get easier to work with when they start your project.

4. **The variety of styles and materials available.** Each company works with a limited variety of styles and materials. Some companies specialize in a particular style: country, contemporary, formal. Most companies offer a limited variety of materials as well. You may want to explore several styles and materials before settling on a particular one.

5. **The quality of the workmanship.** As you begin to shop around, you will see the variation in quality. Look at drawer construction to see if there are interlocking joints (and glue) or if they are just glued. This is an excellent visual clue to the quality of the workmanship. In quality cabinets, joints will join the other parts of the cabinet, but these are not visible. Joints are much stronger than nails; see if nails are visible on the cabinets.

6. **The quality of the materials.** If the cabinets are wood, look to see if they have many knots and imperfections and if the grains, tones, and color of the wood are consistent. Look to see if the cabinets are painted-indicating the

wood may be a poor grade. If the material is laminate, look to see if Color-Core® (which is the same color throughout) is used so that dark edges will not be seen. Look at the interior of the cabinets; make sure they are plywood or particleboard, the most stable materials for the interiors. Check to see that the same materials are consistently used in all cabinets. Look at the types of hardware (slides, knobs, and handles) used.

7. **The cost of the cabinets.** Just as cabinets come in a wide variety of styles and materials, they also come in wide range of costs. When you are ready to make a decision, make sure you are comparing like products and materials.

8. **The cost of installation.** The dealer who sold them to you should always install the cabinets. Otherwise, if the cabinets don't fit, the dealer and installer will be pointing fingers at each other. The owner is the ultimate loser in that situation.

9. **The availability of accessory items.** Check to see what accessories–knife drawer insets, spice racks, towels racks, pot racks, blackboards, and/or knobs and handles are available. After looking at the cabinets of several companies, you will know what is available and which items you prefer.

10. **The references of the dealer or carpenter.** Ask for recent references. Find out if the cabinets were delivered on time, if the customers received what they thought they were getting, if they were happy with the quality and efficiency of the installer, and if the company was cooperative in returning to fix imperfections or errors.

Cabinet Construction

There are basically two types of cabinet constructions: frameless and framed.

Frameless cabinets (overlay door construction). These cabinets are sometimes referred to as European cabinets. The hinges are always hidden. This type of construction is very often used in contemporary style homes. They always have concealed adjustable, or European, hinges. They are attached to the interior of the cabinet and cannot be seen unless the cabinet is open. Many of the interiors, particularly those on moderately priced cabinets, are made of particleboard. The screws that are used to attach the hinges to the interior of the cabinet often become loose over time and begin to shift because there is nothing to hold on to. Plywood is more stable for the interiors but is rarely used on frameless cabinets. Occasionally the doors even become unattached at a particular hinge area. The hinges are made adjustable so that the door can be put back in line. People are often lead to believe that the adjustable hinge is an added feature. Do not be impressed with this feature; it is a nuisance to constantly adjust hinges. If you are planning to use frameless cabinets, be sure the interior is particleboard or plywood.

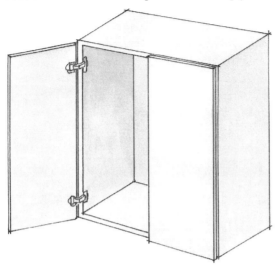

Face-frame cabinets (inset door construction). These cabinets are made with a frame around their periphery. When the door or drawer is attached to the frame, a portion of the frame is visible. The hinges may be visible, semi-visible, or concealed. They are sometimes referred to as American cabinets, which tend to have a more traditional or country look.

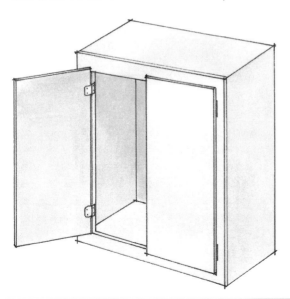

Hinges

The style, weight, and material of the cabinet and door determine which hinge should be used. When you are shopping for cabinets, ask if there are any options in hinge style and finish. Check the hinges in the showroom to be sure the doors open easily. Cabinets generally open on the side, but hinges are also available for hatchback style (top-opening), pocket door, and pull-down doors (although they are not commonly used). Hinges are available in many finishes and, if visible, should be matched to the other hardware in the kitchen as well as to the overall style of the room.

Cabinet Exteriors

The exteriors of cabinets are available in a wide range of materials. Combinations of materials are now common as well as the use of door-less cabinets integrated into the design. All doors should be 3/4 of an inch to 1 inch thick. The thicker the doors, the sturdier they will be.

Solid wood. Solid wood cabinets are available in a wide variety of types: oak, maple, cherry, and pine are very popular. When considering wood cabinets check the following:

- The selection of wood offered.
- The cost of the wood you prefer.
- The grade of wood. A lot of knots, blemishes, and figuring (design) indicate a low grade of wood.
- The uniformity of the color, markings, and grain.
- Choice of stain colors and finishes.
  - If wood is stained dark, the manufacturer may be camouflaging a poor grade of wood.
  - If the cabinet is painted, make sure it is wood or MDF (medium-density fiberboard), not particleboard. Particleboard is not as durable as MDF or wood. Cabinets will take a great deal of abuse, so make sure the materials are strong enough to last.
- Whether there is a recessed or raised panel wood door. Anticipate that the door may develop hairline cracks where the parts meet because of the difference in the natural expansion of wood (caused by changes in temperature and humidity). The cracks will be more visible in painted wood than unpainted. To avoid such cracks, the house should be climate controlled. If you live in a very moist area and the climate is not controlled in your house, do not buy face-frame cabinets. Frameless cabinets will have more flexibility if the cabinets expand. Hard woods

(mahogany, cherry, walnut) are denser and take in less moisture and so are not as susceptible to expansion as soft woods. Some companies offer cabinets with a higher moisture content, which is more suited to certain climates.

- If there is a floating panel on a cabinet (a panel inserted in a groove into the frame, but not attached, to allow it to expand and contract), make sure the entire panel will be stained before it is inserted into the frame. The panel may shrink as a result of changes in temperature and humidity, showing more of the periphery of the panel than it had before.
- Whether the factory will include an ultraviolet protection against fading.

Painted Wood. Check for the following:

- Find out what type of wood will be used. Hard woods are denser, less susceptible to moisture, and less likely to crack. Hard woods are also less likely to dent. If there is a dent in a painted cabinet, the paint will visibly be dented as well.
- Check that all areas of the cabinet will have the painted finish.

Wood veneer. Check for the following:

- The substrate (the base for the veneer) is MDF or particleboard. MDF should be your preference.
- The veneer is affixed well to the substrate and won't easily peel off.
- All outer areas of the cabinet are made of the same veneer.
- The thickness of the veneer is at least .7 or .8 inches thick.

Laminate. Check for the following:

- That it's available in a color, texture, or pattern that you like.
- That all areas of the cabinets will have the same material. This includes side panels, inside doors, and so on.
- What the substrate will be, preferably MDF.
- That the laminate is attached well to the substrate.
- That a minimum thickness of .028 inches is used.

Lacquered.
- This is a multicoated painted finish. The finish can be high-gloss or matte. This coating is added to the cabinet's core material. Scratches can be buffed out of some lacquer finishes.

- To check for quality lacquered cabinets, look to see if the color is consistent over the entire cabinet. Look at the clarity of color and see if the finish is smooth to the eye and to the hand. The look should be like an auto finish.
- The substrate should be MDF.
- If all the edges of the cabinets are finished and sealed, gases from the glues and resins used to assemble the core material of the cabinet can't leak out. This makes lacquered cabinets an excellent choice for people with allergies.

Glass.
- There are various options available in glass, such as tinted, clear, smoked, colored, stained, leaded, sandblasted, and etched.
- These can be used effectively to display favorite china or collections and/or as a decorative element to break up the cabinet area.

Stainless steel.
- Check to see the gauge of the stainless steel. Stainless steel comes in 16-, 18-, and 20-gauge material, with 16 being the best.

Cabinet Interiors

A variety of materials are used for the interiors of cabinets. Commonly, a different type of wood is used on the interior than on the exterior. This is fine as long as you know in advance what interior material you are getting, that the material is consistent throughout, and that it is complementary to the exterior.

The following are some of the materials commonly used on the interiors of cabinets:

1. **Particleboard.** Many inexpensive or moderately priced cabinets have particleboard interiors. They can have a laminate (which can also have a wood coloring) or wood veneer finish. Particleboard works very well in most situations. However, in frameless cabinets, which use screws to hold the hinges to the cabinet and door, particleboard may not be sturdy enough to support the screws, which may loosen over time, causing the doors to shift. This problem will be described in the hinge section.

2. **Plywood.** Expensive cabinets usually have interiors made of plywood with a hardwood veneer, which may be different than the wood on the exterior. This is a very stable material and looks like solid wood. It holds hinges well and is very durable.

Cabinet Design

Many features are available. After looking at various cabinets, you will select those you prefer.

- Recessed or raised-panel cabinets come in a variety of styles. The center panel is either raised or recessed with one or several beading designs and shapes. Thy can be multi-paneled and also have several layers on them.
- Beading (molding) is available in simple or ornate styling. Beading alone (without recessed or raised panels) is often seen on more moderately priced cabinets.
- Two-sided cabinets open from both sides and can be used to divide the room or be put on islands or peninsulas to make access easy from both sides.
- Blackboards (slate or slate paint) can be installed on a panel of a pantry door for family messages or grocery lists. They are very useful as well as being an interesting design feature.
- Cabinet heights may vary from the traditional 36 inches. If the chefs in the house are particularly tall or short, or if they are confined to a wheelchair, the cabinets can be adjusted to a comfortable height. The resale value of the house could be affected, however, if you alter the height substantially. On the other hand, if you plan to live in your house for many years, chances are the new owners will want to renovate the kitchen anyway. Therefore, make the kitchen as comfortable and utilitarian as possible for yourself and your family.
- Appliance garages are available with some cabinets. They are a good feature for people who prefer their small appliances to be out of view. Others prefer them to be more easily accessible and on top of the counter. Another option is to store small appliances in the cabinets,

KITCHEN ESSENTIALS

A blackboard integrated with the kitchen cabinets.

which does require lifting them when needed. Appliance garages can take away from precious cabinet and counter space. Consider your preference before the kitchen is designed. If you do plan to include appliance garages, be sure to have outlets included in them as well.

- Open shelving, bins, and/or drawers are available on most cabinets. There are many options for storing pots and pans, cutlery, dishes, and so on. Evaluate your needs and preferences before shopping for cabinets.

- Paper toweling is something that most people use and want to have in a convenient location. Placement is often overlooked, however, until the kitchen is complete. A dispenser can be put inside or under a cabinet or built into the cabinet. When you are shopping for cabinets, ask the dealer if they offer any options for paper towel storage. It is better to make this choice in the planning stage.

- Baking areas have become more popular recently. If you like to bake and have the space, a great idea is a low cabinet with a cold surface (such as marble or granite) for rolling dough. This is also a useful place for baking and cooking with children.

- Dish-drying cabinets are bottom-less, slotted cabinets used above the sink for drying and storing dishes.

Accessories are available from most cabinet dealers. Insets and special compartments are very useful for storing a variety of kitchen items. Find out which accessories are available from the various companies you speak with. The following is a partial list of some available options:

- Vertical dividers for trays.
- Breadboxes. Request a metal inset that will keep the bread fresh and the crumbs in one place. This should be removable for cleaning. Don't put the breadbox next to the dishwasher; the moisture could make the bread mold quickly.
- Trash bins: regular and recyclable.
- Knife insets for drawers.
- Silverware insets for drawers.
- Spice racks or insets for drawers.
- Pantry insets.
- Pullout cutting board. Be sure it can be removed for cleaning, particularly if you plan to use it for cutting meats.
- Tilt-down compartment for sponges.
- Towel bar inset.
- Racks for cleaning supplies.

- Lazy Susans are used in corner cabinets to make use of difficult space. Items often fall off, however, and there is still some wasted space. These shelves are excellent, however, for storing large platters and other oversized items.
- Cookbook holders.
- Stemware racks.
- Wine racks.
- Pullout baskets or bins for storing a variety of items.
- Storage cabinet for mops and cleaning supplies.
- An elevator shelf, which rises to counter height and lowers into a base cabinet to hold small appliances.
- A stepladder that pulls out of a toe-kick panel.

Cabinet Drawers

Drawers can be used for storage of a multitude of items. Many insets are available to store items such as spices and knives. Large drawers can be used to store pots and pans and smaller ones to store cooking utensils and a variety of dishes. Lined drawers are available for storing bread and other food items. Drawers get a great deal of use, so they must be well made to hold up over time. Table 7-1 lists those aspects of drawers to look for and those to avoid.

Table 7-1 Drawer Construction

Look For	Avoid
1. Drawers that are constructed of a plywood bottom (1/4 to 3/8 inches thick) and hardwood sides (1/2 to 3/4 inches thick). Laminated MDF or HDF (high- and medium- density fiberboard) can be used for laminated cabinets.	1. Particleboard drawers.
2. Drawers with four sides. A separate panel should be attached for the front of the drawer.	2. Drawers with a fourth side that doubles as the drawer front. This design is not as sturdy as four-sided drawers.
3. Drawers with interlocking joints, such as dovetails, or dowels.	3. Drawers that are stapled or glued.

Slides

Slides are on the sides or bottoms of drawers and help the drawer to easily open and close. Slides come in several varieties. When selecting your cabinets, be clear about what kind of slides will be used on the pullout drawers or shelves. Avoid cabinets that have a single slide; select those that have two, either undermount or sidemount.

1. **Undermount slides.** These are generally used on more expensive cabinetry and are installed in pairs underneath the drawer or shelf. They allow the drawers to be wider and to hold more weight.
2. **Sidemount slides.** These are attached to both sides of the cabinet shelf or drawer. The size of the drawer is more limited, as well as the amount of weight the sidemount slides can support. These runners are typically used on less-expensive cabinets.

Both styles of slide come with either 3/4 extension or full- extension runners. The full-extension variety is preferable because these slides allow you to get to items in the back of the shelf or drawer. Slides are also rated for different weights. Some runners will hold 30 to 40 pounds; others will hold up to 75 pounds. This is an important feature if you plan to use the drawer or shelf to store a small, but heavy, appliance or if you have small children who might want to try and get into a drawer.

It is best to look at the slides and check to see that the drawers move easily and silently.

Handles

Handles come in a large variety of styles, finishes, sizes, and colors. They should be consistent with the style of the kitchen and coordinated with the other metals in the room. As mentioned earlier, if the cabinet you want doesn't offer handles that you like, ask the dealer if there are any alternatives. If not, ask for a discount and find your own handles elsewhere. Purchase your own handles if you feel it will make a big difference in the appearance of the cabinets. If possible, shop for handle options so that you will have an idea of what you like before you settle on cabinets.

Purchasing Cabinets

Get bids from several sources-carpenters and cabinet dealers-before making a decision. When you have found cabinets that you like, have the sales company make a plan for you. The plan will offer their ideas on the best use of your space. Usually, this is a free service, but sometimes there is a fee if you decide not to buy from them. If you don't hire them, you probably won't be able to keep the plans, but you will nevertheless have a better sense of what you want. You should plan to make a small sketch of the plan when you leave the designer. (A space has been left in the Notebook at the end of this book for a sketch on each dealer page.)

Once you have seen the designs of several companies, you may decide that you like the style, quality, and costs offered by one company, but not necessarily their proposed design. You should have them alter the plans to meet your new insights and negotiate the best possible price. After meeting with several kitchen contractors, we decided to remove one door, one window, and one island from our original architectural plans. We settled on our "perfect" plan only after exploring many kitchen alternatives.

When you order the cabinets, you will be given a final plan with a contract and payment schedule. Most companies will require a percentage of their fee when the contract is signed (usually 50%), another percentage when the cabinets are delivered (usually 40%), and the final payment when the installation is completed (usually 10%). Be sure to review the contract and plans carefully. Even if you have reviewed the plans with the dealer, review them again carefully and question any part of the plan that is not clear. The dealer should explain why the kitchen was laid out in a particular way. If you have a question about any aspect of the plan, ask the dealer before the contracts are signed. Often people are surprised or disappointed when after the cabinets are installed, they appear different than they did on the plan.

Countertops

When selecting countertops, you will find a large variety of materials to choose from, ranging from very expensive to moderately priced, and from extremely durable to quite delicate. You will make a selection based on your budget, the durability you require in your household, and the appearance you prefer. While you are shopping for countertop materials for the kitchen, you should also be looking for materials for the bathroom and other areas of the house where you might want stone, solid surfacing, or other counter and floor materials. The best way to decide what you want to purchase is by looking at all of the options.

Look at various materials and find out as much as you can about each. When you have found a material that you like, look at as many variations as possible and compare prices. Find the best variation at the best price, from the most reliable supplier. Wherever possible, get a sample, even if you have to leave a deposit for it. Every dealer labels varieties of stone with different names. My designer sent me a beautiful variety of limestone. I called several local stone dealers to locate that particular variety. Nobody seemed familiar with that label. I did manage to find it locally with an entirely different name. The best way to compare products that might have different names is to have the product with you. It is important here, as with all of the other products you are shopping for, that you keep good notes on prices and descriptions. You will find the products you prefer at a better price if you are knowledgeable.

Table 7-2 includes information about the most commonly used materials for countertops.

Table 7-2 Countertops

Material	Examples	Cost	Advantages
Laminate	Solid Core laminate	$$	Price Stands up to moderate heat. Easy to clean. Not likely to break dishes. Available in a large variety of colors, patterns, and textures
Ceramic Tile		$ $$-$$$$	Resistant to knife cuts. Tiles can easily be replaced. Resists scratches. Most heat resistant.
Concrete		$$	Can form any kind of edge. Can be any thickness. Can be tinted many colors.
Stone	Marble Granite Slate Soapstone Limestone	$$$-$$$$$	Surface scratches and stains can be polished out. No grout lines. Some stone (granite) won't burn.
Solid Surfacing	Corian Avonite Surrel (Laminate)	$$$-$$$$$	Resistant to cuts, scratches, and stains. Burns, cuts, and scratches can be polished out or pieces replaced. (Save the piece removed from the sink for possible patching.) Large variety of matte and glossy finishes. No grout to keep clean. Seams are usually invisible.
Solid Surface Veneer	Wilsonart	$$$-$$$$	Less expensive than solid surfacing, with many of its advantages.
Stainless Steel		$$$$	Doesn't chip, stain, or burn. Has an industrial look. Can be renewed with polishing.
Wood	Butcher block Teak	$$ $$$$	Can be used for cutting. Has a warm look.

Alternative applications

There are a variety of ways to individualize your countertops. Here are a few suggestions:

1. Traditionally, countertops are from 3/4 inch to 1 1/4 inches thick. Most materials can be ordered in thicker slabs (1 1/2 to 2 inches) or thinner slabs.

Disadvantages	Type of sink to be used
Easy to scratch or cut. Scratches will collect dirt. Can be easily scorched. Cannot be repaired. Plain laminate leaves a brown seam (which is not so on solid core laminate.)	Drop In
Grout is porous and absorbs stains easily. (Consider using a dark grout, which won't show stains as much.) Glassware dropped on it will break more easily than on other materials	Drop in Tile in
Porous, difficult to sanitize even if sealed. Glassware dropped on it will break. May need several seams if large.	Drop in Tile in Under counter
Expense of materials and installation. Visible seams. Glassware will break if dropped on it.	Tile in Under counter Integral
Expense. Glass will break if dropped on it. Needs work to keep it clean.	Drop in Under counter Tile in Integral mount (available from some solid surfacing companies.
The expense of fabricating this material makes it almost as expensive as solid surfacing though still a bit less.	Drop in Integral
Has a cold appearance. Suppliers are limited - may have to be custom-made to fit. May show scratches. Expense. Hard water causes water stains.	Integral mount-fabricated in one piece with the counter. Drop in
Requires maintenance: oiling and resurfacing. Porous: difficult to sanitize. Susceptible to heat and water damage.	Drop in

2. For an interesting, unique look, use more than one material for the counter-tops in the kitchen. One material can be used on the island, if there is one, and another material on the rest of the counters. If it is a very large kitchen, you might consider a third material. Marble is often used for a baking area because it is cold and excellent for rolling out dough.

3. Drain boards (next to the sink) can be integrated into some counter materi-

als, such as solid surfacing, stone, and stainless steel. This prevents your having to use ugly plastic drain boards and is a wonderful feature if you are using a material that lends itself to this application.

Back splashes

The back splash is the area above the counter top and below the cabinets. You need to choose the material for this area when you are choosing the counter material. You may opt to use either an alternate material or the same material for the back splash as for the counter. Whatever material you pick should be easy to clean and non-staining. Stainless steel, solid surfacing, and laminate work particularly well when they are fabricated with the counter. Back splashes may be 4 inches or go up to the bottom of the cabinet above. You can explore some other possibilities for the backsplash:

1. Using the counter material with a different application, such as altering the color or pattern of the material.
2. Using a novelty material, such as a mirror, colored glass, or novelty ceramics.
3. Using a painted design on tile.

Sinks

Kitchen sinks come in many colors, materials, and mounting styles. After you have

Table 7-3 Kitchen Sinks

Material	Cost	Advantages
Porcelain-enameled Cast Iron	$$	Resistant to scratching and staining. Available in colors.
Stainless Steel	$-$$$	Doesn't chip or stain. Very durable.
Solid Surfacing	$$$	Countertop and sink can be integrated – having no seams to accumulate dirt. Resistant to staining. Can be scoured. Scratches can be easily removed.
Quartz Resin Composite	$$$	Doesn't chip or stain. Scratches and stains can be rubbed out.
Fire Clay	$$$-$$$$	Scratch resistant. Durable-won't fade, rust, or discolor.
Stone -Soap stone -Slate -Granite	$$$$-$$$$$$	Stains and scratches can be polished out. With a stone counter there are no visible seams.
Copper-Weathered & Shiny	$$$$$$$	Appearance.

selected the countertop, you need to explore your sink options.

Installation or mounting type

Before you choose your sink, you have to choose your countertop. Your sink selection may be limited by the countertop material.

Drop-in or self-rimming. This sink is dropped into a hole in the counter. The sink has rolled edges, which sits on top of the counter top.

Undercounter or undermount. The sink is attached below the level of the counter. The advantage of this type of mounting is there are no seams to collect dirt, so they tend to stay cleaner. This type of mounting also keeps the attention on the counter rather than on the sink, which is an advantage if you are using a beautiful stone. There is also a bit more counter space because there is no lip to take up space on the countertop.

Tile-in or flush mount. The sink sits high to meet and be flush with a standard tile. It is then grouted to give it a finished look.

Integrated. The sink is joined to the countertop so that it appears continuous. It can be fabricated out of either one piece of material or two materials that are fused.

Table 7-3 shows the various materials that are used for sinks, the advantages and disadvantages of each, and available mounting types.

Disadvantages	Mounting available
Enamel can chip away. Heavy to mount.	Self-rimming. Tile in. Under-counter.
Hard water causes spotting. Material can dent & scratch. Thin-gauge stainless steel may sound tinny.	Self-rimming. Under-counter.
Expense.	Under-counter, tile-in, or integral mount. Self-rimming.
Tend to have a plastic appearance.	Self-rimming. Under-counter.
Expense. Not available in all designs.	Undercounter. Tile-in.
Expense.	Undermount. Self rimming. Tilein.
Expense.	Undercounter. Tilein.

Hole configurations

Hole configurations are pre-cut in some sinks and can be custom-cut on-site in others. Holes are used to incorporate various features into the sink. Some of the available features that you can select from include:

- Soap dispenser.
- Hot water dispenser.
- Separate sprayer.
- Water-purification spout.
- Chilled water dispenser.

Additional considerations when shopping for a sink are discussed below.

Sink size. The size of the sink will be determined by the available space. I recommend getting the largest sink possible so that you are able to clean large pots and platters.

Interior configuration. Sinks divided in a variety of ways are very popular. My preference is an undivided sink, which makes cleaning large items easier.

Number of sinks. Many people opt to have two sinks in a large kitchen so that two people can work at food preparation or so that one can be used for food preparation and the other for cleanup. It is all a matter of priorities. I prefer one sink and more counter space. If you do want to have two sinks, consider using a different material for the second sink for added visual interest. While shopping for sinks, consider whether you want an additional sink in the butler's pantry, laundry room, or bar.

Farm sinks. Farm sinks have become very popular and are available in a variety of sizes and designs. They have a terrific country look, but limit the usage of undersink sponge compartments, which have become popular. They are available in cast iron, fire clay, stainless steel, copper, and soapstone.

If you are renovating the kitchen and have decided to replace the sink, make sure that you will be able to find a sink that will fit the space. Consider that if you install a new sink you may have to replace the countertop as well.

Appliances

The average homeowner will keep her or his appliances for a very long time. Be careful to select those that will function well, that look attractive, and that are easy to maintain. Be sure that you select the appliances before ordering the cabinets, so you can be assured they will fit.

The best way to become familiar with the vast variety of appliances on the market is to shop at appliance stores, look at appliances on the Internet, collect brochures on the various products, and just generally become familiar with what is available. You can then select those products that best suit your needs.

I bought one of the new General Electric Monogram stoves. It came highly recommended by the salesman. I had my heart set on a Viking, but was convinced that the GE stove was a better product. The idea of purchasing an American product was appealing. The GE name behind the product gave me confidence that I was buying dependability and service.

Shortly after the stove was installed, I found out that I had to disassemble the sides of the oven to clean it. After a short investigation, I discovered it was the only stove that I could find that had to be disassembled to that extent. I called GE to complain. The service department told me that I should have read the manual, and the CEO of the company apologized for the inconvenience but refused to do anything about the problem. So, for obvious reasons, I highly recommend doing a great deal of research into reliability, maintenance, the warranty, and so on, so that you are not disappointed later.

You could call or write to several companies to receive brochures on appliances that interest you. Many of the magazines listed in Appendix B offer easy access to information from various appliance companies. Another efficient method is to get the information you need on the Internet. Many of the appliance companies have their own Web sites, which you can locate via one of the browsers. Homeportfolio (www.homeportfolio.com) offers a great deal of information on appliances as well as most other items for the kitchen and the rest of your home. A few other web sites with information about appliances are: Improvenet (www.improvenet.com), B4Ubuild (www.b4ubuild.com) – which has links to large and small appliance web sites. These sites are very helpful in educating the consumer about the abundance of different appliances available. Spend time reviewing appliance web sites, as well as the other sites listed.

After collecting information, you should visit stores so you can actually see the various products. Ask a lot of questions about maintenance, warranty, and features. Ask for recommendations and reasons for salespeople's preferences. Then make an educated decision about which appliances to purchase based on your own priorities: quality, price, ease of maintenance, color, and so on.

Consider your family's individual needs, your budget, and available space. We had the space, so we decided to add a small refrigerator in the island for our children. This eliminates constant opening of the larger refrigerator and provides easy access to healthy snacks that they can get themselves. Consider whether you want additional refrigerators in other parts of the house, such as in a butler's pantry, bar area, or master bedroom. Another option is two dishwashers to handle an abundance of dishes. If you have a large kitchen, consider using some of the many com-

Figure 7-1 Form for Getting Appliance Bids

Name	
Address	
Telephone	
Fax	
Name of store	
Salesperson	
Address	

Please fill in prices and return as soon as possible.

Appliance	Style	Price	Availability
Stove			
Refrigerator			
Microwave oven			
Dishwasher			
Compactor			
Range hood			
Instant hot			
Washing machine			
Dryer			

mercial appliances, which are heavy-duty and may work proportionally better in the room because of their generally large size. Think about whether you prefer a stove with an oven, or a cook top and wall oven setup. If you have a bad back, leaning down to take a heavy turkey out of the oven could cause unnecessary strain.

Select the appliances that you like and have them worked into the rest of the plan. Plan for the proper outlets for the large and small appliances while the architect is developing an electrical plan.

If you are renovating an existing kitchen, and decide to replace an appliance, be sure that you will be able to find a replacement that you like, that will fit into the space. Another issue to consider is the depth of the existing appliance. Make sure the flooring will meet the new narrower model. Investigate all of these issues before starting a kitchen renovation.

Once you've selected appliances, you should prepare a bid sheet of all the items you're planning to purchase (see Figure 7-1). Then solicit prices from several suppliers by mail or fax. Once you've received the bids, try to negotiate the best deal you can on all of the items from one source.

Some of the less popular appliances you might consider are:

- Food warmers.
- Warming drawers.
- Refrigerated drawers.
- Wine coolers.
- Ice makers.
- Trash compactors.

Ventilation Systems

Ventilation is necessary to remove the cooking fumes and smoke from the kitchen. The effectiveness of a ventilation system is determined by the cubic feet per minute (cfm) of air it removes. The higher the cfm rating, the more powerful the system. There are two types of ventilation systems:

- A re-circulating system is generally used in apartments and condominiums. The smoke is filtered and the air is pumped back into the room.
- A ducted system is more commonly used for houses. The smoke and fumes are expelled to the outside through a system of ducts. There are two types of ducted systems:

• Hooded systems have either an internal fan inside the hood or an external fan mounted on the outside of the house. If there will be a range hood, try to let the architect and GC know where it will be situated as early as possible, so that the proper duct work can be done. When you select a hood, make sure it is at least 6 inches wider than the cooktop so it will be able to capture the fumes and smoke. The optimum distance from the cooktop to the bottom of the hood is 21 inches to 30 inches. If you are planning on putting a cooktop on an island or peninsula, consider that a hood may obstruct the view across the room. If this will be a problem, another option would be to use a down-draft system. If a hood is selected, it should be no higher than 30 inches above the cooktop to be effective. The rating for a hooded fan should be a minimum of 150 cfm for a standard cooktop. The rating should be much higher for commercial-style cooktops, for cooktops over an island, and for cooktops with an added grill. There is a large variety of hoods available, so check out the many options.

• Downdraft systems have grills or vents mounted on the cooktop, which pull the smoke and fumes outside. The ducts are often run along the floor or inside cabinet toe kicks; they therefore have to be planned in the initial layout of the kitchen. This type of system is generally not as effective as a hooded system but is often chosen for its unobtrusive appearance.

Lighting

Be sure there is sufficient lighting for cooking, eating, working, and socializing in the kitchen at all times of the day. Lighting specialists are the best people to evaluate and recommend your lighting needs. Most retailers that sell lighting supplies have a lighting expert on staff and do not charge extra for the service if you buy your lighting supplies from them. Once you find a retailer who will make professional recommendations, bring them your kitchen layout and let them plan the lighting for you. The lighting will fall into the following three categories.

Task lighting. This is the most important kind of lighting in the kitchen because it provides illumination for work surfaces: over the sink, range, countertops, island, and table. Recessed lights-ceiling mounted or in soffits under the cabinets-are good sources of task lighting. Other types of lighting include track lights, wall fixtures, and ceiling fixtures. Decorative pendant fixtures or chandeliers work well over tables and islands for lighting up the area while adding variety to a lighting system that may include mostly recessed lights.

Ambient lighting. This is the general lighting achieved with natural daylight or a variety of light fixtures. It can also be used to create a mood in the room. Uniform light throughout the room can be achieved with recessed, track, wall, or ceiling fixtures. Putting all of the fixtures or an individual fixture on a dimmer (or rheostat) can set a particular mood. Remember to put lighting in a walk-in pantry (if there will be one), with a light switch on the wall outside of the pantry, on the handle side of the wall.

Decorative or accent lighting. Decorative lighting is used to accent a painting, a piece of furniture, an entranceway, a favorite object, or an architectural feature. The light should be three times more intense than that used for general lighting. This can be achieved with a variety of fixtures, including recessed or track lights with eyeball fittings.

The amount of lighting you need will depend on the size of the kitchen, the amount of daylight the kitchen receives, and the configuration of the design. Review the kitchen plans with a lighting consultant so that he or she can suggest the most efficient use of fixtures and recommend the newest design options.

Electrical Lines

Once you have selected the design for the kitchen, make a list of the electrical lines you will need for:

- Telephones.
- Television.
- Computer.
- Small appliances.
- Large appliances.
- Instant hot water (requires an outlet under the sink).
- Disposal (also requires an outlet under the sink).

If possible, you should review the plans with the local inspector to find out where outlets have to be placed to comply with local building codes. We completed an island and then discovered we had to add several outlets. Before the construction begins, plan the location of all switches and outlets so they are convenient and unobtrusive.

Flooring

Have the floor laid before the cabinets and appliances are installed. That way, the flooring will be installed over the entire floor and you will still be able to use it even if you decide to renovate the kitchen later. In addition to being practical in case of future renovation, having the cabinets on top of flooring also creates a better seal than flooring which just meets the cabinets. Also, if an appliance has to be repaired or replaced, it will be easier to remove the appliance on level flooring that covers the entire floor. Consider the following factors when selecting flooring:

1. **Comfort on the feet.** Some materials have more "bounce" and are easier on your feet. If you will be doing a great deal of cooking, certain floorings (such as hard stone floors or uneven tile floors) could be uncomfortable. If your kitchen will be merely decorative, any material will do.
2. **Safety from slipping.** Be sure the material you select is not slippery. Liquids spilled on the floor add to the danger of an already slippery surface.

3. **Maintenance.** Find out how the flooring will have to be cleaned-the simpler the better.

4. **Appearance.** The flooring should work with:
   - Other elements in the room.
   - Floorings in adjacent rooms.

5. **Cost.** There is a wide range of costs, from vinyl tiles, which are relatively inexpensive, to antique ceramic tiles, which are very costly.

6. **Substrate floor** (if renovating).
   - Can it hold the weight of a particular material, or will it have to be reinforced?
   - Does it need to be replaced?
   - Is there room to lay a particular material that is thick or requires mud laying?
   - Will the door (it there is one or more) clear this material?

7. **Renovating the current floor.** If you are renovating an existing kitchen, it is possible to refashion an existing floor. You could paint a pattern on an existing wood floor, for example.

Possible flooring materials (further info in Chapter 8, Bathroom Essentials):
- Concrete-stained and sealed or scored to look like tile.
- Linoleum, rubber, and vinyl.
- Stone.
- Wood.
- Clay tile.
- Ceramic tile.
- Glass tile.

Window Treatments

It is not uncommon to leave windows bare. Unless you are concerned about privacy or too much light, there is no real need to put anything on windows. Shades and curtains will add warmth and a decorative element. Consider alternative treatments for the kitchen windows. Valences (horizontal decorative fabric treatment used on windows) are often used to add accents to the window without obstructing the light. Shutters can be used on the entire window or just the lower portion-to let in light while creating a degree of privacy. Herb gardens and flower gardens can be set on shelves across the inside of the window to make a practical and colorful addition to the room. The window treatment should relate to the style of the kitchen and coordinate with the other colors and textures used in the room.

Furniture

The furniture you select for the kitchen will depend on the size of the room, your budget, and the look you want. Always try to use furniture you already own, even if it means painting or refinishing it. Consult with the interior designer (if there will be one involved in the building or renovation) or the kitchen planner during the planning stage for recommendations about the type of furniture you might use. Always consider durability, particularly if there are children in the house. Use fabrics on cushions and throw pillows that coordinate with the other patterns and colors in the room.

If there will be a kitchen table or breakfast nook, decide on the placement and size of the table before construction begins so that one or several light fixtures can be planned above it.

Consider having a window seat included in your plan if you have the space. Window seats add a warm touch to the room, create an added place to sit, and can be used for additional storage. Cushions for the seat can be coordinated with chair cushions, curtains, and the like later on.

Sofas and easy chairs create a relaxing sitting area in the kitchen where family members and friends can keep the cook company. Fabrics and throw pillows also can coordinate with the other materials and colors in the room.

Consider incorporating a freestanding antique, vintage, or contemporary armoire for storage or display. A desk can serve as a work area for paying bills or as an office. Found objects, such as empty barrels or trunks can serve as interesting tables to accompany casual seating.

Some terrific furniture and accessories can be bought through catalogs. Save catalogs and pictures of items from various publications that you think might be appropriate for your room when you are ready to furnish it.

Wall Applications

On walls where there are no cabinets, appliances, or furniture, consider some of the many possibilities in wall applications. Painting is always an option with a multitude of choices. Murals can be painted on the wall, as well as designs that emulate the look of tile. I recently saw portions of a wall painted to look like brick exposed through old stucco. Faux painting can be used to give the room a variety of special looks. Wallpaper can be used in an endless variety of colors and patterns. Only your budget and imagination will determine your limitations.

Pot Racks

Pot racks are available in many styles, from undercounter metal shelves to hanging racks. Pots and pans take up a great deal of space in the kitchen, so be sure to consider their placement when your plans are being developed. Discuss this option with whomever will be laying out the kitchen. Some companies that sell cabinets offer options to meet this need.

Otherwise, a variety of metal shelving and racks can be purchased separately from restaurant supply companies and kitchen supply retailers.

Additional Design Ideas

Here are some interesting design ideas I ran across while I was researching options for my own kitchen. Maybe some of them will appeal to you.

1. Plan for open shelving to display collections. Those that are relevant to the kitchen such as teapots and cookie jars look particularly good.

2. A friend of mine used facades of French bibliotheques (a cabinet with glass doors, originally designed to store books) as shelved storage and display areas. This can add a wonderful touch in a French country type kitchen.

3. Ceiling beams add a warm touch to the kitchen.

4. Assorted pottery and baskets add a great look to a country kitchen.

5. Seating banquettes can be used for dining, storage, and as a room divider.

6. A half beaded wall can be a nice trim in the kitchen.

French bibliotheque doors used over recessed shelving.

There are so many areas to explore when putting together the kitchen. Take the time to look at as many options as possible. You will be spending a great deal of time in the kitchen; try to create a room that you and your family will enjoy spending time in.

CHAPTER 8

Bathroom Essentials

Like the kitchen, the bathroom is made up of many elements, which come together to create a room that will look appealing and function well for you and your family. This chapter is not meant to be an exhaustive study of bathroom design but an outline of the elements to consider when building or remodeling a bathroom.

Preliminary Considerations

The design of the bathroom will depend on the following basic considerations:

1. **The size of the space.** Although not totally restrictive, the size of the space will put limitations on the items you can include and the functions the room will serve. Creativity can change even a small space into an attractive and functional one.
2. **Your budget.** Fixtures, faucets and bath accessories are available in all price ranges. Your budget will determine which items and materials you opt to use.
3. The design of the room will be determined to a large extent by who will be using it. Consider if it will be used by adults, children, persons with disabilities, older adults, or by guests, and whether it will be used by one person, shared by the whole family, or used only occasionally (perhaps in the case of a powder room).
4. **Its functions.** Bathrooms today are multifunctional. In addition to their regular functions, they can also serve as exercise rooms, dressing rooms, spas, and

sitting rooms.

5. **Your style preferences.** There are numerous design possibilities to suit any style, from hi-tech to Victorian and from country to contemporary. Before deciding on a particular style, look through some of the many specialty magazines and books listed in Appendix B for inspiration and ideas. The room should be designed to appeal to your personal preferences and should coordinate as much as possible with adjoining rooms in the house.

6. **Whether this is a new construction or a renovation.** If you are building a new house or doing a major renovation, you may have unlimited options for the size and design of the room. If you are remodeling just the bathroom, you will be limited to the existing space. It will be possible, however, to change even a small bathroom into a more functional, attractive one with material, fixture, and lighting changes. Try, however, to keep the fixtures in the same location to save on plumbing costs.

7. **Safety.** Many accessories are available to make the bathroom safe, particularly for children, persons with disabilities and older adults:

■ Grab bars should be placed in the shower near the entry and inside the stall, approximately 40 inches high. They should also be placed next to the bathtub. They should be easy to grip, slip-resistant, and capable of supporting 300 pounds.

■ Toilet seats should be equipped with anti-slam mechanism to protect little fingers. Medicine cabinets should be locked and out of the reach of children. Sturdy step stools should be provided for children so they can reach adult-size sinks.

■ Privacy locks should be used that can be quickly and easily opened from the outside in case of emergency.

■ Slip-resistant materials and surfaces should be used in wet areas.

■ Lever-style door handles are easier for children and the disabled to grab.

■ Night lights should be put in the bathroom to avoid falls.

■ Many fixtures are available for the disabled or older adults, such as special toilets with grab bars and higher height units from the floor. There are several Web sites which could be helpful in finding resources for making bathrooms safer, such as www.specialtyconstructions.com offer a variety of products (such as barrier free bath and shower systems) for people with special needs. They also renovate kitchens and baths and build entire houses for people with disabilities and/or older adults.

• www.akerplastics.com are manufacturers of showers and tubs for people with special needs. You can e-mail them through their web site to find a dealer near you.

• www.toilevator.com offers platforms which can be used on any floor mounted toilet and raises a standard 14-inch toilet three and a half inches, making it ADA (Americans with Disability Act) accessible at 17 1/2 inches high.

• For further information on universal design, accessible housing in general and products for residential use, contact The Center for Universal Design, at 800-647-6777 or go to their web site - www.design.ncsu.edu/cud.

8. **Privacy.** If more than one person will be using the bathroom at a time, consider putting an enclosure or a full- or half-wall partition around the toilet. Placing a toilet in an alcove sometimes creates adequate privacy. Saloon doors can offer easy access with some degree of privacy as well. Some people prefer to put the toilet in a separate room with a door; pocket doors (doors that come out from a "pocket" or space in the adjoining wall or walls) allow privacy without taking up a great deal of space. For baths and showers, you can create a private space with glass blocks or by taking advantage of corners or alcoves.

Planning the Design

If building the bathroom will be part of a new construction or major renovation, an architect will most likely design the space and the GC will supervise the subcontractors working on the bathroom, along with the other parts of the house.

If you are remodeling just the bathroom, you should consult with an architect or a certified bathroom designer (with a CBD-a certification by the National Association of Home Builders). You can contact the National Kitchen and Bath Association, listed in Appendix D, for a specialist in your area. You may also have to hire a GC to supervise the plumber, electrician, mason, and painter unless you or the bathroom designer will be doing this yourself.

If you are renovating just the bathroom, chances are you do not have a floor plan of the room and will need to develop one (see Chapter 7, Kitchen Essentials, for directions), noting the locations of the doors, windows, tub, toilet, shower, sinks, built-ins, and heating elements. Before meeting with a bathroom designer, prepare a floor plan and make a list of all aspects of your current bathroom that you like and dislike. Look through magazines, home sections of newspapers, books, and bathroom product brochures. Make a wish list of items you would like included in your new bathroom.

Choosing Room Elements

The following are some of the primary elements to consider when planning the bathroom: walls, flooring, lighting, windows, storage, vanities and counters, and ventilation. These will all have to be coordinated with the fixtures, fittings, and accessories, which will be discussed later in the chapter.

Walls

In bathrooms, where there tends to be a lot of moisture, care should be taken to use the most durable and waterproof materials possible. Interior walls can be made of glass blocks, which will allow light to come through while offering privacy. These can also be used for shower enclosures or for partitions. Table 8-1 lists some of the other available materials for bathroom walls along with the advantages and disadvantages of each.

Several of these materials can be combined in a single bathroom. The more waterproof materials should be used in the "wet" areas of the room. Many colors, textures, shapes, and designs in tiling are available. Consider combining several to create a unique and interesting look.

Flooring

When selecting flooring, consider cost, ease in cleaning, slip-resistance, durability, and appearance. Some building codes require a waterproof floor and baseboard in the bathroom. One material may be used on the entire floor, or two can be used to separate areas if the room is large enough. Table 8-2 lists some of the most popular flooring materials along with the advantages and disadvantages of each.

Lighting

Before planning the lighting, consider the amount of sunlight the room gets from windows and skylights during the day. The room's size and layout will determine the quantity and wattage of fixtures you will need. Lights in the bathroom should be on a dimmer so you can have adequate light for tasks such as putting on makeup and low light for a relaxing soak in the tub. You will need three types of lighting: ambient, task, and accent.

Table 8-1 Wall Coverings

Material	Advantages	Disadvantages
Ceramic and mosaic tile	Available in a wide range of prices; available in plain and patterned designs; durable, washable, and waterproof	Grouting may get dirty or flake off and may need to be redone in several years.
Glass tiles	Attractive.	Expensive; may crack if hit.
Stone and marble (limestone, marble, granite, slate,)-shiny tiles can go on the wall, although not on the floor.	Very durable.	Expensive; scratches are more noticeable on dark colors.
Wood (wood paneling, bead-board, or wood veneer; wainscoting)	Warm appearance; useful for covering uneven wall surfaces; good for insulation.	Must be sealed with a waterproof finish; not waterproof; should not be used behind the shower, tub, or sink.
Paint	Inexpensive; quick to apply. (Use vinyl paint that contains fungicides to restrict mildew growth.)	Not waterproof; cannot be used behind the tub, shower, or back-splash of sink.
Wallpaper	Many choices of color, texture, and pattern to choose from; vinyl-coated wallpapers are the best for this area and are easy to clean.	Not waterproof, least durable—should not be in direct contact with water.
Glass that has been painted on the back	Gives an illusion of space.	Can be broken with hard impact.

Ambient Lighting. Ambient lighting is for general lighting of the room. A variety of fixtures can be used, including a central pendent(hanging fixture), wall sconces, and cove lighting (lights are in a bay). These can be put on a dimmer for varying degrees of light in the day and evening.

Task Lighting. Task lighting is used for areas where you apply makeup, shave, read, or do any task that requires adequate illumination. For the application of makeup, ideal lighting should include lights directed from above and sides of the mirror. Another alternative is overhead sconces used with additional recessed lights in the ceiling. A pull-out lighted mirror is useful for shaving and putting on makeup as well. You will need to have moisture-proof lights above showers and baths for safety. Overhead lighting will be necessary for those who like to read in the tub. (Most building codes require switches to be 5 feet to 6 feet away from any water source.) Task lights include track lights, recessed lights, and sconces.

Accent lighting. This lighting is used to highlight structural features (such as on bathtub platform steps) or decorative features (such as plants or ornaments). For bath and shower areas, waterproof recessed lights are

Table 8-2 Flooring

Material	Advantages	Disadvantages
Stone (limestone, sandstone, granite, slate, marble)	Luxurious looking; durable; easy to clean; large variety of colors and textures.	Expensive; requires a strong subfloor to support the weight. Some stone can stain and must be sealed. Can be cold on the feet in the winter. Smooth finishes should not be used because they will be slippery when wet.
Ceramic tile: porcelain, terra-cotta, quarry, saltillo	Durable, waterproof, easy to clean; available in a wide range of prices; available in many colors, sizes, patterns, and textures.	Cold on the feet; breakables will shatter when dropped on tile. Some tile, such as terra-cotta, requires sealing.
Glass tile	Beautiful, airy appearance; available in a large variety of colors, sizes, and designs.	Material and installation are expensive.; may crack if heavy things are dropped on them.
Wood: The most commonly used woods are oak, maple, cherry, and pine. Decay-resistant woods: cedar, redwood, and teak.	Has a warm look; if polyurethane is used for the finish, the wood will be durable and easy to clean.	Must be sealed to prevent water damage; can swell or warp; softwoods may dent.
Linoleum, rubber, and vinyl	Waterproof, durable, easy to lay; available in a wide range of colors, patterns, and textures.	May discolor if exposed to sunlight; may be slippery when wet, unless they have a textured finish.
Carpeting: Coir, sisal, and sea grass are ideal for bathrooms because their fibers, ordinarily prone to breaking when dry, remain flexible in a moist environment.	Natural fibers can add a special look to the room. Synthetic fiber carpets are warm and soft to walk on.	Other than coir, sisal, and sea grass, carpets cannot be used in wet areas of the bathroom or mildew will grow from the moisture that collects in it.

available to accent the surrounding walls. Although not commonly used, sealed, low-voltage floor lights can be sunk into tiles to illuminate a passageway. These lights are shatterproof and water-resistant, so they can be used in a bathroom.

Windows

It is very pleasant to have natural light coming into the room during the day. When planning the placement of windows in a new construction or major renovation, consider placing the windows high, so there won't be a privacy issue. Skylights are an excellent source of light. If the window will look out on an open field, placement may not be an issue, and you may opt to have limited coverage on the window. If your bathroom window looks out on a busy street, you will have to use a window treatment, install frosted glass, or use glass blocks for privacy. The following are some of the window treatments you may want to consider for the bathroom:

- Wooden shutters work well in the bathroom because they can be angled to let in varying degrees of light while still giving you privacy.
- Shades also work well and are available raised from the bottom or lowered from the top, allowing light in at the top, while giving privacy on the lower portion.
- Blinds can also be angled to allow light to enter while maintaining privacy. Wood blinds are particularly practical in the bathroom and can be coordinated with wood cabinetry.
- Sheer fabrics may not offer a great deal of privacy but will give the room a decorative look.
- Drapes will give more privacy but generally have a more formal appearance.
- Valences give the window a decorative look without obstructing the view.

Storage

You will need storage space for personal hygiene products, cosmetics, extra towels, children's toys, extra rolls of toilet paper, and so on. The size of the bathroom will determine the amount and type of storage you will be able to have. When you are planning the bathroom, consider where you might like to put in recessed shelving and cabinets, so they can be roughed in before the drywall is installed.

Decide what items you would like to store in closed units and which should be easily accessible on open shelves. Storage can be moveable, built in, recessed, or in a closet. Frequently used items should be in open, easily accessed locations. Here are some possible storage options:

- Open shelving is an alternative to closed cabinets and drawers. If you are using narrow shelves for bottles or small objects, try to find shelving with safety bars, which can be decorative and also make the shelf safer.
- Built-in cabinets can be custom-made in a wide variety of colors, sizes, and materials.

Ideas for displaying towels.

■ Free-standing storage units can be purchased in specialty stores, large hardware chains, or catalogs.

■ Drawers are an excellent way to store many small items and to keep them out of sight.

■ Baskets of varying sizes can be used for towels or small objects such as makeup.

■ Closets are a great place to store towels and smaller objects as well. You can use any number of types of small containers (such as wicker and plastic).

- Free-standing furniture such as an armoire, chests of drawers, or dressing tables add special warmth to a bathroom.
- Wheeled trolleys that can be moved around the room will give you flexibility as well as storage space. Some have pull-out drawers, some have open shelving where you can put wicker or plastic containers of varying sizes.
- Hooks can be used for robes and towels. You can use single hooks, multiple hooks, or a series of hooks, which come on a backing of varying lengths. There are also racks, originally used in classrooms for jackets, that have a line of several hooks. Some of them also have an upper shelf, for additional storage. You can find these racks in antique stores.

Vanities and Cabinetry

Vanities and cabinetry can be either pre-made or custom-made. They can be used to hold the sink or as dressing tables. Some vanities come with countertops; others must be custom-made. Make sure all countertops are designed without sharp edges to avoid injury in the bathroom. A variety of materials are available for countertops. Your selection will depend on the durability you require, your budget, and your personal preference. Table 8-3 indicates the materials available, as well as the advantages and disadvantages of each.

Pulls and knobs on the vanity drawers or cabinets should coordinate with the other materials (i.e. metals) in the room. A large variety of styles, sizes, and colors are available. Take the time to look at many options.

Mirrors

Mirrors are necessary in the bathroom for grooming: putting on makeup, shaving, and so on. If more than one person will be using the bathroom at the same time, and if there is enough space, it's nice to have several mirrors. A variety of styles are available in antique and contemporary designs. Your options include:

- Wall mirrors.
- Decorative mirrors-stable or adjustable.
- Full-length mirrors.
- Free-standing mirrors.
- Magnifying mirrors.

Table 8-3 Countertops

Material	Advantages	Disadvantages
Plastic laminate and veneer	Protected with layers of lacquer or resin; large variety of colors, patterns, and textures; water-resistant and easy to clean.	Heat and abrasive objects will damage the surface.
Solid surfacing (such as Corian)	Durable and seam-free, needs little maintenance and can be molded to be integrated with the sink and backsplash; large variety of colors.	Expensive; intense heat and heavy objects dropped on it can cause damage.
Stone	Durable and has a beautiful natural appearance.	Expensive; requires professional installation; some stones are porous and require sealing; can become scratched or stained if subjected to acidic or oil-based products.
Stainless steel	Durable, chemical resistant, waterproof; can be integrated with a sink	Will be damaged if sharp or abrasive materials rub across the surface.
Glass: laminated, sandblasted, and frosted	Allows light to shine through; gives an airy appearance	Expensive; can be broken with heavy impact (should not be used in a children's bathroom).
Wood	Attractive and easy to install.	All woods must be sealed with polyurethane. Any standing water will damage the wood; can warp or crack if subjected to direct heat.
Cast-concrete: pre-made or poured onsite.	Inexpensive; has a contemporary look.	Must be sealed to avoid staining; must be custom-made.
Ceramic tile (including glass mosaic chips and terra-cotta)	Waterproof, durable; available in a wide range of colors and finishes.	Grouting attracts dirt and may be difficult to clean. Grout may need to be resealed periodically.

Ventilation

Exhaust fans are required by code in bath and shower areas in most locations. Plan for fans that not only meet code but are sufficient to reduce moisture (which will control mildew). Ventilation needs to be quiet and powerful enough to eliminate moisture and odors quickly. The system should vent to the outside whenever possible. The NKBA recommends the following formula for evaluating the minimum size of the system required: length times width times height (cubic space) times 8 (changes of air per hour) divided by 60 minutes, which will equal the minimum cubic feet per minute (CFM).

Today there is a wide range of styles, materials, and colors to choose from in all categories: toilets, bidets, sinks, baths, showers, and even urinals, which were recently designed for home use. Try to check out as many options as possible before making a choice. After you have selected the fixtures, you will have to coordinate them with the fittings.

Toilets or Water Closets

When selecting a toilet, consider color, style, size, material, and type of flush you prefer. Most toilets are made of vitreous china, which is available in a wide range of colors and designs. Until recently, stainless steel toilets were only used commercially, but they are now available for home use as well. Toilets come in one-piece, two-piece, and wall-mounted designs with hidden tanks (inside the wall). Wall-mounted designs have the added advantage of leaving open floor space. Typically, toilets are 15 inches off the ground, but some 17-inch models are now available. Three types of flush systems are available:

- **Gravity-fed siphon flush.** This is the most commonly used-flush system; this type of flush uses the weight of the water to wash waste away.
- **Pressure-assisted systems.** A cartridge in the tank mixes air and water to create a powerful flush. Although these are highly efficient, they tend to be noisy when operated.
- **Electrically powered toilets.** These have a pump inside the tank, which assists the water in washing away waste. They are quiet and efficient and use less water than the other types of systems.

A variety of specialty toilets are available, including the following:

- Hydraulically operated seats, which lift and lower automatically for persons with disabilities and for older adults.
- Soft-closing seat systems, which prevent toilet seats from slamming down on little fingers.
- Integral air-intake systems, which either extract toilet odors or filter and return the air.
- Heated seats, personal-hygiene systems, and automatic air deodorizers. These are sometimes used when there is no room for a separate bidet.

BATHROOM
ESSENTIALS

■ Toilets with concealed exterior trap ways provide a smooth flat surface for easy cleaning where dust may collect. They also give the fixture a more contemporary appearance.

Bidets

Bidets are usually situated near the toilet so they can be used in sequence. Some toilets offer bidet features for those that don't have the space for both units or prefer to have both fixtures in one. Bidets come in two styles: vertical spray and horizontal spray.

Urinals

If there are many men in the household, you may want to consider installing a urinal. Urinals are generally used in commercial areas, but they are available for home use as well.

Sinks or Lavatories

If more than one person will be using the bathroom at the same time, it is a good idea to have two sinks (also called basins) if you have the space. Sinks are available in three styles:

■ **Pedestal.** Pedestal sinks come in a variety of heights, ranging from 29 inches to 36 inches. They generally take up less space than some of the other styles but lack storage and counter space.

■ **Wall-mounted.** Wall-mounted sinks, like pedestal sinks, take up less space than some of the other styles but also lack storage and counter space. They can be hung at any height, which is an advantage for people in wheelchairs who need the open space under the sink.

■ **Vanity.** Vanity sinks have the advantage of counter space and storage but reduce the floor space in the room. The standard height for vanities is 31 inches or 32 inches, but taller ones are available on some models.

Several types of sinks can be installed in a vanity:

■ **Self-rimming.** The sink has rolled edges and sits on top of the

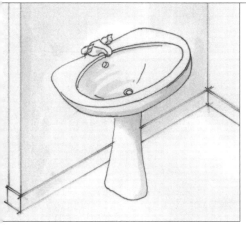
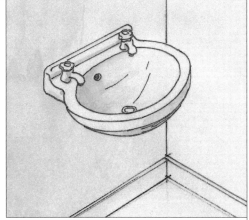
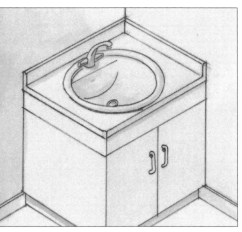

Examples of sink
options – pedestal, wall
mounted & vanity.

countertop.

- **Under-mount.** The sink is attached below the level of the countertop.
- **Integral.** These sinks are made from the same piece of material as the countertop. They are easy to clean because there are no seams. If, however, either part is damaged, both have to be replaced. These can be made from solid surfacing, stainless steel, and stone.
- **Vessel-style.** These sinks are available in a variety of shapes, sizes, and colors. This type of sink is placed in a hole that is made in the vanity or put on a stand or pedestal. Unusual pedestal stands are available for vessels in wrought iron and wood or they can be custom-made. Antique wash stands and other types of new and antique furniture can be used as well.

Sinks are also available in a variety of materials, which are listed in Table 8-4, along with the advantages and disadvantages of each.

Table 8-4 Sinks

Material	Advantages	Disadvantages
Vitreous china	Most popular; durable, easy to clean; wide range of colors that can coordinate with other fixtures in the bathroom.	Could crack or chip with heavy impact.
Glass: Most glass has an aqua-tint. If you want warmer tones, you can purchase glass with burnished finishes (such as gold, platinum, or copper.)	Unique design.	Expensive; heavy impact can cause cracks.
Stainless steel: available in satin, linen, and mirror-polished finishes	Strong, lightweight, easy to clean; stain- and erosion-resistant	Can be scratched by heavy use and abrasive cleaners. Can spot from soap and hard water.
Polished brass and copper	Unique design; can match other specialty fitting in the room.	Require a great deal of maintenance.
Hardwood: Oiled hardwoods can be carved into bowls	Unusual design; holes can easily be drilled for faucets and waste outlets.	Must be oiled regularly to prevent splitting and are difficult to clean.
Stone	Luxurious looking and can be integrated with the countertop; burns can be smoothed out and polished.	Expensive.
Ceramic: Made by potters and commercially	Unusual design.	May not be durable.
Enameled cast iron	Easy to clean, durable.	They are heavy and need a strong support system.
Solid surfacing (such as Corian)	Very durable; can be integrated with the countertop; good selection of colors.	Expensive; may chip if struck by a heavy object.

Showers

Not too long ago, a shower was merely an enclosure and simple showerhead. Today, you have the option of custom-made showers with body sprays, a variety of shower heads, waterfalls, and so on, as well as oversize proportions-all of which make showering a totally relaxing experience.

Showers are available in four basic types:

■ Prefabricated units are available in acrylic or fiberglass. These come with a base, walls, and door in a wide range of colors, shapes, sizes, and styles.

- Custom-made units are put together by selecting the wall covering, fittings, floor fabrication, and door. The walls of the shower can be made of a variety of materials, listed in the wall covering section of this chapter. Glass blocks can be used for the enclosure. Glass doors or shower curtains can be used for closing off the shower. If the shower is large enough, you may want to consider leaving it open. People sometimes prefer open showers with pitched floors that go to a drain. They give the bathroom an open, airy look. A partition or half wall can separate the shower area from the rest of the bathroom. If you are considering using a shower door, make sure it opens out. Consider the maintenance required for the door you choose: Clear glass enclosures are difficult to keep presentable (showing every smudge and fingerprint); translucent glass is easier to care for.

- Prefabricated shower pans are available in a limited number of sizes and shapes (square, rectangular, and corner designs), in colored acrylic and mineral resin. The shower surrounds are then custom-made.

Relaxation and indulgence rule in this rustic setting with a fireplace, open shower and freestanding bathtub.

- A variety of bathtubs can be used for tub/shower combinations. Specialty tubs, such as free-standing (i. e. lion's paw designs) can be converted to combination fixtures by adding a shower rose(a type of shower head) to dispense water and a shower curtain ring, giving the room a vintage look.

Consider the following when putting in a shower:

- Make sure the floor of the shower is slip-proof; use either a non-slippery material or non-slip mats.
- A 12-inch by 12-inch niche in the wall is excellent for storing soap, shampoos, and conditioner. If possible, design this into the construction plans or at least before the dry wall is installed.
- The minimal dimension for a shower is 32 inches by 32 inches; 42 inches by 34 inches or larger, however, will be more comfortable.
- A shelf or seat in the shower, which should be covered or made with the shower wall or flooring material, is useful for washing or shaving legs.

Bathtubs

Bathtubs can be very relaxing and a wonderful addition to the bathroom. Often, however, tubs are installed and never used. Before you design your bathroom, decide if you will use the bathtub or if the space could be put to better use-for storage, a sitting area, or exercise equipment.

If you decide to put in a tub, try some out (with your clothes on, of course!) in the store, to see which one feels the most comfortable. A variety of sizes and colors are available in standard and oversize tubs. Some towns have a maximum water capacity allowed for bathtubs. Find out what the codes are before shopping for a tub. If you're going to install the tub in a platform, plan to have no more than one step, at least 10 inches deep and 7 1/2 inches high. Make sure the faucets are installed where they can easily be reached from outside the tub.

Specialty tubs are also available in many colors and styles, and come with special features. Some of the specialty tubs available are:

- Spa baths. Spa baths have a series of pinholes that air is pushed through to give a soft foaming effect. With this type of system, essential oils can be used and cause no harm to the mechanism.
- Whirlpool baths. These have several jets from which the water is pushed out with a stronger force. Baths come with several configurations and numbers of, usually, adjustable jets, which can be directed at particular

areas of the body. Manufacturers suggest that no essential oils or chemicals be used in these tubs, to avoid ruining the PVC piping. Some tubs have built-in heaters, which takes pressure off the home water heater.

■ Freestanding tubs. Freestanding tubs such as claw-foot tubs give the room a more vintage look. They are available in a range of materials, styles, and sizes.

Table 8-5 lists the materials that bathtubs are available in as well as the advantages and disadvantages of each.

Table 8-5 Bathtubs

Material	Advantages	Disadvantages
Enameled cast iron	Very durable; comes in a wide variety of colors and styles.	Heavy; have to make sure the floor can support the weight; expensive to ship.
Enameled steel	Lightweight; resistant to chemicals and corrosion.	Chips easily if heavy or hard items are dropped on it.
Fiberglass	Lightweight; easy to install and clean; inexpensive.	Loses its shiny surface and may become dull gray color.
Acrylic	Lightweight; durable; won't fade, crack, or chip. More durable and harder to scratch than fiberglass; slight scratches can be sanded & buffed out.	Needs to be reinforced for rigidity. Abrasive cleaners will damage the surface.
Stone	Luxurious look.	Expensive to purchase and to ship; usually have to be custom-made; floor joists may have to be reinforced to support the extra weight.
Stainless steel	A unique look, can be matched to other metals in the room.	Expensive; must be custom-made.
Wood: cedar, teak, marine ply	Have a unique look; some woods have a pleasant aroma when wet.	Joints can weaken and leak; have to be sealed; can be difficult to clean.

The tub deck and skirt surrounding the tub can be ceramic tile, cultured marble, stone, or solid surfacing veneer. The deck and skirt can be different materials, but the deck and vanity counter should match. While some people build steps to make it easier to get into the tub or because they like the look, they can be dangerous, particularly when wet, and should not be built in unless they are absolutely necessary.

Tubs often come with pre-drilled holes for specific faucet configurations; others must be custom drilled. When you are purchasing a tub, find out what type of fittings you will need to purchase.

Fittings

Fittings - the parts of the plumbing system that are visual - are available in a wide variety of colors and designs.

Select fittings that will coordinate (in style and color) with all of the other fittings in the bathroom and also coordinate with the style of the room, as well as the rest of the house. Check for predrilled holes in sink, baths, and prefabricated showers, which might limit your selection. Many polished and brushed finishes are available: stainless steel, nickel, bronze, antique copper, brass, oil rubbed bronze, and more. Epoxy-coated finishes are available in a variety of colors, which can be matched to the bathroom fixtures.

Some of the available fittings are discussed in the following sections.

Baths and Showers
Depending on the complexity of the bath/shower you are installing, you will have many fitting options. The following are several of them.

Tub fillers. Tub fillers-which are on every tub- mix the cold and hot water, transporting it into the tub. These are available in a variety of lengths, colors, and styles. Some are available to give a waterfall effect.

Anti-scald valves. These valves prevent injury from scalding surges of water. These are now required by code in most areas. The following are two types of anti-scald valves:

- Pressure balance valve. This valve maintains the amount of pressure from either hot or cold water by adjusting the water flow to provide protection against water surges of scalding or freezing water. In the event of a hot or cold water supply failure, automatic safety shut-offs will stop the flow in an instant.
- Thermostatic shower valve. This valve allows the user to preset the desired temperature of the water, which will cut off immediately if the hot or cold water fails. If more than 16 gallons/per/minute of water will be used by a particular showerhead, more than one valve will be needed. The thermostatic shower valve is more expensive than the pressure balance valve.

Shower Faucets. Shower faucets are available in separate controls for hot or cold or with a single-handle control. They should be near the entrance of the shower so you don't have to get wet to turn on the water.

Showerheads. Showerheads, which disperse the water for showering, are available in a wide variety of colors and styles. The showerhead should be at a convenient height for everyone who will be using the shower. Multiple showerheads are convenient if several people will be showering at the same time. Make sure that the water pressure will be adequate.

Steam-bath features. These are available but require the enclosure to be totally closed from ceiling to floor. They require a separate boiler, which can be housed in the bathroom, an adjacent room, or an insulated attic. They can be prefabricated, or the feature can be installed in a custom-designed shower. An automatic turn-off timer and a seat are essential. A steam-bath must be at least 3 feet by 4 feet, but 4 feet by 5 feet is optimal.

Hand shower (or handheld shower). These are showerheads that are attached to the wall with a hook or a cradle, with the exposed hose hung on the wall. They are also available on an adjustable track to accommodate users at varying heights. These are useful for washing animals, children, and those with disabilities.

Body sprays. Body sprays are small heads generally installed in two sets of three sprays on the vertical walls of the shower, each with its own control. They are placed according to the height of the users, to spray an intense stream of water. If several people will be using the sprays, consider adjustable sprays, which can be adjusted to various heights. The pipes supplying the water to this type of system should be upgraded from the typical 1/2 inch to at least a 3/4 inch or larger pipe (depending on the fixtures selected). Drains may also have to be larger to accommodate added water from the additional fixtures.

Spray bars. Spray bars are vertical bars with many small openings mounted on the wall of the shower, providing an intense spray of water.

Diverters. These direct the flow of water to the bath, shower, or hand shower at the rate of flow and temperature you desire.

Flow valve. The flow valve controls the amount of water to bath, shower, or hand shower. This valve works each control individually.

Sinks

Fittings generally are at the rear of the sink. They can, however, be mounted on the wall behind the sink, with the plumbing hidden in the wall. There are even fittings which come out of an integrated mirrored cabinet on the wall, above the sink. Fittings come in numerous colors, shapes, sizes, and styles. Remote sensors are available that automatically turn on the water to a preset temperature without anyone having to touch the faucet. Ceramic-disc valves are now standard in sinks and baths. The majority of faucets use this mechanism to eliminate dripping faucets and difficult-to-turn handles; they regulate the flow and temperature of the water. The ceramic-disc valve replaced compression valves (which have washers) in most faucets. Other, less-popular, valves include ball faucets and cartridge faucets.

With the exception of undermount sinks, most sinks have predrilled holes for faucets and spouts. If there are no holes in the sink, you can direct the installer to put them where you want on the counter or on the wall behind the sink (which is possible with some types of faucets). Three types of faucet are available:

Single-hole faucets. These are used with sinks or vanities with just one predrilled hole. They can have a single faucet (usually connected to the spout) or two with a spout.

Center-set faucets. There is a spout and a hot and cold faucet in one base; the distance is always 4 inches from the center of the hot water faucet to the center of the cold water faucet.

Widespread faucets. The two valves and spout are separated on the sink. They go on sinks with predrilled holes 8 inches to 12 inches from the center of the hot valve to the center of the cold valve. This allows more flexibility in placing the faucet on the sink.

Specialty faucets. Specialty faucets are available that are infrared hands-free activated (by four AA batteries) and deliver water for a maximum of 30 seconds and only while hands are in the flow area. These faucets are excellent for water conservation. Several wall mounted novelty spouts and faucets are also available.

For toilets, trip levers can be purchased in the same colors as the other fittings in the room.

Accessories

The following items are typically used in the bathroom. Some are necessary, such as towel racks; others are luxury items, such as saunas. You will decide which ones to purchase based on your budget, space, and lifestyle.

Necessary Items

Medicine cabinets

Plan for medicine cabinets before the architect completes the working drawings, so that room is left between studs for recess mounting. If two people will be using the bathroom, it is a great luxury to have two medicine cabinets. If the cabinets will be accessible to children, install safety locks.

Holders and dispensers

If possible, try to plan recessed areas in the wall adjacent to sinks, tubs, and showers, for storing soaps, shampoos, and conditioners. If this is not possible, consider one of the many holders or dispensers available. Cup, soap, and toothpaste holders are available either wall-mounted or freestanding. If space is an issue, holders will free up counter space. Toilet-roll dispensers should be within easy reach of the toilet. Freestanding holders and built-in holders are available for storage of additional rolls.

Towel racks

A place to put towels is essential in the bathroom; a place to store additional towels is a luxury (they can be stored in any additional storage areas that can be created-either in built-in shelves or in freestanding units). Towel bars or rings should be located near baths, showers, and sinks. Alternatives to traditional towel holders are fixtures with a series of hooks where towels can be kept in a more casual manner. These can be homemade with a plank of wood and dowels or purchased in a specialty store. Or you can use the antique racks that were originally used in school coatrooms. If there is a shelf on top, you can use it to store additional towels or other items. Some sink fixtures are available with towel racks. When planning a sink in a countertop, such as stone or concrete, a towel rack can be included below the slab.

Towels

Towels can be used not only for their intended use, drying off, but also as a decorative, colorful element in the room.

Hooks

Hooks are useful on the backs of doors or near showers for hanging bathrobes or towels.

Waste baskets

These can be placed in one or several areas of the bathroom, depending on the size of the room. They can be coordinated with soap dishes, toothbrush holders, and glasses.

Hampers

Hampers can be built into the wall or be freestanding. A variety of styles are available, from more traditional hampers to large baskets. Hampers can also be placed in dressing rooms or bedrooms if space is an issue.

Toilet brushes

These can be put in freestanding holders or in housings attached to the wall near the toilet.

Scales

Scales are available in a variety of colors and with a variety of features. If you are one of those people who likes to weigh yourself daily, try to arrange for a spot for the scale where everyone won't be tripping over it.

Luxury Items

Heated towel bars

These should be situated close to the bath or shower. They are available in a variety of finishes (baked enamel, chrome, nickel, satin nickel, gold plate, brass) and a variety of designs. They are available in water-heated or electric models.

Heated floor

The heating element must be installed before the flooring is laid. Heated floors are particularly welcome when the floors are made of cold materials, such as stone or ceramic. The heating system can be installed in defined areas and turned on when needed.

Philip John Franz, Architect / Photographer: Philip Jensen-Carter

A deep soaking tub completes this spa style bathroom.

Freestanding furniture

If you have the space, you may want to have chairs or stools in the bathroom, or a dressing table where you can sit to put on your makeup. The bathroom is also a great place to put armoires and chests. They can be used for storage or display; antique pieces, in particular, will add a special warmth to the room. If you have the space for a sitting area, an easy chair or couch offers a relaxing place to sit after a bath or if you just want to relax in a private area. Banquettes can be built into a corner of the room or used as a partition, with cushions coordinating with the other colors and textures of the room.

Whirlpools

A whirlpool is expensive to install and takes up a great deal of space. Consider whether this is something you will use. Codes require a door or panel to provide access to the pump for repair or replacement. Make sure the panel is put in an accessible place, close to the pump.

Saunas

Saunas use dry heat and are said to relax, cleanse, improve circulation, relieve tension and have other additional attributes. A sauna takes up a lot of space, so unless you have a large bathroom and feel sure you will use it, you're probably best off not installing one.

Steam rooms
Steam rooms use moist heat and are said to relax, cleanse, and revitalize. They are said to be economical environmentally, using only about a gallon of water. Steam rooms can be built in any shower, but the walls have to go from the ceiling to the floor. A seating area is also necessary when you are using the sauna. Prefabricated units can be purchased. Some companies offer a port, to be used for adding an aroma to the water, to further enhance the experience.

Novelty shower panels
These are available in an assortment of configurations, with such features as water-falls, body sprays, showerheads, hand showers, body sprays (jets), and seats. Some are electronically controlled (some are not) to select options (waterfall, jet, and so on), flow speed (such as pulsating), and water temperature, and can also be set to turn off after a set amount of time.

Soaking baths
A shell within a shell, deep-soaking tubs have an overflow rim and a recirculation system whereby the bather is submerged in a full tub of water with the water continually cascading over the edge. Most of these tubs have special air jets that generate tiny effervescent bubbles. Optional features available on these tubs are light ports transmitting a progression of warm and cool colored lights and faucets with water flowing into the tub from the ceiling. These tubs are said to provide a relaxing experience.

Shallow basin spa sinks
Suitable for creating a spa within the home, shallow basin sinks, made of vitreous china, provide a working surface for the homeowner. Some models actually feature a raised flat surface flush with the sink's edges, so that when water hits the surface it slides off and into a channel surrounding the sink. These sinks can be paired up with accessories such as porcelain bowls (open- or closed-bottom) that can be set upon the raised flat surface and used for everyday hygiene or for preparing spa treatments.

Ceiling beams and Posts
These give a rustic, warm look to the room.

Fireplaces
Fireplaces are not common in bathrooms but can be a great luxury. If your fireplace is woodburning, as opposed to gas, you will need room to store a small amount of wood.

Washer/dryer

If you have the space, keeping your washer and dryer in the bathroom can be quite convenient.

Television or radio

It is a great luxury to have a television for watching the news in the morning while you are getting ready for work, watching a movie while soaking in the tub, or watching while relaxing in the sitting area if there will be one. Plan to put outlets (and cable connections) where you will want to use the television. If you plan to put an audio system in the house (which will be discussed in Chapter 9), consider planning for the installation of speakers in the bathroom as well.

Magazine and book racks

For people who like to read in the bathroom, a variety of decorative magazine racks are available. In the planning stage, consider building an open shelf in the wall, covered with the material used on the rest of the wall. This is an excellent way to have a place for books and magazines without sacrificing floor space.

So many wonderful design options are available for the bathroom. Look through the many available bathroom books (Appendix C) and magazines (Appendix B) to find inspiration for your own project. Look at materials, fixtures, and fittings on Web sites and in stores to find the options that appeal to you.

Notes

CHAPTER 9

Selecting Systems for Your Home

To assure the sustained value of your new home or renovation, consider installing systems that contain the latest technology. Systems such as water quality and security make your house safer; lighting, telephone, and central vacuum systems add to the convenience; while an audiovisual system adds pleasure and entertainment to your life. New systems are on the market every few years. You can't possibly keep up with every innovation, but you can try to stay as current as possible and select systems that can be expanded in the future as your needs grow, your budget increases, and technology expands. Evaluate and prioritize the systems, if any, you will want to incorporate into your home.

People often don't plan for systems when they're doing the initial plan of the house. By the time they think about installing these systems, their budget may be used up and the Sheetrock may already be up-making the task more difficult. You may not want any of the following systems, but you should be aware of their availability and decide whether to include them when you are in the planning stage of your project.

We will cover the following systems in this chapter:

- Water quality
- Security
- Lighting
- Audiovisual
- Telephone
- Central Vacuum

Finding System Suppliers

The best way to find out who supplies the various systems is to:

- Ask the contractors working on your job.
- Ask the architect.
- Ask the interior designer.
- Look for advertisements in local newspapers and magazines.
- Check the yellow pages.
- Ask family and friends to make recommendations.
- Check the Internet.

Whenever possible, try to deal with local suppliers. This shortens the trip they will have to make to service your account. Local vendors also have a stake in the community and do not want to alienate their local customers. This obviously doesn't mean, however, that you should automatically eliminate a dealer who has a great reputation but is outside of your community.

Systems are sometimes complicated to purchase because they may involve many components. It may be difficult to compare the quality and various components of some systems, such as audiovisual, where different components and brands may be recommended.

Follow these general rules:

- Interview several suppliers in each of the systems categories. For an audiovisual system for example, keep clear notes on what components each supplier will include. Meet with several suppliers and then define what you want. Formulate a list of your preferences. There is a section in the Notebook for entering this information.
- You might have to set up several meetings with each supplier to review

the options you have selected with each system. Each supplier of audiovisual equipment, for example, might recommend different components and different systems. After speaking with several suppliers, decide on the mixture of components and systems you prefer.

■ Try, if possible, to evaluate every bid in terms of unbundling (or breaking down) the costs of materials, labor, profit, and overhead. The bid will most likely come in as a composite bid, which includes all of the above. Many suppliers or contractors will not be willing to break down the cost. If they are, however, it will help you to understand what you are paying for. You will most likely have to select the contractor based on the price he gives you and then evaluate it the best way possible. Go back to each of the suppliers; get their prices on the components you have selected. Be sure that you are very clear on what is included in the bid. Many suppliers sell the same products or the equivalents. Be sure that when you have made your final selection, you have compared apples to apples and pears to pears.

■ Call references on all the suppliers and find out about how efficiently they work, how easy they are to deal with, and how quickly they follow up on problems.

■ If possible, obtain written bids from at least three contractors in each area. Some AV companies, for example, will not bid jobs. They will ask for a retainer and will design a system according to the customer's requirements. If you find excellent recommendations on a particular company, you may consider not bidding out this type of system. You must feel comfortable with a company and have a clear agreement on budget allowances if you consider such a situation.

■ Get a letter of agreement on every system you decide to install. Be sure you are getting at least a one-year warranty on labor and all manufacturers warranties. For an audio system, in particular, you may want to include a reasonable number of hours for learning to use the system, as they are sometimes difficult to operate. It is not uncommon to put such a system in, only to find that you can operate only half of its functions.

With all systems, consider not only their prices, but also the professionalism of the supplier, recommendations by others, and service polices. Become educated before making a decision. Very often, one bid is much less expensive than the others. If the bid is substantially less, you are probably getting less. If it seems too good to be true, it just might be. Everyone wants to get the best possible price, but try not to squeeze the contractor so hard that he will do shoddy work or run to the next job without completing yours (because there is more profit in the other job.) The relationship between you and the contractor will only work well if both parties are happy with the deal.

Preparing the House for Systems

Consider wiring the house for some of the systems (audiovisual, lighting, telephone) even if you do not want to put the systems in immediately. The cost, inconvenience, and mess associated with adding the systems later can be huge. The cost of installation for the tubing for the central vacuum system and the wiring for the telephone, AV, lighting, and security systems will be quite small while your house is under construction, in comparison to the cost of installation later on. Just having the wiring and tubing installed could add value to your home, if you should decide to sell it.

If you are working with an architect, make sure the specifications (specs) include the types of wiring and installation you will need down the road. If you are working directly with the electrician, make sure to give him or her this information as well. The following is a list of things to request when planning the wiring of the house:

- All wires and cables should be "home run." This indicates that the wiring for each telephone jack, television jack, and so on goes directly to the main panel (which is generally in an out-of-the-way location). Many electricians have been wiring with a "loop run" technique, which takes the cable from one television jack to the next and ultimately causes interference and "snow."
- All communication wires should be category 5 (watch for category 6, 6+, and 7.) All cable should be RG-6 Coaxial cable (not RG-59). Two RG-6 Coaxial cables should be run to each TV wall plate so that one wire receives video (such as a movie playing in a VCR) and the second wire can distribute the picture to other TVs in the house.
- Consider including a fiber optics wire to the bundle of wires in some locations. If you will have wiring going across your property or to the outside, fiber optic wire will not short out when it gets wet, as copper wire will. It can be used for telephones, video equipment, and contact closures such as electronic doors or gates.
- Consider putting an extra conduit from an unfinished basement (if you have one) to an unfinished attic (if you have one) for future need. The conduits (a tube or pipe that is designed to carry electrical wires or cables) should be capped at both ends to adhere to most local fire codes.

Electronic technology is developing so rapidly that it is worthwhile to prepare your home for any additional wiring that might be necessary in the future.

■ If you have, or plan to have, several computers in the house, consider putting in a computer network system. One computer can serve as the "hub" (which can be a dummy computer with a security program on it) attached to several "ports." You can then use a DSL (digital subscriber line)or a cable modem, which allows remarkably faster access to the Internet and could possibly save on the cost of paying a service charge for several individual lines. The security program will prevent someone from breaking into your computers through the DSL or cable line, which is on all the time. DSL is now currently being used in businesses as well as in private homes. It is recommended, however, for people who are doing business at home and use the Internet on a regular basis. It is very efficient and becoming more competitively priced.

To find out if this service is available in your area or to get additional information on this service, call 877-DSL-NET1 or access their Web site at www.DSL.net. The local cable company can install the wiring for the cable modem, and DSL can install the outside wiring for DSL. The local telephone company or electrician can install the inside jacks for the DSL while installing those used for the telephone. Be sure all wiring and cable are installed in areas where you might consider putting a computer. Again it is less costly to install before the house is completed than after. Be sure that when you hire an electrician, he or she is giving you a price on the work done in the way outlined above and that you are comparing "like" bids.

To Integrate Systems or Not to Integrate Systems

People often believe in integrating several systems, such as audiovisual, telephone, security, and lighting. There are advantages to tying them together:

■ Functions can be more easily integrated when one contractor installs them all.

■ There is only one person to deal with if there are problems. The person who sold you all systems should be accountable.

■ An integrated system requires fewer keypads on the wall.

■ One person is doing the installation instead of many.

- Owners save time in checking references for one dealer instead of several.

But there are also reasons to keep them apart:

- It is more difficult for a layperson to determine which part of the system is faulty. If there is a problem, one might not be able to tell which component is causing the problem in an integrated system.
- When you purchase an integrated system, it is sometimes difficult to determine what you are paying for each system. Dealers don't always itemize the various components.
- Often you are getting a more professional individual or company when you hire people to do one system. Someone who puts in phone systems all day long, for example, is more knowledgeable about phones than someone who occasionally puts them in. If you do opt to hire a multi-system supplier, be sure to check references on all systems that you will purchase from them.
- The multi-system company may contract out some systems. When you separate the systems and hire individuals, you know who is doing the job and you can check on their individual references.

If you are interested in installing a home automation system (an integrated system, which may include audiovisual, security, and lighting), contact the following Web sites to find qualified installers in your area.

Organization	Web Site
Home Automation Association	www.homeautomation.org
Custom Electronics Designers and Installers Association (CEDIA)	www.cedia.org

Water Conditioning Systems

Whether you build or renovate a house in an area with municipal water or well water, it is important to have the water analyzed. You have to make sure you are drinking the healthiest possible water and that you are not bringing contaminants into your home, which could cause harm to you, your family, and the structure of your home. So even if your house is on municipal water, you should have the water tested and treated. If the water is staining the fixtures, has a color or an odor, these are signs there is a problem with the water.

People who are living in areas with municipal water systems have fewer concerns about the water than people on well water do. The Environmental Protection Agency sets standards that the local government is required to adhere to. Municipalities are required to check the water and treat it on a regular basis. All states require the publication of the results of water testing once a year. You can request a copy of this report any time.

You should consider several conditions if you are on municipal water (or town water):

■ There are no minimum requirements for hard water in municipal water supplies. The hard water can then be treated in the home by adding a water softener to the water at the point of entry or POE, which refers to treating all the water that enters the house.

■ It is also possible for contaminants to enter the system from the water source or from the water main lines themselves. You should add a filter at the point of usage, or POU, which in the home is most often the kitchen sink. The cost for testing can be significant, and many of the contaminants can appear soon after the water is tested. A local water specialist, who is familiar with the water supply and knows what the possible contaminants might be, should either tell you if it is prudent to test the water or should design a filtration system that will remove the contaminants indigenous to the local water supply. These are the contaminants you need to test for:

■ **Lead.** Lead is generally removed by the municipality but enters the water from solder joints in old plumbing in the pipelines, which predate 1986. If there are young children in the house, you should consider removing even low levels, as lead has been linked to learning disabilities in young children.

■ **Cryptosporidium and Giardia (Cysts).** These are parasites (living organisms). They come from fowl, which migrate to reservoirs and defecate in the waters. The organisms are part of the fecal matter. Most municipal water systems cannot filter them out because of the small size of the parasites. Cysts pose a significant threat to people with immune impairments and are commonly linked to serious digestive problems. It is very costly to test the water for Cysts in particular. It is prudent therefore to install a water-filtration system that will filter 3 microns or less if you have digestive problems or immune deficiency disorders because of the serious threat they pose. The cost is generally less for the installation of the system than for the cost of testing the water.

- **Asbestos.** Asbestos is a fibrous mineral that contaminates the water and enters the system from the water main pipes. Asbestos has been linked to lung and other forms of cancer.
- **Chlorine.** This chemical is pumped into the system for sterilization. It produces an objectionable taste and odor, along with drying of the skin.
- **Trihalomethanes (THM).** THMs are VOCs, or volatile organic compounds. They are by-products of the chlorine that is pumped into the system. The chlorine has a chemical reaction with the organic matter, causing THMs to develop. THMs have been linked to bladder and rectal cancer.

The local/state governments vary in their requirements for the testing of water in houses with existing wells or new wells. The state of Connecticut requires all homes that are sold or refinanced to have bacteria and chemical testing done on the water. If an infant is adopted, the state requires these tests plus one for lead in the water. Requirements vary among all the states and local townships, so you must check with the local board of health to find out what the requirements are in your area. The federal government established the Safe Drinking Water Act, which determined the maximum amounts of various impurities (maximum contaminant level or MCL) that may be tolerated in a potable (drinkable) water supply.

The water should be tested when you plan to live in the house and use the water, not while the house is under construction. Several conditions that occur in the water supply must be addressed immediately. Some of these conditions are:

Bacteria

The EPA requires all municipalities to test for bacteria before issuing a Certificate of Occupancy. The bacteria most often found in water are coliform and E.Coli. The EPA has set the requirement at 0 colonies-as a minimum level. Every 2 years, the water should be retested for bacteria.

Treatment. Initially, the well system should be shocked by chlorine. If this is not successful, there should be continual treatment of the water with an ultraviolet light system or chlorine feed.

Hard water

This is water that contains calcium and magnesium, which is measured in grains per gallon (gpg). Classifications for the degree of hardness are listed in the following table.

Soft water	0 to 1.0	GPG
Slightly hard water	1.1 to 3.5	GPG
Moderately hard water	3.6 to 7.0	GPG

Hard water	7.1 to 10.5 GPG
Extremely hard water	10.6 or more GPG

Samples of hard water can also be reported in mg/L (milligrams per liter). Soft water would be 0-75 mg/L, moderately hard water would be 75-100 mg/L and extremely hard water would be anything over 150 mg/L.

The minerals have several negative effects on the water supply in the house:

- They will oxidize precipitate (come out of the water) when they are exposed to heat and will crystallize, turning solid, and forming scale on faucets, drains, coils on boilers, and so on, impeding the passage of water.
- They will prevent soap from lathering and from being used effectively.
- They will cause white spots on dishes washed in the dishwasher.
- Bathtub rings will appear along with soap scum.

Treatment. An ion exchange process will take care of the problem of water hardness. The hardness is absorbed by an ion exchange material, and a chemically equivalent amount of sodium is released into the water. When the supply of sodium in the exchanger is exhausted, flushing a strong salt solution through the tank restores it. After the salt and the hardness are rinsed down the drain with fresh water, the softener is ready for another softening cycle. A holding tank must be kept supplied with sodium, which dissipates at a level consistent with the amount of hardness in the water. It will remove the calcium and magnesium. Salt substitutes (such as potassium chloride) are recommended for people on sodium-restricted diets or for people concerned with their sodium intake.

Sediment

Sand, clay, minerals, small rock and gravel naturally occur in wells. It causes the deterioration of household fixtures and abrasion of pipes and fixtures. It also builds up a pollution source to contaminate water in the tank. The sediment can clog icemakers and irrigation systems. Seals on toilets will deteriorate and eventually leak from corrosion caused by the sediment in the water.

Treatment. Filter the water to remove the sediment with particulate filtration. Have the water tank flushed once a year.

Iron

Iron is measured in parts per million (ppm) and when present in the water at levels of 0.3ppm or higher may cause brown or rust-colored staining on plumbing fixtures and clothing. The U.S. Public Health Service recommended limit for iron content is .3 ppm. Iron may be present in water in either of two forms or in some cases a mixture of both. A water supply containing soluble iron (ferrous) may be perfectly clear when it is drawn from the household tap, but after the water has been exposed to the air for several minutes, the well-known reddish brown sediment will appear. It is this insoluble form (ferric hydroxide) that causes the troublesome stains.

Treatment. Limited amounts of iron will be removed from the water with an ion exchange process through the use of a water softener. Larger amounts must be removed by using a filtration system using an oxidizing filter or a solution dispensing system feeding chorine, followed by a clarifying filter. Green Sand Filtration with potassium permagnate is another system, which has been successful in removing the iron.

Iron bacteria
This is not a common problem. It is most common, however, in old well systems and in water with high levels of iron. Iron bacteria thrive in iron-bearing water supplies, using the iron as an energy source. They clog and foul the plumbing lines and appliances that use water. They stain fixtures and clothing.

Treatment. Treatment involves chlorination to kill the bacteria, followed by filtration to remove the residue.

Manganese
This mineral is not as common in water as iron, but when it is present it usually is accompanied by iron. The results are similar in that it causes black staining. The recommended limit for manganese in the water is .05 ppm.

Treatment. Treatment is similar to that of iron.

Acid water
Acidity in water is measured as a pH value. The pH value is measured on a scale of 0 to 14, with 7 being the neutral point. pH values below 7 indicate acidity, with 0 most acid; pH values above 7 indicate basicity (with no corrosive tendency), with 14 most basic, or alkaline. Acid water, or low pH water, shortens the life of iron and copper plumbing and causes pinhole leaks in them. It also causes rusty or blue/green stains on plumbing fixtures along with excessive corrosion. Exorbitant concentrations give the water an objectionable "soda" taste, and the water may cause undue drying of skin and hair. Acid eats into copper pipes, fixtures and valves, depositing copper and lead (which are carcinogens) into the water.

Acidity	Level of pH	Treatment
Slightly acid	6.8 to 6.9	Phosphate crystal cartridge.
Moderately acid	6.0 to 6.7	A neutralizing filter or a

		solution-dispensing system feeding a neutralizing compound.
Extremely acid	4.0 to 5.9	A solution-dispensing system feeding a neutralizing compound.

Treatment. The corrosive water is passed through a neutralizing (calcite and corsex) filter bed. Often, neutralized water becomes hard during the filtering process (depending on the acidity or hardness of the water.) A water softener may have to be installed after the filter is in place. Another method of treatment is adding a feed pump, which injects soda ash. A water softener will not be necessary, but this system may require more maintenance.

Hydrogen sulfide

The presence of the gas hydrogen sulfide causes the water to have a rotten egg odor. This gas increases the corrosive activity of water, and in extremely high concentrations it may be toxic. It may also cause black stains on silverware or cause the silverware to tarnish. Hydrogen sulfide usually occurs in the hot water only and is generated by the hot water heater (the annobe in the water.) Look for water heaters that have an aluminum annobe instead of a magnesium annobe (which encourages the growth of a bacteria which gives off hydrogen sulfide.)

Treatment. The first procedure is to treat the well with shock chlorination. If the problem is not cleared up, chlorination with an automatic chemical feed pump, followed by filtration to remove the residue may be necessary.

Turbidity

This cloudiness in the water is due to very small solid particles such as sand, silt or clay, which tend to float because of their low weight.

Treatment. A fine filter material will remove the turbidity.

Total dissolved solids (TDS)

This is measured in parts per million (ppm) and includes the total amount of minerals dissolved in a water supply. This term comes from the original method of testing, which consisted of evaporating the filtered water and weighing the solids, which remained. These solids come from rock that dissolved in the water. At high concentrations, the TDS may leave a white residue on various surfaces, including faucet tips, when the water evaporates. Excessive amounts can cause a noticeable mineral or salty taste and if there is a high concentration of sulfate, it could have a laxative effect as well. The Federal Drinking Water Standards on TDS is 500 ppm.

Treatment. Reverse osmosis is the most effective treatment.

Sodium and chloride (salt)

Although sodium and chloride are the components of salt, they are not necessarily present together in equal amounts due to many factors that affect these elements at their source. When salt is dissolved in water, the sodium and chloride separate into two elements.

Sodium

The EPA advises that the maximum contaminate level is 250 mg/l. Twenty-eight milligrams per liter of water is advised for people with high blood pressure. Two thousand milligrams of total sodium intake per day is advised for people with high blood pressure. Levels exceeding 28 mg/l (liter) are issued an advisory by labs that test water.

Treatment. There are two methods of treating high levels of sodium in the water. The simplest and least-expensive method is reverse osmosis. Distillation is another method, whereby a heating element boils the water to steam and the vapor is collected. The solids remain in the container and have to be removed. This is a costly, higher-maintenance method.

Volatile organic compounds (VOC)

These are byproducts of gasoline derivatives, oil byproducts, and solvents. There are many contaminants within this group. This is a potential problem, particularly in commercial or industrial-type areas. High concentrations of VOCs are linked to organ damage and cancer in humans. The test for VOCs is expensive, so it should only be used in suspicious areas.

Treatment. Treatment is dependant on which contaminants are found in the water. Treatments vary from carbon filtration to aeration systems.

Waterborne radon

Radon enters the water supply via decaying radium in the soil and bedrock surrounding the house. The radon gas is introduced into the air when faucets, showers, washing machines, and so on are in use. The prolonged exposure to radon, distributed throughout the house, poses a risk of lung cancer and a lesser risk of stomach cancer. The Safe Drinking Amendment Act was signed into law by President Bill Clinton in 1998 and became law in 2000. This charges the EPA's Office of Ground Water and Drinking Water (OGWDW) with setting federal standards or MCLs for radon and several other contaminants that the government previously ignored. The proposed MCL for radon is 3000pCi/L. (Picocuries per liter is the measurement used for concentrations of radon in water and air.)

Treatment. There are two methods of reducing waterborne radon:

■ Granular activated carbon (GAC) filtration system. The GAC system absorbs radon from the water without the use of mechanical components. When properly installed, this method will remove 90% to 95% of the radon. Although this system is less expensive than the aeration system, there are drawbacks to this type of system. It must be closely maintained to avoid the buildup of radionuclides, which emit radiation. The carbon in the system must be replaced annually to avoid the reduction of effectiveness and the increased chance of bacteria growth from the absorption of organics. The EPA doesn't recommend using this system for radon levels any greater than 5,000 pCi/l (liter). The health department of each state, however, has its own requirements.

- Aeration system. There are four main types of aeration equipment: diffused bubble, spray, tray, and packed tower. The agitation and percolation created by aeration releases the radon from the water where it can be vented safely to the outdoor air. Water is passed through a series of chambers, which separate the radon from the water and vent the radon outside through a 2-inch vent line. The cleaned water is then repressurized using a shallow well jet pump and a small well tank. This system will not only reduce the radon 99+% but will also eliminate volatile organic compounds (VOC) and neutralize acidic water. It requires maintenance on an annual basis to avoid bacteria growth. It is noisy and more costly than the carbon system but is more effective and versatile than the GAC system.

You can take samples of the water yourself and bring them to a private laboratory or the local health department for analysis. There are special procedures for collecting the water, which you will have to become familiar with. You will save money, however, by doing the collection yourself. If you use a water-conditioning service, they will collect the water for you and advise you of your options in conditioning the water as well. To locate a water professional, check the phone book, talk with your GC, ask neighbors in the area who may be experiencing water problems, or contact the Water Quality Association at 800-749-0234 or via e-mail at info@mail.wqa.org for recommendations of WQA certified water- conditioning specialists in your area. For additional information on water contaminants and water treatments, access their Web site at www.wqa.org.

Most water-conditioning contractors can test for radon. However, this is a relatively new area and should be addressed by a prequalified specialist. Call Radon and Water Control Systems at 800-343-8304 or check out their Web site at www.radonandwater.com to find out which contractors or testing firms in your area test and condition air- or waterborne radon. You can also obtain information from the National Environmental Health Association (NEHA), which operates a certification program for contractors offering radon measurement and mitigation services at 800-269-4174 or e-mail them at www.radonprog@aol.com.

If you decide to have a security system in your home, it should be planned for in the early stages of designing the house. The wiring for the security system should be installed before the drywall is put up in new constructions and renovations so the wiring can be hidden. Wireless alarm systems are available for installation in existing homes. The cost of labor for the installation of this type of system is less expensive; however, the cost of equipment is higher. Wireless alarm systems are usually used in existing homes that are being retrofitted or for areas that are difficult to secure with wired systems, such as high skylights.

Most contemporary security systems are central monitoring systems, which means that an outside station is keeping track of security problems that occur in the home. Older systems had alarms that went off if there was an intruder, but only the neighbors would hear the alarm. If the house happened to be in an isolated location or if nobody heard the alarm, the alarms accomplished nothing.

Components of a Monitoring System

The following are the various components that make up a security or monitoring system.

- **Exterior or perimeter monitoring sensors.** This type of protection is accomplished through the use of magnetic contacts, which are installed on windows, exterior doors, and garage doors. The contacts vary with the differences in windows and mountings (surface and recessed.) The mounting will depend on the preference of the individual security company and the cost of the system. More expensive houses will usually warrant the cost of recessing and concealing the contacts. The size and color of the contacts vary as well. This part of the system is turned on when the family is at home (referred to as the "home mode") or away.

  If a contact is broken between the door and the doorframe (when the door is opened) or the window and a sill (if the window is opened), an emergency signal is sent to a central station, which has a 24-hour monitoring service. This may be handled by the company itself or may be contracted to another company. The central station will attempt to

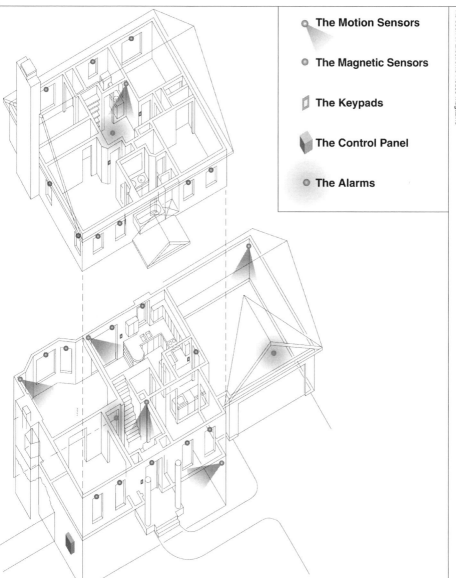

As seen in Electronic House Magazine

The Motion Sensors

The Magnetic Sensors

The Keypads

The Control Panel

The Alarms

verify the alarm and, if necessary, will get help from the police or fire department. For this potential emergency, as with all the other possible emergencies, the "contact list" (people who have keys and whose names have been given to the security company) is called after the police or fire department.

■ **Motion Detectors.** These are the second level of protection and are the interior sensors. The passive infrared protector (PIR) is strategically positioned and is designed to detect the body heat of an intruder moving through the room. This works as a backup to the exterior protection system. These are generally activated in the "away mode," when the family is away from the house. Motion detectors can also be placed outside the house to detect a car moving in the driveway or someone moving outside the home.

- **Fire protection features.** Smoke detectors may be required by local code. Some areas have code requirements for automatic fire sprinklers. Some areas have special requirements for houses adjacent to open areas where wildfires can occur. When there is a security system in the home, the smoke detectors are generally tied into the system. The smoke detectors that are wired into the alarm panel are functioning whether the security system is on or off.

  If the alarm system detects smoke, it will set off an alarm. The system then goes through a verification stage and resets. If there is still smoke, the alarm goes off a second time. It will then transmit a signal to the central office via the telephone, which will contact the fire department. Local smoke detectors make noise, but if no one is in the house to hear the noise, the house can burn down. A fire alarm system that is tied into a security system will send a message to the central station, which contacts the fire department even if the residents are not at home. Some systems have the option of a radio or cellular backup system to transmit the signal to the central office, in case the telephone is not operating.

- **Security Lights.** When a conduit is installed for outside lights, an additional conduit can be added for a sensor that will automatically turn on lights as a car or person nears the house.

- **Control panel.** This is a large metal cabinet that connects to all the sensors and keypads in the house. It can activate the sirens or lights and can send emergency messages to a central station over a telephone line or radio link. The control panel is usually put in a closet or other out-of-the-way location.

- **Keypad.** The keypad allows the user to arm and disarm the system, check the status of each zone in the house and send an alarm to the police or fire department. There is a panic button for potentially dangerous situations. The user can change the alarm code, test the backup battery, and program various features on the system using the keypad.

- **Siren.** All systems require at least one siren; some systems have several, depending on the size of the house. Typically, sirens will give off distinctive sounds for fire and burglary conditions. Voice sirens are also available.

- **Carbon monoxide sensors.** These sensors sound internal alarms and also activate an audible alarm on the control panel if a high level of carbon monoxide is detected.
- **Freeze sensors.** If low temperatures threaten to damage the plumbing elements and appliances that contain water, an alarm is set off on the control panel.
- **Flood sensors.** These sensors are used in areas of the home or property that are susceptible to flooding. An audible alarm is set off on the control panel, alerting the inhabitants of rising water levels. This gives them the time to save valuable property before it is ruined. This sensor also alerts the central station so they can call for help.
- **Key ring remote controls.** These can be used to arm or disarm the system from as far as 100 feet away from the house. This type of control can also report emergencies and provide push-button lighting control.
- **Hand-held remote controls.** These can be used to report emergencies, provide push-button lighting control, and allow you to arm or disarm the security functions from anywhere in the house.
- **Closed circuit TV.** This allows you to view and monitor selected locations in the home or in outside areas.
- **Telephone interface.** This feature, available on some systems, allows the owner to turn the system on and off, obtain the status of the system, and perform any alarm functions from any touch-tone telephone in the world.

Additional Security Measures All Homes Should Have

The following are additional precautions that should be taken to insure the security of your home.

- **Door locks.** Install a single cylinder deadbolt, operated by a key from outside and a thumb-latch inside. The lock's backplate (or strikeplate) should be secured to the doorframe (or jamb) with long screws.
- **Alarm system decals and signs.** These should be easily visible to anyone nearing your house.
- **Exterior Lighting.** Make sure the exterior of the house is well lit. Always replace burned-out outdoor lights quickly.

Methods of Transmitting Signals from the House to the Central Station

Most companies will offer one backup service or the other. You will have to decide if you want one of these services based on availability and cost.

- Telephone transmission. Signals are sent from the home to the central monitoring office over telephone wires. A local sounding device should be installed to go off if the telephone lines are disturbed or cut.
- Radio transmission. Radio transmissions serve as a backup system in case the house loses telephone service or the telephone lines are cut. Signals are sent directly to the central monitoring station if the telephone lines are damaged. There must be a radio link in the area for the security system to be able to offer this service.
- Cellular transmission. Cellular communicators serve as a backup system as well. Cellular transmissions travel further than radio transmissions do, but installation is also more expensive. The cost for the service should be the same.

Things to Consider When Selecting a Security System

When doing your research on security systems, speak with representatives of several companies and request a written quote from each. After reviewing all quotes, decide which components of a system you want. Call for references on all of the companies. You may want to recall some representatives and have them alter their proposals. When it comes time to make your decision, consider:

1. The cost of the system and the monthly payments.
2. Your rapport with the salesperson.
3. The reputation of the company.
4. The reliability and location of the central station.
5. The service policy and warranty.

You also want to consider whether you should purchase or lease a system and whether you should do business with a small, local company or a large, national one.

Purchasing versus leasing a system

When deciding whether to purchase or lease the equipment, consider the following:

- The initial up-front cost will be more when purchasing, but the monthly monitoring costs will be lower.
- If you lease a system and decide to change providers, the company may pull out the system. If you purchase the system, the equipment belongs to you. Most systems are adaptable to other companies you may decide to use.

Small Company versus Large Company

The first consideration in selecting a security system is whether you prefer a large national or a small local company to install and monitor your system. The following are some of the advantages of each:

Small Company

- The service is faster.
- The company is more familiar with local ordinances and codes.
- There is probably more cooperation in interpreting local ordinances and codes by local authorities.
- There is more personal contact. People tend to stay in the same place for a longer time in a smaller company. Therefore, you are more likely to speak to the same person over time for all company-related problems: service, billing, and installation.
- Smaller, local companies tend to be more accommodating. They are more likely to be available 24 hours a day and make service calls on weekends and holidays.

Large Company

- Larger companies have the ability to offer tested new products and services that smaller companies may not be able to offer.
- Larger companies deal with more suppliers than smaller companies so that they can offer a larger variety of equipment.
- Pricing is usually lower with a large company.
- Large companies generally offer better warranties.
- Most large companies have their own central stations and do not contract this work to another company.
- If there is ever a reason to sue a carrier, you are more likely to win a

case against a large company that does its own monitoring. (All Central stations must carry E & O- Errors and Omissions- insurance in the event of loss.

■ All services are handled under one roof: sales, billing, service, installation, and monitoring. The customer can call one number for all problems.

Here are some national companies to look into:

ADT Security Services	800-238-4636	www.adt.com
Brinks	800-874-8891	www.brinks.com
Honeywell Inc.	800-328-5111	ww.honeywell.com/HomeSecurity
Protection One	800-738-4255	www.protectionone.com

Many local companies offer security systems. They can be found through referrals, the builder, or in the phone book. Another option is to contact the National Burglar and Fire Alarm Association (NBFAA) at 301-907-3202 or access their Web site at www.alarm.org for a listing of member companies by location.

Lighting Systems

Lighting systems are designed to "gang" lights together on stations or keypads, which control several lights, from one location. Lighting systems are most often used in new constructions or major renovations. There are however, systems that can be retrofitted into preexisting homes are available as well.

There are basically four types of systems available: line carrier, low-voltage, line-voltage/low-voltage combinations, and radio- frequency.

Line Carrier Systems

The line-voltage system is the simplest system to install and one that is generally retrofitted in preexisting houses. With this type of system, existing wiring can be used. The system is wired with standard wall box dimmers with one extra wire, which can be installed later to control the other dimmers. The master control switch can control up to 22 dimmer pads. This system requires no special wiring or central processing unit and can be used to create a particular "scene" (an industry term), meaning various lights are at a particular intensity at a given time. It is possible to have several lights go on and off or dim in whatever way you like. Some systems have handheld remote controls so you can turn the lights off and on without getting up.

Advantages of the line carrier system

- **Convenience.** You can create a "scene" in a room, turning several lights on or just one or two, with a pad or remote control.
- **Labels.** Some switches can be labeled indicating which light each switch is operating.
- **Expense**. This system is less expensive than all of the other systems listed here.
- **Motion detectors.** These sensors, typically used outside, put on lights when they sense motion.
- **Occupancy sensors.** These sensors turn the lights off when no one is in the room; they detect lack of motion while conserving energy.

Disadvantages of the line carrier system

- **Flexibility.** This system is not as flexible as any of the other systems in controlling lighting paths. When the wiring is installed, you must decide which pad will control which fixture. Once the wiring is complete, this cannot easily be changed. The fixture is hotwired to the pad, which controls it. With low- voltage systems (discussed in the next section), you have the flexibility of changing configurations as your needs change. In that system, the fixtures are hotwired to a central control box and so the configurations can be altered to meet current needs.
- **Features.** Some systems may not offer many of the features available on other systems, such as astrological clocks, which alter the time the night lights go on with the change in season or length of the day.
- **Reliability.** Lights will not always go on because the signal can get contaminated. Ask the lighting specialist about using spread-spectrum technology. (Instead of sending the signal over one frequency, it breaks up the signals and broadcasts them over a number of frequencies, recombining the signals at the receiver end.) This technology reduces the contamination and makes the system more reliable, although not as reliable as the other systems in the following discussion.

Low-Voltage Systems

The most flexible type of system is the low-voltage system. This system must go into a new construction or major renovation so that the house can be pre-wired with low-voltage wire. This system can perform numerous functions.

Advantages of the low-voltage system

- **Convenience.** You can put all the lights on in the house or just one. It can also interface and control the audiovisual system, HVAC systems, pool controls, drapes/blinds, touchscreens, sensors, alarms, and more. Heated driveways and heated floors can also be tied into the system. All of these systems can be accessed and controlled by telephone.
- **Aesthetics.** It avoids wall clutter caused by putting multiple light switches all over the house.
- **Security.** It allows you to put all lights on in the house if you hear noise, and there is a vacation button to alternate the lights if you are away. A remote control is available to put lights on in the house from the car so you don't have to walk into a dark house.
- **Flexibility.** This system allows scene control. The buttons can be changed to accommodate different needs at a later date.
- **Astronomical clock.** The lights can be set to go on at dusk and off at dawn; the lights adjust to the changes in season everywhere in the world.
- **Ease of installation.** Once the contractor installs the low voltage wiring in the house, any combination of functions (in terms of lighting and other controls) can be attained.
- **Switches.** Switches are labeled. The system makes it easy for the family and guests to know which switches to use for which lights. This can be particularly useful in homes with many lights in a room.
- **Motion detectors and occupancy sensors.** Closets and front doors, for example, can have sensors so that lights will go on when the doors are opened. These features are available for security, as well as for conserving energy.

Disadvantages of the low-voltage system

- **Expense.** These systems tend to be costly.
- **Programming.** Most systems have to be programmed by a factory trained individual. Some home owners may be able to do the programming themselves, if they are computer savvy.

Line Carrier/Low-Voltage Combination Systems

This type of system is typically put into new constructions but can be retrofitted to certain homes (with attics and crawl spaces). It is more expensive than a line-voltage system but less expensive than the low-voltage or radio-frequency systems. The controls in each room can be linked, offering more flexibility than a line-voltage system but not as much as with the low-voltage or radio-frequency systems.

Advantages of the line carrier/low-voltage combination system

- **Convenience.** There is some flexibility in creating a scene and in selecting the lights you want on or off.
- **Security.** You can put all lights on in the house if there is an unexpected noise in the house, and there is a button for alternating the lights if you are on vacation.
- **Astronomical clock.** The lights can be set to go on at dusk and off at dawn; the lights adjust to the changes in season everywhere in the world.
- **Switches.** Switches can be labeled.
- **Expense.** This system costs more than the line-voltage system, but less than the low-voltage and radio-frequency systems.
- **Motion detectors and occupancy sensors.** These features are available for this system.

Disadvantages of the line carrier/low-voltage combination system

- **Flexibility.** This system is not as flexible as the low-voltage or radio-frequency systems because it can only control what it is wired to. In the other systems the entire house is covered.

Radio-Frequency Systems

The most recently developed lighting system uses radio-frequency communication. It has all the advantages of the low-voltage system and can be retrofitted into an existing house without rewiring. Wall stations (keypads) and/or master controls are used. This system has the same disadvantages, however, as the low-voltage system in terms of expense and programming.

Special Features Available on Low-Voltage and Radio-Frequency Systems

These systems have many available features. Although they may add tremendous convenience, some may be more than you actually need, such as features that program coffeepots. You should find out your options on particular systems and decide which ones you would like to have while the system is being programmed.

Here are some of the possibilities:

- **Motion detectors.** These put the lights on when you enter a room and when a car, person, or animal nears your house.
- **Modems.** Modems can be added to the system, which allow the factory to reprogram systems that have malfunctioned (if the dealer is away and unavailable to reprogram the system). The dealer uses these as well to make needed changes by remote.
- **Preprogrammed conveniences.** Buttons on the keypads can be programmed to serve different functions, at different times of the day.
- **Motion detectors and occupancy sensors**. These are available on low-voltage and radio-frequency systems.
- **Keypads.** A variety of colors and styles are available for the keypads.

Things to Consider When Selecting a Lighting System

If you plan for your lighting system in the early stages of your project, you will have the time to speak with the representatives of several available systems. Consider the following before making a decision:

- **New or existing structure.** There are limitations on your selection if you are retrofitting an existing house.
- **Budget.** Most of these systems are expensive, making this a major consideration.
- **Reputation of the dealer.** Make sure the dealer will be available when you need installation or service. Be sure the salesperson is selling you the latest system available so that you are able to get service and parts in 10 years.
- **Company.** Buy your system from a company that has been around for

several years and will be available to support your system in the future.

■ **Family Needs**. Select a system that has features you will enjoy using and that suits your family.

The company or representative selling the system are responsible for doing the following:

■ Evaluating the specific needs of the house.
■ Designing the system and discussing the options with the home owner.
■ Supplying the equipment.
■ For low-voltage and radio-frequency systems, the representative is additionally responsible for programming the system.
■ Troubleshooting, if there are problems or alterations to be made.

Electricians can easily install the wiring for lighting systems, which should not cost more than the installation for basic lights.

For low-voltage lighting systems, however, the installation and wiring may cost slightly more.

To locate a lighting specialist in your area, you can contact the American Lighting Association at 800-274-4484 or access their Web site at www.americanlightingassoc.com.

You can also directly contact several of the companies that offer lighting systems:

Company	Telephone	Web Site
Lightolier	800-526-2731	www.lightolier.com
Litetouch	888-548-3824	www.litetouch.com
Lutron	800-523-9466	www.lutron.com
Vantage	800-555-9891	www.vantagecontrols.com

Audiovisual Systems

If you are very handy and also knowledgeable about audiovisual equipment, you can probably shop around, buy components at a discount store, and install a simple system inexpensively. However, for those of us who are not that handy or knowledgeable about audiovisual equipment, it is important to find the most capable, knowledgeable, reliable person or company to help select and install a system. The equipment and systems are becoming so sophisticated, you should consider wiring the house for an excellent system even if you don't plan to put one in right away. You can put systems in, in stages or merely prepare the house for the time when you might decide to add one. Before considering any system, consider your budget, lifestyle (will everyone be listening to the same music or will each person be listening to different music?) and the size of the area the system will cover.

Selecting an Audiovisual Company

If possible, interview several AV suppliers and consider the following before making a decision:

1. It is best to look for a company that has a showroom. Most often, those with showrooms or stores have been successful at the business. It also gives customers the opportunity to see and hear various available components. If there are problems in the future, you know there will be someplace to address them. If an AV company comes highly recommended and they have no showroom, consider them, keeping in mind the possible pitfalls.
2. Make sure they have insurance. If an installer is injured and has no insurance, the owner could be responsible.
3. Make sure the representative is knowledgeable about the latest technology. This is a rapidly changing area. You should find a dealer who is aware of the latest technology even if you don't choose to incorporate it into your home.

In addition to the methods of locating dealers listed above, you can also contact CEDIA (Custom Electronic Design and Installation Association) at 800-669-5329 or access their Web site at www.cedia.org for names of affiliated companies that work in your area.

The Parts of an Audiovisual System

There are three parts to purchase for an audiovisual system, all of which should be supplied by the same company:
- Equipment.
- Installation and programming.
- Follow-up and service.

Equipment

The equipment necessary for an audio/visual system includes various components, as well as controls to run those components. There are several methods or systems for running the components (CD) player, DVD player, and so on) in your home. Consider which system you prefer before purchasing the components.

Systems to run the equipment. There are several ways to install systems into the house so that you can listen to the radio, CD, and so are. The following are two types of systems:

■ Multi-room. With this type of system, different rooms can have sound made by one component; everyone in the house must be listening to the same sound source: radio, CD, and so on. Keypads or electric eyes, with remote controls and volume control knobs control the sound. A receiver alone can usually be used to control this type of system.
    •This type is less expensive than a multiroom/multizone system (below).
    • Not all multiroom designs use volume controls or keypads in each room.

■ Multiroom/multizone. All the rooms in the house can be listening to sounds from different sources or the same source. For this type of system, you would use a control processor and keypad for each room that will have sound; each room has its own amplification. Here are the advantages of this type of system:
    • Users have more control in terms of selecting what they want to listen to.
    • Other systems, such as security, telephone, lighting, and drapery can be tied into this type of system.
    • In more elaborate (and expensive) systems, you can have bi-directional communication. The keypad would then give you such information as what CD is playing, what radio station is on, what the volume of the sound is, what satellite station is on, or what the base and treble settings are.
    • All the components can be controlled with a menu-driven system such as a touch screen on the wall or wireless touch screen on the desk. One touch screen can be used or several in various rooms.

    Here are the disadvantages:

    • These types of systems are generally much more expensive.
    • The system requires space to house all the amplifiers and pre-amplifiers,

along with all the additional components.

A multi-room system can be converted to a multi-room/multi- source system later on if the wiring was put in place before the walls were closed up. If the wiring has not been put in place, it is possible to retrofit the wiring later, usually causing a great deal of damage to the walls, depending on the competency of the installer. If, however, you don't want to retrofit the wiring, you can add a radio-frequency touch-screen master controller to operate the various components in each room.

Components. Most of the AV companies generally use higher-quality components that are not found in local electronics stores. You need to find an AV company that is authorized to service the components they sell. Since many of the components will be names most people are unfamiliar with, they will need to see several AV companies and try to become aware of the various products, along with reading trade publications, which are listed in Appendix B of this book.

Most often, the house has a centralized equipment location. Some people opt to keep the components and amplifiers in one location and the media-room components in a separate location.

- **Keypads.** These are available in a variety of price ranges and styles. They vary in the functions they perform. Some are used for simple input; others talk back and give the user a great deal of information.
- **Amplifiers.** Consider both wattage and current when selecting an amplifier. Additional wattage will not necessarily mean louder sound. When you combine wattage and additional current (high- current amplifier), you will end up with better sound at all volume levels. This is one of the areas where systems vary considerably in price and performance.
- **Preamplifiers.** With certain audio systems, separate components, or "separates" (preamplifiers, amplifiers, and tuners), are used in lieu of a receiver. This allows the buyer to choose the specifications of the individual components.
- **Speakers.** There are hundreds of manufacturers of speakers. Either trust your designer or ask to listen to several. Ask to hear what is recommended and inquire about the warranty. Three types of speakers are available:
  - In-wall
  - Freestanding/Bookshelf
  - Outdoor

- **Subwoofers.** There is a great variety to choose from here as well. Ask the designer for recommendations, listen to several of them and ask about the warranty.
- **Tuners.** There is not a great deal of variation in tuners unless you get to the broadcast-quality level. The dipole antenna, which usually comes with the tuner, is the most important component if you want good reception. Antennas should be bought separately for better reception.
- **CD changers.** Look at all the options. You can choose 1-, 5- ,6-, 100-, or 300-disc players. The larger capacity players are very popular with multi-room installations because one never has to touch their discs once they are loaded into the system. Be sure to buy a numeric keypad to select which disc you want to play. Trying to use the next disc arrow 49 times to get to the disc you want can be an exercise in frustration.
- **Cassette decks.** These components are becoming less and less popular, but those who own a large collection of cassette tapes may opt to include a deck in their system.
- **Laser disc players and DVD (digital video device) players.** These components greatly improve viewing quality. DVDs are quickly replacing the VCR in most home theatres.
- **Film screens.** If you decide on this option, buy only a tab-tensioned or rigid-mounted screen. If the screen is not held rigid, it will affect the focus of the picture. The other option is a manual screen, which is more portable and less costly but will not stay rigid if there is a breeze. Tab-tensioned are sometimes motorized but generally fixed, as are rigid-mounted screens.
- **DLP (digital light processing).** These are projectors used in home theaters. They are currently becoming smaller, more reasonably priced, and create a very bright picture.
- **Televisions.** Six types of televisions are available:
  - **CRT (cathode ray tube).** This is the most commonly used type of TV and does not require that the light in the room be controlled. There is a limitation, however, on the size of the screen, which cannot exceed 36 inches (measured on the diagonal).
  - **Plasma display.** This technology was originally designed for computer screen but is becoming more and more popular for the home television market. Televisions with this technology are available in 42-inch to 61-inch screens and are sought after because of their excellent picture and their narrow size, making them conducive for areas that might otherwise be difficult to put a television, such as over a fireplace. They have been very expensive, but prices are gradually coming down.

A plasma display television used over a fireplace.

• **LCD (liquid crystal display) systems.** This is another system that was developed with computer technology. These televisions are also very thin and are available in 5-inch to 30-inch screen sizes. They are not as commonly used as plasma display televisions because of their size and because the quality is not as good. They have to be viewed straight on to avoid having the picture fade out. These systems are quite expensive but are becoming less so with time. They are usually used in kitchens and bedrooms where their size may not be an issue.

• **Rear-projection systems.** These systems can have larger screens: 39 inches to 70 inches. They do not require a separate screen but may be difficult to incorporate into the room comfortably because they are quite large. They are best viewed straight on. As you begin to watch "off axis," or to the side, the picture gets progressively darker until you cannot see any picture at all. With this type of TV, you need to control the lighting in the room.

• **Separate projector system.** This type of system offers the highest-quality picture with no limitation on the size of the screen. They tend to be 60 inches to 120 inches, but they can be larger. These screens are designed to reflect back any light in the room and will therefore fade out the picture if there is light present. It is critical to this type of system that the light be controlled in the room. These systems tend to be expensive because of the cost of the projector, the screen, and the installation of both components.

Have a professional discuss all the available options with you. There are always new televisions, with new options, on the market. By 2006, all television stations are supposed to broadcast a high-definition signal in addition to an analog broadcast. Currently, high-definition TV is very expensive and there are limited signals being distributed, but the prices will continue to come down when this type of broadcast becomes more common. Converter boxes will also be available for anyone who wishes to use the TVs that they own.

• **Digital satellite systems (DSS).** Digital satellite systems are becoming increasingly popular. Although they require the installation of a satellite dish on the roof, they greatly expand viewing options and quality. Various program packages are available and must be ordered from program providers: DirecTV® and Dish Network™.

Controls for the Media room system.

1. **Universal Remote Control.** This should have the macro feature, which encapsulates all procedures necessary to operate the media room. These remotes tend to be expensive, but they allow the user to perform several functions with the press of one button, such as turning on the television and closing the curtains. These remotes have labels, which most do not, so the user doesn't have to remember what button operates what function.

2. **Touch screen.** This works in a similar way to the universal remote control but is more user-friendly. It incorporates the macro feature. Each function has an icon or graphic, so you can identify functions. If the touch screen doesn't function properly, the system still operates.

Home Theaters

Often the term home theatre is used incorrectly. Some companies advertise cabinets called home theaters, others use the term for anything that plays a movie. The term was actually coined to describe a reproduction of the professional cinema experience. The sound and appearance should simulate that of going to the movies. Typically, one button is used to dim the lights, close the drapes, lower the screen, start the movie, and even make the popcorn. A touch screen or a sophisticated remote control generally controls the system. This type of system is a great luxury and one that owners will have to select as a priority if it fits their space and, most of all, their budgets. Before purchasing a system, be sure you know:

- Whether the dealer capable of installing the type of system you are buying. Be sure to check the dealer's references and portfolio of past installations.
- What type of system you are getting.
- What components you are getting.
- How many speakers will be installed.
- How many hours of training you will get.
- What the warranty will be on the components and installation.

Installation and Programming of Audiovisual Systems

You should begin to plan the system at the early stages of the construction. The wiring should be in place before the drywall is installed. The wires should be the last wiring installed before the walls go up (so other workers will not disturb or cut them.) Speaker and equipment placement should be planned with the interior layout of furnishings.

An entire system doesn't have to be put in immediately. The house should be pre-wired with 12-conductor wire (for later versatility) or conduits should be installed from the control room, home-run, to the areas where you may want lighting or AV equipment. Built-in speakers may be installed in preparation for a system to be installed later on. Be sure the speakers are wired with 12-, 14- or 16-gauge audio wire, which is UL approved, oxygen-free. Electrical wire is meant to transmit electricity (60 Hz), and audio wire is specifically designed to carry the frequencies that relate to music (20 Hz-20, 000Hz); therefore, the audio wire will make the music sound better. If you will have keypad controls for the audio system, you will need control wire, which should be category 5, or the multi-conductor, stranded, and shielded wire specified by the equipment manufacturer.

If you plan to pre-wire the house for the future, be sure you have a clear diagram of where all of the wires are and what wires were installed. It is possible to forget this information, and you would then be forced to start ripping apart the walls (which you definitely won't want to do).

Make sure that the company that installs the system is prepared to program it and spend the time to instruct you on how to use it.

When you sign a contract with the company you purchase the system from, make sure that it is noted how many hours they are willing to spend with you so that you can be assured of being able to work the system.

Telephone Systems

Telephone systems are used for multiple line use and/or for an intercom system and doorbell (although it will not sound like a bell, but an alternate telephone ring). It integrates the phones so they can be tied in with fax machines, answering machines, Internet access, cordless phones, modems, and door intercoms.

Reasons to Put in a Telephone System

1. The large size of the house requires an intercom system to:
   • Communicate with others in the house.
   • Alert people in the house of pending phone calls.
   • Page the entire house in order to locate people and let them know they have a call or that they are needed, for dinner for example.
2. Room-to-room hands-free intercom is required because of small children or the elderly in the house.
3. The owners of the house require multiple lines and would like the convenience of putting calls on hold.
4. You can selectively choose which lines will ring in particular rooms and at what time they will ring.
5. The door phone and intercom allow you to find out who is at the door by just picking up the telephone.

Components of a Telephone System

The components you select will be determined by the size of your house as well as your needs and those of your family. You may opt to have a traditional doorbell on your door, rather than having it connected to your phone system. Find out what is available on the system so you can decide on optional components. Some of the optional components are:

- Control unit (often referred as the KFU-Key Service Unit).
- Stations (phones).
- Door-answering module.
- Door speakers.
- Answering machine.
- Cordless extension phones.

Things to Consider When Selecting a Telephone System

Before selecting any phone system, consider the following:

1. **Aesthetics.** You want to find phones that are unobtrusive and available in neutral colors.
2. **Ease of use.** You want to find phones that are not difficult to operate.
3. **Dealer's references.** Check to see that other clients were satisfied with the system, installation, instruction, and follow-up.
4. **Guarantee.** Most systems offer at least a one-year manufacturer's guarantee, which should be serviced by the installer who sold you the system.
5. **Manufacturer.** Select a well-known company that will be in business in several years in case there is a problem with the equipment and the dealer is no longer available.

It is important to consider future needs when installing a telephone system. Be sure to put in enough jacks and outlets to anticipate family changes. Children's beds are often moved when they get older. They may also need to have their own computers some time in the future. The cost of adding the wiring and outlets is tremendous when it is done after construction is completed, and it takes a great deal more time to do the job. Depending on the situation, it could damage walls and make a mess in the house. It is therefore a good idea to put wiring everywhere when you are building or renovating your house, while the roughing-in is being done, so that you are prepared for the addition of modems for computers, fax machines, answering machines, or additional telephones.

People are often intimidated by all the features that phone systems provide. All systems are designed for commercial use and therefore provide all that is needed in an office setting. If homeowners decide to put in this type of system, they need to concentrate on the functions that will work in their homes. The system provider should design the system to work for the individual home and let the homeowner know what features are available for future needs.

All wiring installed in a new or renovated home should be category 5, 6, 6+ (or the newer category 7 wiring, which will be needed in the future for high-technology computers). This wire is slightly more expensive than regular wire, but it should have no effect on the cost of the labor for installation. It allows you to network high-speed data, as required by all Internet services. Every wire must be home-run (terminating at a central location in the utility area).

When you are selecting a system, be sure you know how many jacks will be installed and how much time the dealer will be willing to spend with you so that you can learn to operate the system.

Several available systems are:

- Panasonic
- Lucent Partner
- AT&T
- Soho

Central Vacuum Systems

A central vacuum system is a stationary type of canister vacuum cleaner, which is usually mounted in the basement or garage. The hose inlets are mounted in the walls, and 2-inch PVC pipe is installed to carry the dirt-laden air to the central power unit. A 30-foot hose allows the user to reach every part of the house to effectively clean it. It is easier and less expensive to install a central vacuum system in a new house, but it is possible to install in an existing house by snaking the tubing through the walls, as an electrician would snake electrical wires. If the system will be installed in a new house, the inlets and tubing should be installed before the drywall is installed.

These are some of the advantages of a central-vacuum system:

- They are generally quieter than other vacuum cleaners.
- They remove more dust and dirt than most portable vacuums, keeping it from recirculating in the house, particularly if the exhaust air is vented outside. A healthier living environment results.
- Many people feel they are easier to use than conventional vacuum cleaners.
- Because they are stationary, they usually have larger and more powerful

motors than those in a portable vacuum cleaner.

How to Select a System

The following are some of the factors to consider before selecting a central-vacuum system:

- Cost. The cost will vary between systems.
- Reliability of the dealer. Find out how long the dealer has been in business. Ask for references and call several of them to find out if they showed up for the installation on time, were careful with the installation and were willing to correct errors or exchange faulty parts when necessary.

Components of a Central Vacuum System

The following are the components to consider when purchasing a central vacuum system.

Power Unit

This is a stationary canister, which is generally mounted in the basement or garage and contains the motor. The motors in a large percentage of the central vacuum systems have been manufactured by Ametek Lamb Electric. They produce several different motors, which differ in cost, performance, and reliability. Select a specific motor based on:

1. **The size of your home.**
2. **The air watts of the machine.** Air watts is a specification that rates the output power of the vacuum cleaner rather than its input power. It is based on suction with airflow as measured at the vacuum cleaner inlet. Air watts is the number that indicates what dirt the motor is picking up. The higher the air watts, the better the pickup of the vacuum cleaner. This is a combination of:
- **The CFM, or cubic feet per minute, of air.** This is the unrestricted airflow, which is measured at the vacuum cleaner inlet.
- **The water lift (or sealed vacuum rate).** This is the technical standard defining the strength of a vacuum system's suction. It measures how high a given system can lift a column of water, expressed in inches. The

System design: M&S Systems / Illustration: Rob Leanna

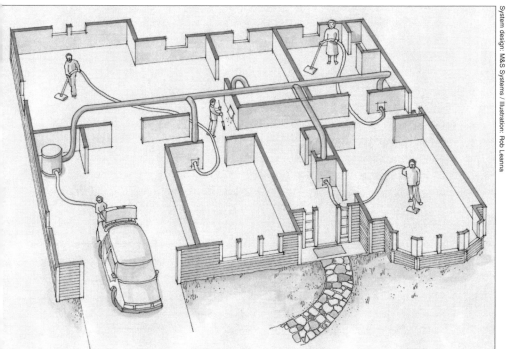

A central vacuum system.

higher the number, the more powerful the vacuum system.

3. **The system of venting.** One of the biggest advantages of central vacuum systems is that they remove dust and dirt to completely outside living areas and do not recirculate particles back into the air. Once dirt is in the power unit, the filtration system takes over to trap it for permanent removal. To further eliminate the possibility of dirt recirculating through the motor exhaust air, most units can be vented to the outdoors, just like clothes dryers. But even if the unit is installed to vent indoors, any dirt that escapes the power unit is in the garage or basement-well outside the living areas.

The noise of the air discharge can be reduced by installing a muffler on the air-discharge pipe going outside. This is an optional, inexpensive feature.

4. **Motor size.** This is a less important issue, although one you may want to consider. Motors typically are available in two sizes: 5.7 and 7.2. The 7.2 vacuum motor is more durable and offers a longer life expectancy than the 5.7 motor.

5. **Motor stages.** Often, three-stage motors are put in the more expensive

systems. However, three-stage motors tend to burn out more quickly, shortening the work life of the motor. There are two-stage motors that have higher airlift than three-stage motors. If a two-stage motor can be found with higher air watts, it should be considered preferable.

Wall Inlets

Generally, one inlet is installed for every 550 feet to 700 feet of living space, using 30 feet of hose. The homeowner (or installer) can generally determine valve locations by taking a 30-foot length of string and stretching it around the room and around corners to assure that the hose will reach the entire home, including draperies and shelves.

Most inlets have low-voltage contacts that mate with the hose to enable the user to switch the main power unit on and off from the hose end in their hand. There are special inlets (Hayden's SuperValve and Canplas hose inlet valve are two such valves) that incorporate a receptacle to supply the household voltage via the hose to the power nozzle. Inserting this hose into the wall energizes the system. The older method of attaching a power nozzle was to insert the hose and then plug a 6-inch cord attached to it (pigtail connection) into a standard electrical outlet. This type of connection is still used when adding a system to an existing house. Since many system manufacturers have these valves available with their systems, be sure to ask about it when having a system installed in your house.

Two-inch OD (outer diameter) Schedule 20 thin wall PVC tubing

This tubing connects the wall-mounted hose inlet valves to the main power unit.

Hose

The design and quality of the hoses varies with the systems. Most standard hoses are 30 feet, but they are also available in 25-foot and 35-foot lengths. All hoses come with an inlet adapter at one end and a curved wand on the attachment end. Hoses vary, however, in diameter. They are available in both 1 1/4-inch and 1 3/8-inch diameters.

Features

Some or all of the following features are available from the companies that supply central vacuum systems:

- ■ On-off buttons activate the power unit from the hose handle.
- ■ 360-degree swivel handles minimize kinks in the hose.

- Hoses with a110-volt wire within the hose can operate an electric power brush.
- Crushproof hoses are available from most vacuum companies, but they tend to close off the air and lose suction when you pull it around a corner if the system is not planned properly. These hoses weigh about 5 1/2 pounds, about 4 pounds less than the wire and vinyl reinforced hoses, making them easier to use. Wire and vinyl hose designs are a popular alternative, however, to crushproof models.
- Hose socks cover the hose and protect the woodwork and furniture, and reduce twisting.

Cleaning Attachments

Various attachments, in a variety of sizes, can be attached to the hose. Not every company carries every attachment. Some of the available attachments are as follows:

- Bare floor brush.
- Upholstery/curtain brush.
- Crevice and ceiling nozzle.
- Dusting brush.
- Rug brush.
- Carpeting brush.
- Furniture dusting brush.
- Garage and car care kit.
- Hose and attachment caddy.

Optional Accessories

Several optional accessories are available on most central vacuum systems. The following are some that you might be interested in purchasing:

- Automatic dustpans are inlet ports that flush-mount to the wall or cabinet kickboard. A foot switch activates (and deactivates) a suction created by the central vacuum system and the dirt is then swept into it. Most are available in black, white, or almond and can be added to an existing system or a new system.
- ExtenVac ™ is a long and flat tool that reaches under appliances and low furniture.

- Mini-accessories are used for hard-to-reach and fragile cleaning jobs, such as electronics, computers, and decorations.
- Turbine-driven carpet brushes are attachments used primarily for deep cleaning carpets. The power in this brush is derived from a turbine rather than a motor, and the power to drive the brush roll works off the airflow of the system. These are less expensive and less powerful than electric carpet brushes. It is recommended that these be used with hoses that are 1 3/8 inches in diameter.
- Electric power brushes are attachments used for deep cleaning carpets. They incorporate a revolving brush roll with an electric motor, which adds to the power of the cleaning system and creates a higher performance. Although higher performing, electric power brushes are generally a bit more costly because the installer must run the 120-volt wires at each of the wall inlets.
- Monitors are available that let you know when to empty the cans and when to schedule maintenance or service.
- Water and fireplace ash vacs use 51/2-gallon interceptor cans. This feature serves the dual purpose of acting as a water vac and using a fire-retardant filter with a pickup nozzle to remove ash from a fireplace.

Methods of Separating the Dirt

Several types of filtration system are available.

Bag and filter dirt separation

Many central vacuum systems use a filtration bag to remove and dispose of accumulated dirt. An important consideration in maintaining optimum performance is changing the bag regularly. If bags are not changed when needed, filters clog. Problems caused by clogged filters include loss of suction, which reduces cleaning efficiency. There is a substantial difference in bag size between models, with larger capacity units requiring bag changes only every several months. Because bag and filter replacement can be expensive over the lifetime of the system, many homeowners prefer cyclonic units.

Cyclonic separation

These systems usually use no changeable bags or filters, although some units do offer a removable non-disposable filter. Dirt-laden air is brought into the cylinder in a spinning, rotating fashion where gravity separates the heavy dirt from the air stream and deposits it into the dirt receptacle. When it's full, the receptacle can be detached and emptied. While bagless cyclonic separation units do save money on periodic bag changes, it can be a dirty, cumbersome job to carry and dump the receptacle when it is full. The receptacle must also be checked periodically to be sure that it is not full.

Permanent self-cleaning cloth filter

This filtration system employs self-cleaning cloth filters, which are permanently mounted in the power unit and cannot be changed. The vacuumed dirt falls into the receptacle and is emptied in the same way as the cyclonic system. There are permanent self-cleaning cloth filter units that are also cyclonic. Some manufacturers say the motor and filter are kept cleaner with this filtration system, creating better performance by the unit. The filter can, however, also reduce the airflow through the motor, which can add resistance and reduce overall performance. This system is also less expensive because there is no need to buy replacement filters.

After speaking with representatives of most of the companies, I would assume that most of the systems work very well. You will have to speak with representatives of several companies, however, to decide which system you will be most comfortable with.

Installation

Some companies will install their own systems; other companies will give you a good discount for installing the system yourself. There are several ways to arrange for installation:

- Buying the system with installation provided by the dealer.
- Buying the power unit from a local dealer and installing the system with a DIY (do-it-yourself) kit.
- Buying the system from a local dealer and hiring a local installer.
- Buying directly from a central vacuum cleaner company that you have accessed from the Internet. A local installer can be found by referrals from the Internet or from the vacuum company.
- Other professionals working on the house, the builder, electrician, plumbers, and so on, may be able to install the system.

Warranty

Look for a company that offers at least a 5- or 6-year warranty on the repair or replacement of defective parts and a 3-year warranty on defects in accessories.

Here are several companies to look into:

Company	Telephone	Web Site
Air Master	800-525-2055	www.builtinvacuum.com
Air Vac	800-366-6874	www.mssystems.com
Astro-Vac	800-546-3729	www.astrovac.com
Beam Industries	800-369-2326	www.beamvac.com
Broan Ltd.	800-548-0790	www.broan.com
Budd	800-245-2833	www.buddvac.com
Duo Vac	800-453-5353	www.duovac.com
Easy Flo	800-327-9356	www.easyflo.com
Electrolux	800-243-9078	www.electroluxusa.com
Eureka	800-282-2886	www.eureka.com
Filtex	800-366-6874	www.mssystems.com
FloMaster	800-525-2055	www.buildinvacuum.com
Galaxie	800-238-2294	www.galaxie-vac.com
Hayden	800-501-5018	hayden.ca
Hoover	800-891-5696	www.hoovercompany.com
M & S Systems	800-877-6631	www.mssystems.com
Modern Day	800-525-2055	www.builtinvacuum.com
Nutone	800-463-2358	www.nutoneinfo.com
Silent Master	800-525-2055	www.builtinvacuum.com
Silent Partner	800-546-3729	www.vacumaid.com
Vacu-flo	800-822-8356	www.vacuflo.com
Vacu-Maid	800-546-3729	www.vacumaid.com
Zenex	800-248-8221	zenexvacs.com

You can now see how complicated some of these systems are in terms of components and selection. Allow plenty of time to investigate each system carefully.

So many terms are thrown around in the process of constructing a house that it is sometimes difficult for the layperson to understand what is being said. I thought it would be helpful to have an extensive guide to keep with you so you can quickly look up the terms. I hope you find the list relevant and the explanations understandable. Good luck!

AIA
The American Institute of Architects.

allowance
The amount of money provided in the contract by the general contractor or builder, for the homeowner to purchase certain items or products that they have not pre-selected. Items that are not provided by the allowance will be paid out of pocket.

amp (ampere)
A unit that measures the amount of electricity that flows through a wire.

anchor bolt
A bolt set into the concrete foundation that connects to the walls of the house. These are required in some areas with seismic activity to keep the house stable in an earthquake.

apron
The horizontal piece of window trim attached to the wall, just below the stool.

asphalt
A byproduct of refining crude petroleum, used for paving and waterproofing.

awning window
A single window hinged at the top, which swings outward.

backfill
Excavated or imported soil used around the foundations or in filling a trench.

backhoe
An excavating machine with a shovel at one end and a hoe at the other end.

balloon frame
A wood frame in which studs are continuous from the sill to the roof. This method of framing is rarely used in new construction.

baluster
One of several vertical poles that supports the handrail of a stair hand railing.

balustrade
The railing formed by the newel post, balusters, and handrail.

baseboard, or base molding
A molding consisting of strips of wood used to cover the joints between the floor and the adjoining walls.

base coat
The first coat of paint put on drywall.

base plate
A horizontal wood piece that serves as the bottom tie in a stud wall partition.

batten
Narrow wood strips that are used to cover joints in outside walls.

bay window
A window projecting outward from the wall of the house.

beam
A horizontal supporting structural piece made of wood or metal.

berm
A mound of earth or pavement used to control the flow of surface water.

bearing wall
A wall that supports the ceiling, floor, or roof above it.

bid
A statement of the price at which a contractor or supplier will off services and/or supplies.

biscuit joint
A joint formed when rectangular notches are cut out of two

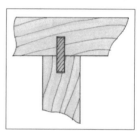

pieces of wood and put together with a compressed wood "biscuit," which expands and creates a tight joint.

blind-nailing
Nailing through wood so that the nailhead does not show. Often used in tongue-in-tongue and groove flooring.

brick veneer
A facing of bricks used as exterior siding. It does not carry any load other than itself.

breezeway
A covered passage between the house and a detached structure.

BTU
British thermal units. The quantity of heat required to raise the temperature of one pound of water one degree Fahrenheit.

builder-grade materials
Typically, the least-expensive, lowest- quality materials available.

building code
Regulations established by state and local governments stating the minimum standards for construction.

building permit
A release issued by the local government allowing construction or renovation to begin.

bulldozer
An excavating machine on tracks, with a steel blade that can be raised or lowered attached to the front. It is used to move earth from place to place and to shape the grade.

bullnose
A rounded outside edge of a step, tabletop, or counter.

cable
An electricity conductor made up of two or more wires contained in a covering.

cantilever
A projecting beam supported at only one end.

cap
Anything that tops another member: a column, door cornice, molding, and so on.

casing
A molding used to trim door and window frames; a pipe used for well drilling.

casement window
A side-hinged window that swings in or out.

catch basins
A structure for catching and retaining surface drainage over a large area, in which sediment may settle.

cathedral ceiling
A high, open, gabled ceiling.

caulking
The compound used to make joints or seams weatherproof or waterproof or to make them smooth.

certificate of occupancy
A certificate issued by the building department stating that the house has been built in accordance with the local building code and zoning ordinance, and may be occupied.

chair rail
A molding placed on the wall at chair-back height to protect the wall from damage.

change order
A document describing alterations or additions to the original contract between the owner and the general contractor.

chipboard
A board made from wood chips glued together under pressure.

circuit
The path traveled by electric current from a source to an appliance or fixture and back to the source.

circuit breaker
A switch that automatically breaks the electric circuit when a short or overloading occurs.

cladding
A covering over a lesser-grade or vulnerable structure or

material to make it more durable.

clapboard
Thin, horizontal, overlapping boards of graduated thickness used as exterior building siding.

clear
A term used in wood grading systems to describe the best grade of material, with fine texture, no knots, and few imperfections.

code
A federal, state, or local ruling, law, or regulation that stipulates building safety and health requirements.

collar beams
Beams used to tie rafters together.

column
A vertical loadbearing post, pillar, or strut.

compressor
The part of the air-conditioning or heat-pump unit that compresses the refrigerant gas so that it can absorb heat.

concrete
A mixture of sand, gravel, water, and Portland cement that dries to a hard consistency.

conduit
A tube or pipe designed to carry electrical wires or cables.

contraction or control joint
The grooves placed in a concrete slab to which cracks in the structure will gravitate, maintaining the structure's integrity and appearance.

convenants
Restrictions or requirements placed on the builder or homeowner by homeowners' associations, architectural

review boards, or subdivisions.

coping
A continuous protective covering or cap along the top of a masonry parapet or wall, designed to protect the masonry from water damage.

corbel
A piece of wood or masonry projecting from a wall used to support some part of the house above it.

corner bead
A strip of metal designed to protect a plaster or drywall corner.

cornice
The exterior trim of a structure at the meeting of the roof and wall.

countersinking
Screwing or nailing the head of a fastener below the surface of the wood to conceal or protect it.

coverage code
A code adhered to by the local area that specifies what percentage of the property can be used to construct a home or other structure.

cricket
A small roof for diverting water.

crawl space
An enclosed shallow space below the first floor of a house or porch, or in an attic.

crown molding
Decorative trim placed where the interior wall and ceiling meet.

cupola
A small-domed structure rising above a roof.

cured
When a material, such as

concrete or mortar, is dry.

dado
A section of a wall that extends from the baseboard to the chair rail.

dado cap
A molding used to finish the top of a dado.

damper
A valve installed inside an air duct to regulate the flow of air.

deadwood
Pieces of wood nailed to the frame of the house, to which the sheetrock is attached.

dead load
The weight of permanent parts (not furniture, people, etc.) of a structure that must be supported by other parts of the structure.

dentil molding
A type of crown molding with an even pattern of little squares and blank spaces.

distribution panel box
A metal box, used in an electric system, containing the fuses or circuit breakers.

dormer
A vertical structure projecting from the slope of a roof and containing one or more windows.

double-glazing
Two panes of glass set in a single frame, trapping air between them for insulation.

double-hung window
A window consisting of two sashes; the windows slide vertically.

dovetail joints
A joint that locks in a zigzag pattern and resembles the feathers of a dove.

dowel
A pin made of wood or metal that is used to reinforce or hold two joining pieces of wood.

downspout or leader
A vertical metallic tube that diverts the rain and melted snow from the roof to the ground or to a drainage system.

drainpipe
A perforated plastic or clay pipe embedded in gravel or crushed stones and put around the footings to drain away the subsurface water and keep the lower level of the house dry.

drip cap
A protective molding set on top of a window or door casing to divert rainwater.

drywall, sheetrock, gypsum board, or plaster board
Boards consisting of a gypsum core faced with heavy paper on both sides and used to cover interior walls and ceilings.

dry well
A pile of stones or gravel buried below the elevation of the footings to collect water from the drainpipe. This water evaporates during hot weather.

duct
An enclosure, such as a pipe, used for distributing heated or cooled air to the living areas of the structure.

easement
A right or privilege that one party has to the property of another that entitles the holder to a specific, limited use of the

property.

eave
The lower part of a roof that overhangs the outside wall.

elevation
A flat drawing of the side of a building or wall.

enamel
Oil-based paint used in areas that are most apt to get soiled.

errors and omissions
Liability insurance generally carried

insurance
by architects to cover errors made in home design or construction.

expansion joint
A joint used between concrete units that allows for expansion and contraction without cracking.

fascia
The flat board enclosing the exterior ends of the rafters of the roof.

fiberboard
A type of building board used for insulation made of reduced fibrous material, such as wood, cane, or other vegetable fibers.

fitting
A plumbing term for any device that connects a pipe to a pipe or a pipe to a fixture.

flashing
Water-resistant material used to protect, cover or deflect water from exterior joints where different slopes meet such as chimneys, skylights, vents, windows and doors, preventing water infiltration.

floating walls
Walls in the basement built to allow movement in the basement floor without damage to the walls.

floor area ratio (FAR)
The ratio used to describe the building's square-foot area to the lot's square-foot area.

flue
An opening in a chimney or vent through which smoke and gases pass.

flying buttress
A horizontal brace that spans from the wall to a supporting abutment and receives the outward thrust of the wall.

footing
A concrete base that sits on the soil to distribute the loads of the foundation walls above it over a wider area of soil than the structure being supported.

footprint
The outline of the foundation of a structure.

forms
Wooden structures made of plywood and two-by-fours used to retain concrete before it sets.

foundation
The part of the structure below the first floor or below grade that supports the entire structure.

framing
A part of construction process that consists of putting together the lumber skeleton of the house.

French drain
A drainage trench filled with loose stones covered with soil sloped in such a way as to carry water away from a structure.

frost line

The depth at which the ground freezes in a particular area.

furnace
An appliance that generates hot air.

furring
The process of putting a space between two materials to achieve a flat surface.

fuse
An electrical safety device that protects the wiring from overheating and becoming a fire hazard.

gable
The triangular end of a house formed by the pitched roof.

gambrel
A roof having two pitches on each of two sides, with the steeper one on the lower portion.

gasket
An elastic strip that forms a seal between two parts.

GFCI
Ground fault circuit interrupter, a safety component of outlets near a water source. The GFCI instantly cuts off the power to an outlet if there is an electric short.

girder
A large or main beam that supports numerous floor joists and heavy loads along its span.

grade
The level of the ground.

grade beams
The structural members, made of poured concrete, that connect and reinforce structural piers.

grading
The process of shaping the surface of a lot to give it the

desired contours.

green
An environmentally friendly product.

grout
A fine cement used to fill the joints or cracks between tiles, between the old and new surface of poured concrete, and around anchor bolts.

gutter
Troughs along the roof eave that collects the rain and melted snow from the roof and diverts it to a downspout.

hardwood
Tough, heavy timber of compact texture taken from deciduous trees, such as oak, maple, and walnut. This does not refer to the hardness of the wood.

header
A structural beam that spans the top of windows, doorways, and other wall openings and carries the load above it.

head jamb
The top of a window or door-frame.

hearth
The slab that forms the base of a fireplace and extends into the room.

heartwood
The older wood at the core of the tree which is dark in color and resistant to decay.

hip
The sloping ridge that forms when two sloping sides of a roof meet.

hip roof
A roof sloped on all four sides.

hopper
A window that is hinged at the bottom and opens in.

hot wire
Any wire that carries electrical current from a power source to an electrical device. This wire is usually identified by black, blue, or red insulation, never white or green.

HVAC
Heating, ventilation, and air-conditioning.

jamb
The piece forming the side and top of a window or doorframe.

joist
The heavy horizontal beam that supports the floor or ceiling.

laminate
A material (layers of paper with phenolie resin), which is fused together under high pressure and heat. It is then glued to the substrate.

latex paint
A water-based paint that is easy to apply and cleans up with soap and water when still wet.

lath
A grid applied to exterior sheathing as a base for stucco.

leaching field
A field of trenches dug into the ground and lined with tile, broken stone, gravel, or sand, used to disburse wastewater from a septic tank into the ground.

lien
A legal claim placed on a property in order to get payment on a debt.

light
An individual pane of glass in a window.

load bearing wall
Any wall that supports the

weight of other structural components.

live load
The people, furniture, and so on that occupy a structure; this does not include parts of the structure itself.

load-bearing capacity
The amount of weight a particular substance (soil, steel, or wood) can withstand without breaking or bending beyond its design.

load-bearing wall
An interior or exterior wall that carries the load of the roof down to the foundation.

locking rabbet
A joint used in woodworking to make a secure fit.

lumber
Wood milled for use in construction.

Mansard roof
A hipped roof with two pitches. The bottom pitch is very steep and the top pitch flatter, so it is usually not seen from the ground.

mantel
The shelf above the opening, or the trim on the sides and top of a fireplace.

masonry
Bricks, stones, concrete blocks, or tiles bonded together by mortar.

masonry board
Waterproof sheet material used on walls instead of drywall as a base for tile.

mechanic's lien
A claim put against a property to satisfy an unpaid bill to a subcontractor or supplier.

melamine
A material that is fused to the substrate under heat and low pressure. The material then becomes part of the substrate. It is scratch-resistant and cleans easily, and is more reasonably priced than laminate.

millwork
Stock and custom-made woodwork in the form of cabinetry, shelving, panels, and molding, shaped or molded in a millwork plant.

miter
A cut or joint at an angle that is more or less than 90 degrees.

mortar
A material composed of cement, sand, and lime, used by masons to bond brick, stone, block, or tile together.

mullion
A vertical dividing piece between two adjoining windows or doors.

muntin
The small piece of wood or metal that holds and separates glass within a window sash. Windows with a single pane may have a snap-in grid to give the effect of muntins.

newel post
An upright post that receives and supports the handrail at critical points on a stair.

nonbearing wall
A wall that supports only its own weight.

nosing
The rounded edge of a tread that extends out over the riser.

oil-based paint
Paint that must be thinned and cleaned up with solvents or paint thinners. It is durable,

has a scrubbable finish, and requires a long drying time. It also has a strong odor.

on center or o.c.
The distance between the centers of two consecutive members in equally spaced framing or reinforcing bars. Standard o.c. is 16 inches or 24 inches.

open stair
A stair not attached to the wall.

paint grade
Lumber intended for use with a painted finish. The quality of this wood is not as fine as stain grade.

parapet
A low wall on the edge of a roof, bridge, or terrace.

parging
The thin coat of cement used to smooth, waterproof, and fireproof foundations, or to finish masonry walls, chimneys, and so on, usually on the exterior.

particleboard
A solid panel formed by compressing flakes of wood with resin under heat and pressure.

penalty clause
A clause put into a contract, with a general contractor for example, which stipulates a penalty if the project is not completed by a given day.

percolation (perc)test
A test that checks the feasibility of a site for a septic system.

perfatape
A wide paper tape applied to sheetrock seams with plasterboard compound or mud.

pier
A vertical structural support

formed by drilling a hole in the earth and filling it with a masonry or metal column.

pitch
The angle of inclination that a roof makes with the slope horizon.

plenum
The space between the suspended ceiling grid and the ceiling. This space often contains mechanical systems.

plumb [AU: plumb?]
An exact vertical line typically determined by using a plump bob, a cone shaped metal weight hung on the end of a long sting.

plywood
A product made of layers if wood veneer bonded together with adhesive.

pocket door
A door that slides into a concealed pocket recessed in the wall.

Portland cement
A hydraulic cement manufactured by a process patented in 1824 used in concrete and mortar.

prehung doors
A door that is delivered attached to the frame.

pressure treated wood
Lumber that has been saturated with a preservative under high pressure, causing it to penetrate the pores, while it is still green. It is the most effective method of treating wood for outdoor use. It is also thought to be extremely toxic.

primer
The first coat of interior or exterior paint.

punch list
A checklist of items to be completed before the final inspection of the house is done.

pvc pipe
Plastic pipe.

quote
A guaranteed price given in advance of work or the purchase of supplies.

rabbet
The groove for a matching tongue, routed out of the face

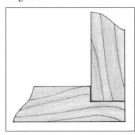

of the receiving material.

rafter
One of a series of parallel sloping beams that support the roof.

rail
The horizontal section of a frame for a panel or door.

R-value
The ability of a material to resist the escape of heat.

register
The facing plate on the wall, ceiling, or floor where supply air is released into the room and where air returns.

regrade
To change the level of the ground.

reinforcing bar or rebar
Bars made of bendable steel, Teflon, and so on set into wet concrete for reinforcement and

to deter cracking.

renderings
A perspective drawing showing what the house is likely to look like.

retainage
The part of the contractors payment that the owner holds back until the project is sufficiently complete.

retrofit
To upgrade a structure using modern materials.

return
The ductwork leading back to the HVAC unit to be reconditioned.

ridge board
The top board of roof that runs horizontally above the rafters.

riser
The vertical piece of a stair between two treads.

rough-in
The installation of all the electrical and mechanical parts that will be concealed by the interior walls.

rough opening
The space defined by framing elements to be faced with trim or to receive a door, window frame, stairwell, or chimney.

saddle
A strip of wood, stone, or metal installed at the step of a door or arched opening to form the boundary for flooring materials (such as tiles, wood, and carpeting.)

saltbox roof
A gabled roof with one slope longer and lower then the other.

sash

The frame that holds glass in a window or door. It may be moveable or fixed.

scale
A deposit of mineral solids on the interior surfaces of water lines and containers, often formed when water containing the carbonates or bicarbonates of calcium and magnesium is heated.

schematic drawing
A rough preliminary drawing used to generate or show ideas, usually made in the early stages of designing.

sconce
A wall-mounted light fixture.

seepage drain
A drain which allows for a liquid overflow to be discharged without causing a flood or creating a standing body of water where none is desired.

semi-gloss
A paint or enamel that when dry has a luster but does not look glossy.

septic tank
A steel or concrete settling tank which receives waste water (from sinks and bathtubs) and soil water (from the toilet) through an inlet pipe. Solid free water flows through an outlet pipe to a drain field where it is distributed over a large area underground.

service panel
A metal box into which the main electric service cable is connected and from which wiring is routed via circuit breakers or fuses.

setback
The minimum distance between a structure and the

property lines, established by the local zoning ordinances or deed restrictions.

shake shingles
Wooden roof shingles, somewhat irregular in width, that weather to a gray color. They are made by splitting rather than sawing the wood.

sheathing
Boards, plywood, or particle wood panels used to cover the wood framing of the roof and exterior walls, and a base for siding.

shed roof
A roof sloped in one direction only.

shim
A tapered, narrow piece of wood, stone, or metal that is slipped under a part of a structure to level it.

sidelights
Vertical, narrow windows used on each side of a door.

siding
The finish layer covering exterior walls.

sill
The horizontal piece of wood or masonry sitting atop the foundation wall and supporting it. Also refers to the horizontal piece forming the bottom frame of the opening into which a window or door is set.

site plan
A drawing of all the existing conditions, including topography, setbacks, and existing utilities, on a lot.

slab
A thick plate made of concrete.

slab-on-grade foundation
A type of basementless foundation made by pouring concrete

directly over dirt with no basement or crawl space.

soffi
Trim applied to the eave, the section of ceiling that drops lower than the main ceiling or the section under the kitchen cabinet. In the kitchen they conceal light fixtures, heating or air conditioning installations or serve as decorative "fillers" between a cabinet and the ceiling.

softwood
Wood from evergreen trees (conifers) such as pines, cedars, and firs. This wood in not necessarily soft.

stain grade
The finest quality of lumber, intended for a stain finish. This wood receives and absorbs stain easily.

stile
The vertical section of a door, window, or cabinet frame.

stool
A flat, horizontal molding installed at the bottom of the window over the apron and extending slightly into the room.

stucco
The cement plaster or concrete applied to the exterior wall or surface of a building as a finish.

strip flooring
Finished floor made of narrow strips of wood (usually hardwood) flooring.

stringers
The sloping sides of a staircase that supports the treads and risers.

stud
One of the vertical members of a wall frame to which sheath-

ing and siding are attached.

subfloor
Plywood or boards nailed to the floor joists to form a base for the finish flooring.

subpanel
A secondary service panel installed to serve a specific zone of a house or added space, reducing the number of circuits and the amount of wiring routed to the main panel or service panel.

substrate
Core materials such as medium-density fiberboard (MDF), or plywood that are used as a backing or base for a veneer or other material, such as ceramic tile.

sump pump
A square, rectangular, or circular structure that collects water and then discharges it with a pump.

supply & return
Ductwork that leads from the HVAC unit to the registers and back to the HVAC unit to be reconditioned.

survey
Measurement to determine the exact boundary lines of a property.

swale
A sloped trough or channel, close to one or several houses, which captures and carries drainage from rain or snow away from the property.

tamping & vibrating
The process of removing air pockets from poured concrete by manual and/or mechanical process.

tap fee
A utility company charge for

hooking up a new home.

tarpaper or roofing felt
A heavy, black, waterproof paper applied beneath roofing and wall siding and sometimes to the outside of foundation walls.

termite shield
A protective shield (galvanized steel or aluminum sheets) placed between the foundation or pipes and the wood structure of the house so as to interrupt the migration path of termites from the ground into the structure.

title insurance
A type of policy issued by a title insurance company after it searches the public record and insures against losses resulting from improperly recorded deeds, forged documents, incorrect marital status, etc.

thickset
A method of installing tiles in a rigid mortar mud bed reinforced by wire.

thinset
A method of installing tiles into mastic, an organic adhesive.

ton (air-conditioning)
A unit of measure that determines how much area an air-conditioning unit can cool.

tongue & groove
Strips of wood milled to fit together; one half has notches cut into it and the other has protruding pieces (tongues) that fit into each other.

transom
A horizontal bar between the top of a window or door and the structural opening; the section above is a transom light or panel.

tread
The horizontal surface of a stair that people step on to go up and down the stairs.

trim
Any finish material placed to provide decoration or to cover the joints between two materials. They are baseboards, cornices, and window and door casings.

truss roof
A joist and rafter system that forms the triangular construction of a roof.

turret
A small decorative tower.

underlayment
A thin layer of material placed over the subfloor to provide a smooth surface for the finish flooring, such as carpeting.

under pinning
The rebuilding or deepening of the foundation of an existing building to provide additional or improved support.

U-value
The measure of the rate heat passes through a material or combination of materials.

vapor barrier
A layer of material or paint applied to the wall or floor to retard or block the passage of moisture and its eventual condensation. It is commonly used on the outside of a foundation, under a roof, and on the warm side of a wall or ceiling.

variance
Permission granted by a local government body, such as the zoning board, to do something contrary to local building ordinances because that ordi-

nance would cause a hardship.

v-cap
A piece of ceramic tile used at the edge of a counter to prevent liquids from running off.

veneer
A protective or decorative non-structural facing, such as brick, stone, or Formica veneer.

viga
A large pole beam used to support the roof of Southwest adobe houses.

volts
The measurement of power that comes through the power line.

wainscoting
A facing of wood or other material applied to the lower portion of an interior wall for decorative or protective purposes.

water table
An underground aquifer or the upper-most level of ground water.

weather-stripping
Thin strips of insulation, usually with a sticky side, that insulates around windows and doors to prevent cold-air infiltration.

weep holes
Gaps left in masonry to drain water and moisture trapped behind it.

wetlands
An area of land that is characterized by a saturation of water, sometimes having swamps and marshes.

zone
A branch of a heating and cooling system that has its own thermostat and pump or fan.

Magazines

Magazines	House Price Range			Location of House			House Styles				
	Modest	Moderate	Luxury	City	Suburbs	Resorts	Traditional	Regional / Special	Modern	Eclectic	All
American Bungalow	•	•	•		•		•	•			
Architectural Digest			•	•	•	•					•
Art & Antiques			•	•							•
Atlanta Design Resources			•	•	•				•		
Audio Video Interiors		•	•	•	•	•					•
Best New Small Home Designs	•				•						•
Best Selling Home Plans from Home Magazine	•	•			•	•					•
Better Homes and Gardens		•			•						•
BH&G Beautiful Baths		•	•	•	•		•			•	
BH&G Beautiful Bedrooms		•	•	•	•						•
BH&G Beautiful Kitchens		•	•		•		•			•	
BH&G Beautiful New Homes		•	•	•	•	•					•
BH &G Bedroom &Bath		•			•						•
BH&G Country Style		•		•	•		•	•			
BH&G Decorating		•	•	•	•					•	•
BH&G Designers Showcase		•			•					•	•
BH&G Do-It-Yourself		•					•	•		•	
BH&G Garden Deck & Landscape		•									•
BH&G Garden Ideas & Outdoor Living		•		•	•						•
BH&G Garden Shed			•	•	•					•	
BH&G Home Planning Ideas		•		•	•					•	
BH&G Home Plans		•			•						•
BH&G Home Products Guide		•			•						•
BH&G Kids Rooms	•	•	•	•	•		•	•		•	
BH&G Kitchen & Bath Ideas	•	•		•	•		•		•		
BH&G Kitchen & Bath Products Guide		•			•						
BH&G Kitchen Planning Guide	•	•	•		•		•		•	•	
BH&G Landscape Solutions		•		•	•						•
BH&G Paint Decor		•		•	•						•
BH&G Quick & Easy Decorating		•		•	•						•
BH&G Remodeling Ideas		•		•	•		•		•	•	
BH&G Simply Perfect Walls With Style	•	•	•	•	•						•

Area of Concentration of Magazine				Areas of the House Covered by the Magazine					Review New Products	Focus of Magazine		Product Info Easily Avail.	Floor Plans	Frequency of Publication	Contact
Interiors	Exteriors	Landscapes	Gardens	Kitchens	Bathrooms	Bedrooms	Common Areas	Entire House		New	Renovated				
•	•	•	•	•	•		•		•	•	•		•	4	800-350-3363
•	•	•	•					•	•	•	•			12	800-365-8032
•							•			•	•			11	815-734-1162
•	•	•	•					•	•	•		•	•	1	800-810-8810 x202
•								•	•	•	•	•	•	12	800-333-8849
•	•							•		•			•	9	800-235-5700
•	•							•	•	•		•	•	6	800-322-6797
•	•	•	•					•	•	•	•	•	•	12	800-374-4244
•					•			•			•	•	•	1	Newsstand
•						•		•		•	•	•	•	1	Newsstand
•				•				•		•	•	•	•	1	Newsstand
•	•							•	•	•		•	•	4	Newsstand
•					•	•		•	•	•	•	•		4	Newsstand
•	•	•						•	•	•	•	•		2	Newsstand
•								•	•	•	•	•		6	Newsstand
•								•		•	•	•		6	Newsstand
•	•	•	•	•	•	•	•	•			•	•	•	4	800-247-0078
	•	•						•	•	•	•	•		4	Newsstand
	•	•						•	•	•	•	•	•	2	Newsstand
	•	•						•	•	•	•	•		4	Newsstand
•	•			•	•		•	•	•	•	•	•	•	6	Newsstand
•								•		•		•	•	4	Newsstand
•	•							•	•	•	•	•		2	Newsstand
•						•		•	•	•	•	•		1	Newsstand
•				•	•			•	•	•	•	•	•	6	Newsstand
•				•	•			•	•	•	•	•		2	Newsstand
•				•				•		•	•	•	•	1	Newsstand
		•	•							•	•	•		1	Newsstand
•							•		•	•	•	•		4	Newsstand
•							•		•	•	•	•		4	Newsstand
•	•	•						•	•		•	•	•	6	Newsstand
•							•		•	•	•		•	1	Newsstand

Magazines	House Price Range			Location of House			House Styles				
	Modest	Moderate	Luxury	City	Suburbs	Resorts	Traditional	Regional / Special	Modern	Eclectic	All
BH&G Simply Perfect Window Treatments	•	•	•	•	•						•
BH&G Simply Perfect Color Schemes	•	•	•	•	•						•
BH&G The Best of BH&G Home Plans		•	•	•	•	•					•
BH&G Traditional Style		•	•	•	•		•				•
BH&G Window & Wall Ideas		•			•						•
California Homes			•	•	•	•					•
Canadian Gardening (C)		•		•	•						
Canadian Home Planner(C)		•		•	•						•
Canadian Homes & Cottages (C)		•	•		•		•		•		
Canadian House & Home(C)		•	•	•							•
Cape Cod & Islands Home		•				•		•			
Century Home (C)	•	•	•	•	•		•				•
Charlotte Design Resources		•	•					•			
Chesapeake Home		•	•	•							•
Coastal Living		•		•	•	•		•		•	
Country Accents	•	•		•	•		•	•		•	
Country Decorating Ideas	•				•			•			
Country Gardens	•	•	•		•					•	
Country Home		•			•		•				
Country Houses	•	•	•		•	•	•	•			
Country Living		•		•	•	•	•		•		
Country Living Dream Homes	•	•	•	•	•						•
Country Living Gardener	•	•	•	•	•	•					•
Country's Best Home Designs		•			•						•
Country Sampler Decorating Ideas	•	•			•						
Country Style Living	•	•		•	•		•				
Custom Designed Interiors			•		•	•					
Dallas Design Resources		•	•	•				•			
Decorator Showhouse		•	•	•	•	•	•			•	
Denver Design Resources			•	•				•			
Design Times			•	•			•			•	
Distinction			•		•		•				

| Area of Concentration of Magazine | | | | Areas of the House Covered by the Magazine | | | | | | Focus of Magazine | | | | | |
Interiors	Exteriors	Landscapes	Gardens	Kitchens	Bathrooms	Bedrooms	Common Areas	Entire House	Review New Products	New	Renovated	Product Info Easily Avail.	Floor Plans	Frequency of Publication	Contact
•								•	•	•	•	•		1	Newsstand
•								•	•	•	•	•		1	Newsstand
•	•							•		•		•	•	6	Newsstand
•			•					•	•	•	•	•		1	Newsstand
•								•	•	•	•	•		4	Newsstand
•								•		•	•	•		4	888-544-0005
		•	•											7	905-946-0893
•				•	•	•			•		•	•		2	416-537-2604
•	•							•	•	•	•	•	•	8	888-567-7366
•								•	•	•	•	•	•	9	800-559-8868
•	•	•	•					•	•	•	•	•		4	800-698-1717
•	•	•	•					•	•		•	•	•	7	800-361-1957
•	•	•	•					•	•	•	•	•		1	800-810-8810 x-202
•	•	•	•					•	•	•	•	•		6	410-628-5750
•								•	•	•	•	•	•	6	888-252-3529
•			•					•	•	•	•			6	800-877-5358
•				•		•	•			•		•		4	Newsstand
	•		•								•	•		4	800-677-0484
•			•					•	•		•	•		8	800-374-9431
•	•							•	•	•		•	•	2	800-322-6797
•	•	•	•	•	•	•	•		•	•	•	•		12	800-888-0128
•								•		•			•	4	800-3226797
	•	•	•						•	•	•	•		6	877-273-2322
•	•							•		•			•	8	800-235-5700
•								•	•	•	•	•		6	904-446-4873
•	•							•		•		•	•	2	888-626-2026
•								•	•	•	•	•		1	Newsstand
•	•							•	•	•	•	•	•	1	800-810-8810 x-202
•	•		•					•	•	•	•	•		2	800-374-8791
•	•	•	•					•	•	•	•	•	•	2	800-810-8810
•								•		•	•	•		6	888-883-3744
•								•		•	•			8	516-843-4669

Magazines	House Price Range			Location of House			House Styles				
	Modest	Moderate	Luxury	City	Suburbs	Resorts	Traditional	Regional / Special	Modern	Eclectic	All
dwell Magazine	•	•	•	•	•				•		
Early American Homes	•	•	•	•	•		•				
Echoes Magazine			•	•					•		
Electronic House		•	•	•	•						•
Elle Décor		•	•	•	•	•				•	
Fine Home Building	•	•		•	•		•	•	•	•	
Florida Architecture			•	•	•			•			
Florida Design		•	•	•	•	•					•
Florida Design's Design Sourcebook		•	•	•	•	•					•
Flower & Garden					•						
Garden Design				•	•						
Gardening Life Magazine (C)		•		•	•						•
Good Housekeeping Do It Yourself	•	•	•	•	•	•					•
Good Housekeeping Home Plans	•	•	•		•	•					•
Home		•			•					•	
Home & Design		•	•	•	•						•
Home Building Cost Guide	•	•	•		•	•					•
Homeowners Resource Guide	•	•	•	•				•			
Home Planner	•	•	•		•	•					•
Home Resource & Design Magazine		•			•		•				
Home Systems		•			•						
Home Theater Magazine	•	•	•	•	•						
House		•	•	•		•					•
House & Garden	•	•	•	•	•		•		•	•	
House Beautiful		•	•	•	•						•
House Beautiful Home Building	•	•	•	•	•	•					•
House Beautiful Home Remodeling and Decorating	•	•	•	•	•	•					•
House Beautiful Houses & Plans	•	•	•		•	•					•
House Beautiful Kitchen & Bath Planner	•	•	•	•	•	•					•
House Beautiful Kitchens/ Baths	•	•	•	•	•	•					•
Houston Design Resources			•	•				•			

| Area of Concentration of Magazine | | | | Areas of the House Covered by the Magazine | | | | | | Focus of Magazine | | | | | |
Interiors	Exteriors	Landscapes	Gardens	Kitchens	Bathrooms	Bedrooms	Common Areas	Entire House	Review New Products	New	Renovated	Product Info Easily Avail.	Floor Plans	Frequency of Publication	Contact
•	•	•							•	•		•	•	6	877-939-3553
•	•		•	•	•		•				•	•	•	8	800-829-3340
•								•	•		•	•		4	508-362-3822
•								•		•	•	•		12	800-375-8015
•				•	•	•	•		•	•	•	•	•	8	800-274-4687
•	•							•	•	•	•	•		12	800-283-7252
•	•	•						•	•			•		2	305-858-7900
•	•							•		•	•	•		4	800-523-3327
•	•							•		•	•	•		2	800-523-3327
			•						•	•		•		6	800-444-1054
•	•	•	•						•					6	800-513-0848
			•						•		•			4	800-559-8868
•	•	•	•					•	•	•	•	•		4	800-322-6797
•	•							•	•	•	•	•	•	4	800-322-6797
•	•			•	•	•			•	•	•	•		10	303-604-1464
•	•	•	•					•	•	•	•	•		6	301-621-4413
•	•							•		•			•	2	800-322-6797
•				•	•		•		•		•	•	•	1	800-233-4707x-135
•	•							•	•	•		•	•	3	800-322-6797
•	•	•	•					•	•	•	•	•		6	914-934-1685
•								•		•		•	•	6	Newsstand
•								•	•		•	•		12	800-264-9872
•	•	•	•					•	•	•				6	631-288-5400
•		•	•					•	•	•	•	•		12	800-234-1520
•			•					•	•	•	•	•	•	12	800-444-6873
•	•							•	•	•		•	•	3	Newsstand
•	•							•	•		•	•		4	Newsstand
•	•							•	•	•		•	•	4	Newsstand
•				•	•				•	•	•	•		2	Newsstand
•				•	•				•	•		•		4	Newsstand
•	•	•	•					•	•	•		•	•	1	800-810-8810 x-202

Magazines	House Price Range			Location of House			House Styles				
	Modest	Moderate	Luxury	City	Suburbs	Resorts	Traditional	Regional / Special	Modern	Eclectic	All
Interior Design Magazine	•	•	•	•							•
Kansas City Homes & Gardens			•	•	•						•
Kitchens		•	•	•	•	•	•	•			
Kitchen Planning Guide		•			•		•			•	
Kitchens by Prof. Designers			•		•	•				•	
Landscapes, Decks and Project Plans	•	•	•		•	•					•
Las Vegas Design Resources			•	•				•			
Les Idees de Ma Maison(C)		•			•	•				•	
Log Homes Illustrated			•		•			•			
Log Home Living	•	•	•	•	•	•					•
Luxury Home Design			•		•	•					•
Martha Stewart Living	•	•	•		•	•	•			•	
Mary Engelbreit's Home Companion	•	•		•	•		•			•	
Metropolitan Home		•	•	•	•				•	•	
Metropolitan Home Plans	•	•	•		•						•
Midwest Home & Garden		•	•	•	•						•
Natural Home	•	•	•	•	•						•
Old-House Interiors	•	•	•	•	•					•	
Old House Journal	•	•	•	•	•		•				
Old House Journal Restoration Directory	•	•	•		•	•					•
Open House		•	•		•		•		•		
Phoenix Home &Garden			•	•				•			
Pool & Spa Living			•		•						•
Popular Home Automation	•	•	•		•						
Ready to Build Home Designs		•			•						•
Renovation Style		•	•	•	•	•	•			•	
Romantic Homes		•			•		•				
San Diego Home/Garden Lifestyles	•	•	•	•	•					•	
Select Home Designs (C)	•	•	•		•	•					•
Signature Kitchens & Baths			•								•
Small House Designs	•	•			•	•					•
Smart Homeowner		•	•		•						•

Interiors	Exteriors	Landscapes	Gardens	Kitchens	Bathrooms	Bedrooms	Common Areas	Entire House	Review New Products	New	Renovated	Product Info Easily Avail.	Floor Plans	Frequency of Publication	Contact
•								•	•	•	•	•	•	15	800-542-8138
•	•	•	•					•		•	•	•		7	800-886-5758 x-16
•				•					•	•	•	•		1	Newsstand
•				•	•		•		•		•	•	•	1	Newsstand
•				•	•				•	•	•	•		1	Newsstand
		•	•						•	•	•	•		4	800-322-6797
•	•	•	•					•	•	•	•	•	•	1	800-810-8810 x-202
•	•			•	•	•	•		•			•	•	10	Newsstand
•								•	•	•		•	•	6	Newsstand
•	•	•						•	•	•	•	•	•	12	800-850-7279
•	•							•	•	•		•	•	1	800-322-6797
•	•		•					•	•		•	•	•	12	800-999-6518
•								•			•			6	800-826-3382
•	•		•	•	•	•	•		•	•	•	•		6	303-604-1464
•	•							•	•	•	•	•	•	3	800-622-6797
•	•	•	•					•	•	•	•	•		6	800-933-4398
•	•	•	•					•	•	•	•	•	•	6	800-340-5846
•	•			•	•	•	•		•		•			4	800-462-0211
•	•	•		•	•				•		•		•	6	800-234-3797
•	•							•	•	•		•	•	1	800-234-3797
•								•		•		•		2	800-635-6319
•			•					•		•	•			12	800-228-6540
									•		•			4	888-768-3222
•	•	•	•					•	•			•		6	800-375-8015
•	•							•	•	•		•	•	4	800-235-5700
•	•		•					•	•	•	•	•	•	4	800-374-8791
•			•	•	•	•	•		•	•	•	•		12	800-829-7830
•	•		•	•			•		•	•		•	•	12	800-233-4707 x-135
•	•							•	•	•		•	•	3	800-663-6739
•				•	•				•		•	•	•	3	800-310-7047
•	•							•	•	•		•	•	1	800-322-6797
•	•		•					•		•	•	•	•	6	207-772-2466

Magazines	House Price Range			Location of House			House Styles				
	Modest	Moderate	Luxury	City	Suburbs	Resorts	Traditional	Regional / Special	Modern	Eclectic	All
Southern Accents			•	•	•		•	•			
Southern Living	•	•	•	•	•	•		•			
South Florida Design Resources			•	•				•			
Street of Dreams			•		•	•					•
Style at Home (C)		•		•	•						•
Style 1900	•	•	•	•	•						•
The Home Magazine (C)		•	•	•	•						•
This Old House		•	•		•		•			•	
Timber Homes Illustrated			•		•			•			
Today's Homeowner		•			•		•				
Traditional Home		•	•	•	•	•	•			•	
Trends		•	•	•	•						•
Unique Homes			•	•	•	•					•
Vacation Homes	•	•	•	•	•						•
Veranda			•	•	•	•	•	•		•	
Victoria		•	•	•	•		•				
Victorian Decorating & Lifestyle		•									
Victorian Homes		•		•	•		•	•			
Washington DC Design Resources			•	•				•			
Woman's Day Additions & Decks		•			•						•
Woman's Day Custom Kitchens & Baths		•			•					•	
Woman's Day Decorating Ideas		•			•					•	
Woman's Day Favorite Home Plans Collection	•	•	•		•	•					•
Woman's Day Gardening & Outdoor Living		•			•						•
Woman's Day Home Remodeling New Product Ideas		•			•					•	
Woman's Day Walls, Windows & Floors		•			•					•	
Woman's Day Weekend Decorating Projects		•			•					•	
Your New Home		•	•		•						•

(C) - Canadian

	Area of Concentration of Magazine				Areas of the House Covered by the Magazine						Focus of Magazine					
Interiors	Exteriors	Landscapes	Gardens	Kitchens	Bathrooms	Bedrooms	Common Areas	Entire House	Review New Products	New	Renovated	Product Info Easily Avail.	Floor Plans	Frequency of Publication	Contact
•		•	•	•	•		•		•		•	•		6	800-882-0183
•	•	•	•					•		•	•	•	•	12	800-272-4101
•	•	•	•					•	•	•		•	•	1	800-810-8810 x-202
•	•							•	•	•		•	•	2	800-322-6797
•								•	•	•	•			8	905-946-0910
•	•							•			•			4	609-397-4104
•	•	•	•					•		•		•		7	Newsstand
•	•	•		•	•						•	•	•	10	800-898-7237
•								•	•	•		•	•	6	Newsstand
•				•	•			•		•		•	•	10	800-456-6369
•	•		•					•	•	•	•	•		6	800-374-8791
•								•	•	•	•	•		6	800-428-3003
•	•							•		•	•			6	800-827-0660
								•	•	•		•	•	2	800-322-6797
•								•	•		•	•		6	800-767-5863
•	•		•	•	•	•	•	•		•	•	•		12	800-876-8696
•						•	•			•	•	•		6	800-877-5354
•	•	•	•	•	•	•	•				•			6	800-999-9718
•	•	•	•					•	•	•		•	•	2	800-810-8810 x-202
	•									•	•	•	•	1	Newsstand
•	•	•	•	•						•	•	•	•	1	Newsstand
•	•	•	•					•	•	•		•		3	Newsstand
•	•							•	•	•		•	•	1	Newsstand
	•		•					•	•			•		3	Newsstand
•	•	•	•					•	•	•		•	•	1	Newsstand
•	•	•	•						•		•	•		3	Newsstand
•	•	•	•					•	•		•	•		2	Newsstand
•	•							•	•	•		•	•	9	800-235-5700

Books

Home Construction

Binsacca, Rich
The Home Building Process: Everything You Need to Know to Work with Contractors and Subcontractors
Home Planners, Tuscon, AZ, 1999.

Buchholz, Barbara B. and Margaret Crane
Successful Homebuilding and Remodeling: Real-Life Advice for Getting the House You Want Without the Roof (or Sky) Falling In
Real Estate Education Company, Chicago, 1999.

DiDonno, Lupe & Phyllis Sperling
How to Design & Build Your Own Home, 2nd Edition
Alfred A. Knopf, New York, 1992.

Kidder, Tracy
House
Houghton Muffin, New York, 1992.

Ferguson, Myron E.
Build it Right! What to Look for in Your New Home, Rev. Ed.
Home User Press, Salem, OR, 1998.

Heldmann, Carl
Be Your Own House Contractor: Save 25% Without Lifting a Hammer, 3rd Edition
A Storey Publishing Book, Pownal, VT, 2001.

Locke, Jim
The Well-Built House
Houghton Mifflin, Boston/New York, 1992.

Myrvang, June Cotner & Steve Myrvang
The Home Design Handbook
Henry Holt, New York, 1992.

Nash, George
Do-It-Yourself Housebuilding: The Complete Handbook
Sterling Publishing New York, 1995.

Rusk, John
On Time and On Budget: A Home Renovation Survival Guide
Main Street Books, New York 1996.

Wenz, Plilip
Adding To a House: Planning, Design & Construction
Taunton Press, Newtown, CT, 1995.

Westgate, Alice
The Complete Color Directory: A Practical Guide to Using Color in your Home
Watson-Guptill, New York, 1999.

Youssef, Wasfi
Building Your Own Home: A Step-by-Step Guide
John Wiley &Sons, New York, 1988.

Kitchens and Bathrooms

Ardley, Suzanne
The Bathroom Planner
Chronicle Books, San Francisco, 2001.

Bouknight, Joanne Kellar
The Kitchen Idea Book
Taunton Books, Newtown, CT, 2001.

Grey, Johnny
Home Design Workbooks: Kitchen
DK Publishing, New York, 1997.

Hallam, Linda, Editor
Kitchen Decorating Ideas & Projects
Meredith Corporation, Des Moines, IA, 2000.

Holms, John P. (Editor)
Kitchens & Baths 1-2-3
Meredith Books, Des Moines, IA, 1999

Kimball, Herrick
The Kitchen Consultant: A Common-Sense Guide to Kitchen Remodeling

Taunton Press, Newton, CT, 1998.

Krasner, Deborah, photographs by William Stites
Kitchens for Cooks: Planning Your Perfect
Kitchen
Viking Studio Books, New York, 1994.

Love, Gilly
Making the Most of Kitchens
Rizzoli International Publications, New York,
1997.

Madden, Chris Casson, Photographs by John
Vaughanm
Bathrooms, Inspiring Ideas and Practical Solu-
tions for Creating a Beautiful Bathroom
Clarkson Potter, New York, 1996.

Madden, Chris Casson, Photographs by Michael
Mundy and John Vaughan
Kitchens: Information and Inspiration for Mak-
ing Kitchens the Heart of the Home
Clarkson Potter, New York, 1993.

Pringle, Bella (Editor)
The Kitchen Planner
Chronicle Books, San Francisco, 1999

Sallick, Barbara, and Lisa Light
Waterworks: Inventing Bath Style
Crown Publishing, New York, 2001.

Sawyer-Fay, Rebecca, et al
New Country Kitchens (Country Living)
Hearst books, New York, 1995.

Shaw, Murray
Professional Kitchen Design
Craftsman Book Company, Carlsbad, CA, 1998.

Weimer, Jan
Kitchen Redos, Revamps, Remodels & Replace-
ments: without Murder, Suicide or Divorce
William Morrow, New York, 1997.

Wormer, Andrew
The Bathroom Idea Book
Taunton Press, Newtown, CT, 1999.

Web Sites

The following are the Web sites mentioned in the book. My hope is that you will find some of them helpful.

Appliances

ebuild	www.ebuild.com
B4U Build	www.b4ubuild.com
Homeportfolio	www.homeportfolio.com
Improvenet	www.improvenet.com
Also check individual appliance Web sites.	

Bathroom Safety

Specialty Constructions	www.specialtyconstructions.com
Aker Plastics	www.akerplastics.com
Toilevator	www.toilevator.com

Central Vacuum Companies

Air Master	www.builtinvacuum.com	(800-525-2055)
Air Vac	www.mssystems.com	(800-366-6874)
Astro-Vac	http://astrovac.com	(800-546-3729)
Beam Industries	http://beamvac.com	(800-369-2326)
Broan Ltd.	www.broan.com	(800-548-0790)
Budd	http://buddvac.com	(800-245-2833)
Duo Vac	http://duovac.com	(800-453-5353)
Easy Flo	http://easyflo.com	(800-327-9356)
Electrolux	http://electroluxusa.com	(800-243-9078)
Eureka	http://eureka.com	(800-282-2886)
Filtex	www.mssystems.com	(800-366-6874)
FloMaster	www.buildinvacuum.com	(800-525-2055)
Galaxie	www.galaxie-vac.com	(800-238-2294)
Hayden	http://hayden.ca	(800-501-5018)
Hoover	http://hoovercompany.com	(800-891-5696)
M & S Systems	http://mssystems.com	(800-877-6631)
Modern Day	www.builtinvacuum.com	(800-525-2055)
Nutone	www.nutoneinfo.com	(800-463-2358)
Silent Master	www.builtinvacuum.com	(800-525-2055)
Silent Partner	www.vacumaid.com	(800-546-3729)
Vacu-flo	www.vacuflo.com	(800-822-8356)
Vacu-Maid	www.vacumaid.com	(800-546-3729)
Zenex	http://zenexvacs.com	(800-248-8221)

Locating Relevant Books on Construction, Decorating, and Landscape

Amazon	www.amazon.com
Barnes & Noble	www.barnesandnoble.com
Chapters	www.chapters.indigo.ca
Booksmith	www.booksmith.com

Contractors

National Association of the Remodeling Industry (NARI)	http://www.remodeltoday.com	
Contractors.Com	www.contractor.com	(877-266-8722)
Improvenet	www.improvenet.com	(800-437-0473)
National Association of Home Builders	www.homebuilder.com	
Canadian Home Builders' Association	www.chba.ca	
Service Magic	www.servicemagic.com	(800-474-1596)

Floor Plans

Home Planners Magazine	www.homeplanners.com	(800-521-6797)
Fine Homebuilding Magazine	www.finehomebuilding.com	(800-283-7252)
Garlinghouse Publishers	www.garlinghouse.com	(800-235-5700)
B4U Build	www.B4UBUILD.com	

Home Automation Systems

Home Automation Association	www.homeautomation.org
Custom Electronics Designers and Installers Association (CEDIA)	www.cedia.org

Home Building

B4U Build	www.B4Ubuild.com	
Eplans-The Houseplan Superstore	www.eplans.com	(888-846-8188)
Homeportfolio	www.homeportfolio.com	(800-840-0118)
Improvenet	www.improvenet.com	(800-437-0473)

Lighting Information

American Lighting Association	www.americanlightingassoc.com	(800-274-4484)

Lighting Systems

Vantage	www.vantagecontrols.com	(800-555-9891)

Lightolier	www.lightolier.com	(800-526-2731)
Litetouch	www.litetouch.com	(888-548-3824)
Lutron	www.lutron.com	(800-523-9466)

National Security Companies

ADT	www.adt.com	(800-238-4636)
Brinks	www.brinks.com	(800-874-8891)
Honeywell	www.honeywell.com/HomeSecurity	(800-328-5111)
Protection One	www.protectionone.com	(800-738-4255)

Many local companies offer security systems. Another option is to contact:

The National Burglar & Fire Alarm		
Association (NBFAA)	www.alarm.org	(301-907-3202)
for a listing of member companies by location.		

School Systems

School Reporting Services	www.TheSchoolReport.com.
U.S. Department of Education	http://nces.ed.gov/ccdweb/school/school.asp
USA Citylink	www.usacitylink.com

Information on Universal Design

| The Center for Universal Design | www.design.ncsu.edu/cud. |

Info on a Town or City

| National - USA Citylink | www.usacitylink.com |
| Iplace | www.iplacepro.com |

Water Professionals

| Water Quality Association | info@mail.wqa.org | (800-749-0234) |

for recommendations of WQA certified water-conditioning specialists in your area. For additional information on water contaminants and water treatments, access their Web site at www.wqa.org.

Radon Specialists

Radon and Water Control Systems Inc.	www.radonandwater.com	(800/343-8304)
The National Environmental Health		
Association (NEHA)	www.radonprog@aol.com or	(800-269-4174)
	www.neha.org	

Index

Notebook

Architect:

Telephone:

Fax:

Cell:

Address:

Contact:

Recommended by:

References:

Notes:

Architect:

Telephone:

Fax:

Cell:

Address:

Contact:

Recommended by:

References:

Notes:

Architect:

Telephone:

Fax:

Cell:

Address:

Contact:

Recommended by:

References:

Notes:

Architect:

Telephone:

Fax:

Cell:

Address:

Contact:

Recommended by:

References:

Notes:

Builder:

Telephone:

Fax:

Cell:

Address:

Contact:

Recommended by:

References:

Notes:

Builder:

Telephone:

Fax:

Cell:

Address:

Contact:

Recommended by:

References:

Notes:

Builder:

Telephone:

Fax:

Cell:

Address:

Contact:

Recommended by:

References:

Notes:

Builder:

Telephone:

Fax:

Cell:

Address:

Contact:

Recommended by:

References:

Notes:

Builder:

Telephone:

Fax:

Cell:

Address:

Contact:

Recommended by:

References:

Notes:

Kitchen Company:

Telephone:

Fax:

Address:

Contact:

Hours:

Manufacturers:

Estimated Costs:

Sketches:

Kitchen Company:

Telephone:

Fax:

Address:

Contact:

Hours:

Manufacturers:

Estimated Costs:

Sketches:

Kitchen Company:

Telephone:

Fax:

Address:

Contact:

Hours:

Manufacturers:

Estimated Costs:

Sketches:

Appliances / Store 1

	Store	Price
Refrigerator		
Manufacturer		
Manufacturer		
Manufacturer		
Manufacturer		
Stove		
Manufacturer		
Manufacturer		
Manufacturer		
Manufacturer		
Wall oven		
Manufacturer		
Manufacturer		
Manufacturer		
Manufacturer		
Dishwasher		
Manufacturer		
Manufacturer		
Manufacturer		
Manufacturer		

	Store	Price

Microwave

Manufacturer

Manufacturer

Manufacturer

Manufacturer

Washing machine

Manufacturer

Manufacturer

Manufacturer

Dryer

Manufacturer

Manufacturer

Manufacturer

Manufacturer

Instant hot

Manufacturer

Manufacturer

Manufacturer

Hood

Manufacturer

Manufacturer

Manufacturer

Appliances / Store 2

	Store	Price
Refrigerator		
Manufacturer		
Manufacturer		
Manufacturer		
Manufacturer		
Stove		
Manufacturer		
Manufacturer		
Manufacturer		
Manufacturer		
Wall oven		
Manufacturer		
Manufacturer		
Manufacturer		
Manufacturer		
Dishwasher		
Manufacturer		
Manufacturer		
Manufacturer		
Manufacturer		

	Store	Price

Microwave

Manufacturer

Manufacturer

Manufacturer

Manufacturer

Washing machine

Manufacturer

Manufacturer

Manufacturer

Dryer

Manufacturer

Manufacturer

Manufacturer

Manufacturer

Instant hot

Manufacturer

Manufacturer

Manufacturer

Hood

Manufacturer

Manufacturer

Manufacturer

Countertops

Supplier:

Telephone:

Fax:

Cell:

Address:

Contact:

Material:

Cost:

Material:

Cost:

Material:

Cost:

Material:

Cost:

Countertops

Supplier:

Telephone:

Fax:

Address:

Contact:

Material:

Cost:

Material:

Cost:

Material:

Cost:

Material:

Cost:

Kitchen / Tiles

Supplier:

Telephone:

Fax:

Address:

Contact:

Tile:

Price:

Grout:

Tile:

Price:

Grout:

Tile:

Price:

Grout:

Tile:

Price:

Grout:

Kitchen / Tiles

Supplier:

Telephone:

Fax:

Address:

Contact:

Tile:

Price:

Grout:

Tile:

Price:

Grout:

Tile:

Price:

Grout:

Tile:

Price:

Grout

Kitchen / Stone

Supplier:

Telephone:

Fax:

Address:

Contact:

Stones:

Cost:

Lead time: (*The time it will take to receive the stone*)

Notes:

Stones:

Cost:

Lead time:

Notes:

Kitchen / Stone

Supplier:

Telephone:

Fax:

Address:

Contact:

Stones:

Cost:

Lead time:

Notes:

Stones:

Cost:

Lead time:

Notes:

Bathrooms / Plumbing

Plumbing source:

Telephone:

Fax:

Address:

Contact:

Manufacturer / Cost

Toilets:

Sinks:

Showers:

Bathtubs:

Spas:

Hardware:

Mirrors:

Vanities:

   (kitchen sink):

   (kitchen faucet):

Notes:

Bathrooms / Plumbing

Plumbing source:

Telephone:

Fax:

Address:

Contact:

Manufacturer / Cost

Toilets:

Sinks:

Showers:

Bathtubs:

Spas:

Hardware:

Mirrors:

Vanities:

(kitchen sink):

(kitchen faucet):

Notes:

Bathrooms / Plumbing

Plumbing source:

Telephone:

Fax:

Address:

Contact:

Manufacturer / Cost

Toilets:

Sinks:

Showers:

Bathtubs:

Spas:

Hardware:

Mirrors:

Vanities:

   (kitchen sink):

   (kitchen faucet):

Notes:

Bathrooms / Tile

Tile Supplier:

Telephone:

Fax:

Address:

Contact:

Tile:

Price:

Grout:

Tile:

Price:

Grout:

Tile:

Price:

Grout:

Tile:

Price:

Grout

Bathrooms / Tile

Tile Supplier:

Telephone:

Fax:

Address:

Contact:

Tile:

Price:

Grout:

Tile:

Price:

Grout:

Tile:

Price:

Grout:

Tile:

Price:

Grout

Bathrooms / Stone

Stone Supplier:

Telephone:

Fax:

Address:

Contact:

Hours:

Stone:

Cost:

Lead time:

Notes:

Stone:

Cost:

Lead time:

Notes:

Bathrooms / Stone

Stone Supplier:

Telephone:

Fax:

Address:

Contact:

Hours:

Stone:

Cost:

Lead time:

Notes:

Stone:

Cost:

Lead time:

Notes:

Hardware

Bathroom #1

Shower towel bar	Company	Cost
Hand towel bar	Company	Cost
Toilet paper holder	Company	Cost
Bidet towel holder	Company	Cost
Shower bar	Company	Cost
Knobs	Company	Cost
Knobs	Company	Cost
Soap holder	Company	Cost
Toothbrush holder	Company	Cost

Bathroom #2

Shower towel bar	Company	Cost
Hand towel bar	Company	Cost
Toilet paper holder	Company	Cost
Bidet towel holder	Company	Cost
Shower bar	Company	Cost
Knobs	Company	Cost
Knobs	Company	Cost
Soap holder	Company	Cost
Toothbrush holder	Company	Cost

Bathroom #3

Shower towel bar	Company	Cost
Hand towel bar	Company	Cost
Toilet paper holder	Company	Cost
Bidet towel holder	Company	Cost
Shower bar	Company	Cost
Knobs	Company	Cost

Knobs	Company	Cost
Soap holder	Company	Cost
Toothbrush holder	Company	Cost

Bathroom #4

Shower towel bar	Company	Cost
Hand towel bar	Company	Cost
Toilet paper holder	Company	Cost
Bidet towel holder	Company	Cost
Shower bar	Company	Cost
Knobs	Company	Cost
Knobs	Company	Cost
Soap holder	Company	Cost
Toothbrush holder	Company	Cost

Bathroom #5

Shower towel bar	Company	Cost
Hand towel bar	Company	Cost
Toilet paper holder	Company	Cost
Bidet towel holder	Company	Cost
Shower bar	Company	Cost
Knobs	Company	Cost
Knobs	Company	Cost
Soap holder	Company	Cost
Toothbrush holder	Company	Cost

Powder Room

Shower towel bar	Company	Cost
Hand towel bar	Company	Cost
Toilet paper holder	Company	Cost
Bidet towel holder	Company	Cost

Shower bar	Company	Cost
Knobs	Company	Cost
Knobs	Company	Cost
Soap holder	Company	Cost
Toothbrush holder	Company	Cost

Other Room

	Company	Cost
	Company	Cost
	Company	Cost
	Company	Cost
	Company	Cost

Notes:

Office Checklist

Desk:

Chair:

Built-ins:

Fax machine:

Computer:

Copier:

Filing cabinets:

Other:

Gym Equipment

You need to first measure the space where the equipment will be situated or design a space to fit the equipment you already have.

Space:

Units to be bought:

Store:

Salesperson:

Telephone:

Fax:

Address:

Unit/cost:

Unit/cost:

Unit/cost:

Unit/cost:

Unit/cost:

Notes:

Gym Equipment

You need to first measure the space where the equipment will be situated or design a space to fit the equipment you already have.

Space:

Units to be bought:

Store:

Salesperson:

Telephone:

Fax:

Address:

Unit/cost:

Unit/cost:

Unit/cost:

Unit/cost:

Unit/cost:

Notes:

Interior Designer:

Telephone:

Fax:

Cell:

Address:

Contact:

Recommended by:

References:

Notes:

Interior Designer:

Telephone:

Fax:

Cell:

Address:

Contact:

Recommended by:

References:

Notes:

Interior Designer:

Telephone:

Fax:

Cell:

Address:

Contact:

Recommended by:

References:

Notes:

Floorings

Resource:

Telephone:

Fax:

Address:

Contact:

Material:

Recommended installer:

Notes:

Floorings

Resource:

Telephone:

Fax:

Address:

Contact:

Material:

Recommended installer:

Notes:

Floorings

Resource:

Telephone:

Fax:

Address:

Contact:

Material:

Recommended installer:

Notes:

Carpeting:

Source:

Telephone:

Fax:

Address:

Contact:

Material:

Cost:

Source:

Telephone:

Fax:

Address:

Contact:

Material:

Cost:

Source:

Telephone:

Fax:

Address:

Address:

Material:

Cost:

Carpeting:

Source:

Telephone:

Fax:

Address:

Contact:

Material:

Cost:

Source:

Telephone:

Fax:

Address:

Contact:

Material:

Cost:

Source:

Telephone:

Fax:

Address:

Address:

Material:

Cost:

Furnishings

Furnishings

Swatches

Swatches

Paint Colors

Keep a permanent record of colors so you can have them for touch-ups later on. Remember to label paint cans as well.

Room:

Color:

Company:

Manufacturer:

Room:

Color:

Company:

Manufacturer:

Room:

Color:

Company:

Manufacturer:

Room:

Color:

Company:

Manufacturer:

Room:

Color:

Company:

Manufacturer:

Room:

Color:

Company:

Manufacturer:

Room:

Color:

Company:

Manufacturer:

Room:

Color:

Company:

Manufacturer:

Room:

Color:

Company:

Manufacturer:

Room:

Color:

Company:

Manufacturer:

Room:

Color:

Company:

Manufacturer:

Room:

Color:

Company:

Manufacturer:

Room:

Color:

Company:

Manufacturer:

Room:

Color:

Company:

Manufacturer:

Room:

Color:

Company:

Manufacturer:

Room:

Color:

Company:

Manufacturer:

Room:

Color:

Company:

Manufacturer:

Room:

Color:

Company:

Manufacturer:

Window Treatments

Supplier:

Telephone:

Fax:

Cell:

Address:

Contact:

Kitchen

#of windows

Size of windows

Style of treatment

Cost

Special Trim

Dining room

#of windows

Size of windows

Style of treatment

Cost

Special Trim

Living room

#of windows

Size of windows

Style of treatment

Cost

Special Trim

NOTEBOOK

Den

#of windows

Size of windows

Style of treatment

Cost

Special Trim

Office

#of windows

Size of windows

Style of treatment

Cost

Special Trim

Play room

#of windows

Size of windows

Style of treatment

Cost

Special Trim

Master bedroom

#of windows

Size of windows

Style of treatment

Cost

Special Trim

Bedroom 1

#of windows

Size of windows

Style of treatment

Cost

Special Trim

Bathroom 1

#of windows

Size of windows

Style of treatment

Cost

Special Trim

Bedroom 2

#of windows

Size of windows

Style of treatment

Cost

Special Trim

Bathroom 2

#of windows

Size of windows

Style of treatment

Cost

Special Trim

Bedroom 3

#of windows

Size of windows

Style of treatment

Cost

Special Trim

NOTEBOOK

Bathroom 3

#of windows

Size of windows

Style of treatment

Cost

Special Trim

Bedroom 4

#of windows

Size of windows

Style of treatment

Cost

Special Trim

Bathroom 4

#of windows

Size of windows

Style of treatment

Cost

Special Trim

Bedroom 5

#of windows

Size of windows

Style of treatment

Cost

Special Trim

Bathroom 5

#of windows

Size of windows

Style of treatment

Cost

Special Trim

Office

#of windows

Size of windows

Style of treatment

Cost

Special Trim

Powder room

#of windows

Size of windows

Style of treatment

Cost

Special Trim

Security system:

Telephone:

Fax:

Cell:

Address:

Contact:

Recommended by:

References:

Components included:

Cost:

Notes:

Security system:

Telephone:

Fax:

Cell:

Address:

Contact:

Recommended by:

References:

Components included:

Cost:

Notes:

Audio System

Supplier:

Telephone:

Fax:

Cell:

Address:

Contact:

Recommended by:

Components:

Notes:

Audio System

Supplier:

Telephone:

Fax:

Cell:

Address:

Contact:

Recommended by:

Components:

Notes:

Telephone System

Supplier:

Telephone:

Fax:

Cell:

Address:

Recommended by:

Equipment:

Notes:

Telephone System

Supplier:

Telephone:

Fax:

Cell:

Address:

Recommended by:

Equipment:

Notes:

Lighting System

Supplier:

Telephone:

Fax:

Cell:

Address:

Recommended by:

Notes:

Lighting System

Supplier:

Telephone:

Fax:

Cell:

Address:

Recommended by:

Notes:

Central Vacuum System

Supplier:

Telephone:

Fax:

Cell:

Address:

Recommended by:

Warranty:

System:

Components:

Notes:

Central Vacuum System

Supplier:

Telephone:

Fax:

Cell:

Address:

Recommended by:

Warranty:

System:

Components:

Notes:

NOTEBOOK

Water Purification

Company:

Telephone:

Fax:

Cell:

Address:

Contact:

Recommended by:

System:

Notes:

Water Purification

Company:

Telephone:

Fax:

Cell:

Address:

Contact:

Recommended by:

System:

Notes:

Landscape Professional:

Telephone:

Fax:

Cell:

Address:

Contact:

Recommended by:

References:

Notes:

Landscape Professional:

Telephone:

Fax:

Cell:

Address:

Contact:

Recommended by:

References:

Notes:

Paving Contractor:

Telephone:

Fax:

Cell:

Address:

References:

Cost:

Notes:

Paving Contractor:

Telephone:

Fax:

Cell:

Address:

References:

Cost:

Notes:

Pool Contractor

Telephone:

Fax:

Cell:

Address:

References:

Cost:

What is included:

Cost/service:

Availability:

Pool Contractor

Telephone:

Fax:

Cell:

Address:

References:

Cost:

What is included:

Cost/service:

Availability:

Masonry Contractor:

Telephone:

Fax:

Cell:

Address:

Recommended by:

Estimate:

Comments:

Masonry Contractor:

Telephone:

Fax:

Cell:

Address:

Recommended by:

Estimate:

Comments:

Construction Contractors

Be sure to get the names and telephone numbers of all contractors the GC hired that you might need to contact in the future.

HVAC Contractor

Company:

Contact:

Telephone:

Fax:

Cell:

Address:

Plumbing Contractor

Company:

Contact:

Telephone:

Fax:

Cell:

Address:

Electrical Contractor

Company:

Contact:

Telephone:

Fax:

Cell:

Address:

Roofing Contractor

Company:

Contact:

Telephone:

Fax:

Cell:

Address:

Painting Contractor

Company:

Contact:

Telephone:

Fax:

Cell:

Address:

NOTEBOOK

Warranties

Enter information about the warranties when the contractors are hired or before they leave the job.

Contractors

General contractor:

HVAC contractor:

Roofing contractor:

Other:

Systems

Water Quality:

Security:

Lighting:

Audio / Visual:

Central Vac:

Other:

Maintenance Procedures

Before the general contractor leaves, be sure to write down all procedures you should follow to maintain your home.

Monthly:

Semiannually:

Yearly:

Every five years:

Schools

School:

Address:

Telephone:

Director of admissions:

Interview date/contact:

Notes:

Schools

School:

Address:

Telephone:

Director of admissions:

Interview date/contact:

Notes:

Camps

Camp:

Address:

Telephone:

Contact:

Season dates:

Schedule:

Cost:

Camps

Camp:

Address:

Telephone:

Contact:

Season dates:

Schedule:

Cost:

Meeting Notes

Periodically, you will have meetings with the builder, architect, contractors, and/or suppliers. Keep notes on the meetings for future reference.

Date:

Attendees:

Notes:

Date:

Attendees:

Notes:

Date:

Attendees:

Notes:

Date:

Attendees:

Notes:

Date:

Attendees:

Notes:

Date:

Attendees:

Notes:

Date:

Attendees:

Notes:

Date:

Attendees:

Notes:

Date:

Attendees:

Notes:

Date:

Attendees:

Notes:

Date:

Attendees:

Notes:

Telephone Numbers

Name:

Company:

Telephone:

Name:

Company:

Telephone:

Name:

Company:

Telephone:

Name:

Company:

Telephone:

Name:

Company:

Telephone:

Name:

Company:

Telephone:

Name:

Company:

Telephone:

Name:
_____

Company:
_____

Telephone:
_____

Name:
_____

Company:
_____

Telephone:
_____

Name:
_____

Company:
_____

Telephone:
_____

Name:
_____

Company:
_____

Telephone:
_____

Name:
_____

Company:
_____

Telephone:
_____

Name:
_____

Company:
_____

Telephone:
_____

Name:
_____

Company:
_____

Telephone:
_____

Name:
_____

Company:
_____

Telephone:
_____

Name:

Company:

Telephone:

Name:

Company:

Telephone:

Name:

Company:

Telephone:

Name:

Company:

Telephone:

Name:

Company:

Telephone:

Name:

Company:

Telephone:

Name:

Company:

Telephone:

Name:

Company:

Telephone:

Notes

Notes